Women and Culture Series

The Women and Culture Series is dedicated to books that illuminate the lives, roles, achievements, and status of women, past or present.

Fran Leeper Buss
Dignity: Lower Income Women Tell of Their Lives and Struggles
Forged under the Sun / Forjada bajo el sol: The Life of María Elena Lucas
La Partera: Story of a Midwife

Valerie Kossew Pichanick
Harriet Martineau: The Woman and Her Work, 1802–76

Sandra Baxter and Marjorie Lansing
Women and Politics: The Visible Majority

Estelle B. Freedman
Their Sisters' Keepers: Women's Prison Reform in America, 1830–1930

Susan C. Bourque and Kay Barbara Warren
Women of the Andes: Patriarchy and Social Change in Two Peruvian Towns

Marion S. Goldman
Gold Diggers and Silver Miners: Prostitution and Social Life on the Comstock Lode

Page duBois
Centaurs and Amazons: Women and the Pre-History of the Great Chain of Being

Mary Kinnear
Daughters of Time: Women in the Western Tradition

Lynda K. Bundtzen
Plath's Incarnations: Woman and the Creative Process

Violet B. Haas and Carolyn C. Perrucci, editors
Women in Scientific and Engineering Professions

Sally Price
Co-wives and Calabashes

Diane Wood Middlebrook and Marilyn Yalom, editors
Coming to Light: American Women Poets in the Twentieth Century

Joanne S. Frye
Living Stories, Telling Lives: Women and the Novel in Contemporary Experience

E. Frances White
Sierra Leone's Settler Women Traders: Women on the Afro-European Frontier

Barbara Drygulski Wright, editor
Women, Work, and Technology: Transformations

Lynda Hart, editor
Making a Spectacle: Feminist Essays on Contemporary Women's Theatre

Verena Martinez-Alier
Marriage, Class and Colour in Nineteenth-Century Cuba: A Study of Racial Attitudes and Sexual Values in a Slave Society

Kathryn Strother Ratcliff et al., editors
Healing Technology: Feminist Perspectives

Mary S. Gossy
The Untold Story: Women and Theory in Golden Age Texts

Jocelyn Linnekin
Sacred Queens and Women of Consequence: Rank, Gender, and Colonialism in the Hawaiian Islands

Glenda McLeod
Virtue and Venom: Catalogs of Women from Antiquity to the Renaissance

Lynne Huffer
Another Colette: The Question of Gendered Writing

Jill Kerr Conway and Susan C. Bourque, editors
The Politics of Women's Education: Perspectives from Asia, Africa, and Latin America

The Politics of Women's Education

For Brad Wiley

with our warm best wishes

Jill & Susan

The Politics of Women's Education

Perspectives from Asia, Africa, and Latin America

Edited by
Jill Ker Conway and Susan C. Bourque

Ann Arbor

THE UNIVERSITY OF MICHIGAN PRESS

Copyright © by the University of Michigan 1993
All rights reserved
Published in the United States of America by
The University of Michigan Press
Manufactured in the United States of America

1996   1995   1994   1993   4 3 2 1

Library of Conress Cataloging-in-Publication Data

The Politics of women's education : perspective from Asia, Africa,
    and Latin America / edited by Jill Ker Conway and Susan C. Bourque.
        p.   cm. — (Women and culture series)
    Includes bibliographical references.
    ISBN 0-472-10446-2 (alk. paper)
        1. Women—Education—Political aspects—Asia. 2. Women—
    Education—Political aspects—Africa. 3. Women—Education—
    Political aspects—Latin America. 4. Women—Education—Social
    aspects—Asia. 5. Women—Education—Social aspects—Africa.
    6. Women—Education—Social aspects—Latin America. I. Conway,
    Jill K., 1934–   . II. Bourque, Susan Carolyn, 1943–   .
    III. Series.
    LC2302.P65   1993
    376'.9172'4—dc20   93-20600
                                                            CIP

A CIP catalogue record for this book is available from the British Library.

Acknowledgments

The editors would like to express their thanks to the Ford and Rockefeller foundations for financial support made available to Mount Holyoke College during the initial stages of this effort. This book grew out of the Mount Holyoke College Sesquicentennial conference on World Wide Education for Women, and we are grateful to the many participants in that conference and to President Elizabeth Kennan of Mount Holyoke College for their efforts to highlight the importance of women's education.

This collection was produced under the auspices of the Smith College Project on Women and Social Change and with the financial support of the Esther Booth Wiley Fund for Research. We would like to thank Kathleen E. Gauger, administrative assistant to the Project, for her unflagging efforts in the production of this volume. Finally, the editors express their gratitude to Smith College, to President Mary Maples Dunn, and to LeAnn Fields, executive editor of the University of Michigan Press.

Contents

Introduction
Jill Ker Conway and Susan C. Bourque   1

Part 1: Asia

A Survey of Gender Issues and Educational Development
in Asia
Vina Mazumdar   15

Women's Education in India
Neera Desai   23

Healing the Wounds of Development
Devaki Jain   45

Women's Education in Pakistan
Farida Shaheed and Khawar Mumtaz   59

Work, Education, and Women's Gains: The Korean Experience
In-ho Lee   77

Women's Education as an Instrument for Change: The Case of
the Philippines
Amaryllis Tiglao Torres   105

Part 2: Africa

An Overview of Women's Education in Africa
Dorothy L. Njeuma   123

Enhancing Women's Participation in the Science-Based
Curriculum: The Case of Kenya
Kabiru Kinyanjui   133

Educational Expansion, Cost Considerations, and Curriculum
Development in Zimbabwe
Fay Chung   149

Part 3: Latin America

An Overview of Women's Education in Latin America and the
Caribbean
  Lourdes Arizpe   171

Citizenship and Education in Peru and Mexico: Political
Challenges for the 1990s
  Susan C. Bourque   183

Persistent Inequalities in Women's Education in Peru
  Hernán Fernández   207

Alternative Education for Women in Peru
  Virginia Vargas   217

Education, Race, and Inequality in Brazil
  Fúlvia Rosemberg   223

Part 4: Methodological and Comparative Considerations

The Economics of Women's Schooling
  T. Paul Schultz   237

Rethinking the Impact of Women's Education
  Jill Ker Conway   245

Contributors   259

Introduction

JILL KER CONWAY AND SUSAN C. BOURQUE

In the spring of 1992 the American Association of University Women (AAUW) released its report "How Schools Shortchange Girls," which catalogs the failure of American schools to provide educational equity to girls. The report came as no surprise to those familiar with the long-term struggle to implement and preserve Title IX of the 1972 Education amendment, which was promulgated to secure educational equity on the basis of gender. We have come to see that educational systems are usually microcosms of the gender systems of the societies in which they operate. The function of formal education to instill appropriate behavior and cultural norms, consciously or unconsciously, includes gender-specific messages. Hence, schools, at whatever level, are the vehicles for perpetuating stereotyped or limited views of girls and boys or women and men. But the reverse can also be true. Educational reformers and political leaders also view schools and the education system as vehicles for profound change, as ideal environments in which to develop, promote, and reward new attitudes and behaviors. Nevertheless, as the AAUW report emphasizes, gender equity remains an elusive goal in American education.

This volume is a collection of essays, reflections, and commentary by leading thinkers in Asia, Africa, and Latin America concerned with education as a means to improve women's social and economic status. Some of the authors are academics; others are activists, journalists, or government leaders. All have been deeply involved in expanding educational opportunities for girls, in identifying the obstacles to women's advancement, or in developing programs and policies to make educational opportunities for women play a constructive role in expanding women's leadership and improving their lives.

The concerns raised by these authors bear a striking resemblance to the issues identified in the AAUW report. The past thirty years have brought a remarkable expansion in women's educational access in much of the Third World. Nevertheless, inequality persists not only in access but in educational experience. Just as the authors of the AAUW report discover a "chilly climate for girls" in many U.S. classrooms, the authors in this volume see the need for major reforms in the explicit and implicit content of the curriculum, in the structure of schools, and in our concept of education.

The differences in the societies described in these essays are enormous, from Korea to Kenya, Pakistan to Peru. The cultural and historical differences are reflected in varying levels of economic growth, literacy, and educational access. Furthermore, as the authors point out, class, ethnic, religious, and regional differences make the experience of women within any single country unique.

Nevertheless, a number of similarities are worth noting. First, all of the authors share an appreciation of the importance of educational institutions. They know they are powerful. Though they may play a conservative role when in the hands of conservative authorities, they are powerful agents of change. Thus, each of the authors stresses the need to think systematically about reform, about how to advance a new agenda for teaching, for curriculum materials, and for the transformation of knowledge in both the formal and the nonformal systems.

Many of the authors address the tension between the formal and nonformal educational systems. The nonformal system has been an especially important setting for educational experiments and innovation directed at adult women who were bypassed by the formal system. Because nonformal education is relatively free from many of the bureaucratic constraints of the formal system, it has been a preferred vehicle for feminist and popular groups working to introduce a curriculum more appropriate to the needs of women with limited resources, or a curriculum focused on empowerment, political consciousness, and improved self-esteem. Despite the notable success of many nonformal programs, their relation to the formal state-supported system is a critical but yet unresolved issue. Most of the writers represented in this volume are not willing to withdraw from the formal system. Thus, a central concern for many authors is how the positive aspects of the lessons learned in the nonformal system can be introduced into a system supported through public funds.

Throughout these essays readers will find ample evidence of the unintended consequences of formal education. On the positive side, access to the university has led to the mobilization of elite women and their commitment to reform. Similarly, for women of limited resources access to both formal and nonformal education has been linked to an increased sense of self-esteem and empowerment. Nevertheless, it is equally clear that the persistence of patriarchal cultures and social systems imposes constraints on the educational system as a vehicle for women's liberation. All of the authors note sex bias inherent in the formal school systems, reflected in the curriculum, texts, facilities, teachers, and administration. Girls' access to education has not eliminated the misogynist bias found within Western culture and reflected in educational systems that borrow heavily from the West.

Since the authors of these essays are successful products of formal education, they reflect the capacity of those institutions to produce their own critics and sources of reform. This often gives rise to an ambivalence about educational institutions, an awareness of what they can do combined with an acute appreciation of their shortcomings.

A major theme of the essays is the need to come to terms with the relationship between the educational system and the development model adopted by national political elites. Many, though not all, note the failure of economic development models adopted in the past and stress the need for an educational system that incorporates a new concept of development, one no longer tied to a Western or colonial conception of industrial growth. Many of the authors are searching for a model of national development, based on the unique characteristics and needs of their societies, that would have at its core the development of the full potential of citizens, both male and female. They are also keenly anxious to link the schools and their curriculum to that model of development. This remains a central challenge for educational and feminist reformers. Their task is not simply the reform of the educational system or schools or even the restructuring of gender relations and attitudes; rather, their challenge is to define a program to achieve women's educational equity that can be a fundamental aspect of a new vision for the nation.

Regional Patterns: Asia

The south and east Asian region shows widely divergent patterns of educational access for women. Japan and Korea have achieved levels of access and of literacy equaling and sometimes outperforming those produced by Western systems. By contrast, women have been losing ground in access to education in the Indian subcontinent, despite much publicized and energetically debated national plans for universal education, which are never acted upon.

Within the Asian region the tensions that play about the educational aspirations of women are of two kinds. First, in nation-states that made women citizens as part of the effort to mobilize national populations against colonialism, the question of real participation in the rewards of political and economic life is posed most vividly by women's long-frustrated educational aspirations. Second, whether Confucian, Hindu, Buddhist, or Muslim in ethnic and religious origin, south and east Asian societies have doubts about the benefits of Western-style education, technology, and economic organization. While this ambivalence might be expected of the male beneficiaries of ancient patriarchal systems, many politically aware south Asian women share it. They have been politically mobilized by concerns about the environmental results of industrial development or by questions about whether Western capitalist economic organization and consumerism represent desirable imports.

Women's access to education thus becomes not merely a question of their claim on scarce economic resources but also one that sets in motion a dialectical process of questioning. What is good about traditional values and traditional knowledge? What aspects of Western learning are relevant to our culture and national ambitions? What parts of our system of gender relationships do we value? How do they differ from those in North America and Western Europe?

These questions of cultural politics are posed whenever reformers set about enlarging the formal educational system, and whenever volunteers open another informal educational agency, since Western aid has been dispensed by field staff who often misunderstood male and female gender roles in the cultures in which they operated. Women's protest has been most quickly mobilized around their concern for maintaining the natural environment, which yields many resources for making food, crafts, and popular medicine, including that most precious resource of arid environments, water.

Vina Mazumdar explores the interplay between colonialism and indigenous cultures in southern and eastern Asia and its ramifications in terms of gender roles, arguing that, whatever the agency of education, it is women's exclusion from participation in educational experience that limits their ability to improve their status. Those concerned with ending that exclusion have raised questions about both curriculum content and pedagogy that represent a major contribution to global educational concerns.

Neera Desai describes the history of women's long-postponed quest for education in India and explores why it is that the gap between aspiration and achievement in women's education has widened since independence. She concludes that the abysmal ignorance in which most Indian women live will not be corrected by a benevolent government but, rather, only when women themselves are committed enough to organize to meet their needs.

Devaki Jain, disciple of Gandhi, represents the extreme end of the spectrum of rejection of Western values. As an activist who has devoted her career to projects to improve the earnings of poor rural women, she has come to the conclusion that only a return to a Gandhian notion of simplicity and spiritual discipline will enable Indians to educate themselves to meet the challenges of a continent facing environmental collapse because of misguided development projects.

Farida Shaheed and Khawar Mumtaz describe the ambitious plans for universal education in Pakistan that have been promulgated since 1955. They demonstrate that the reality has been one of such mismanagement that less than 13 percent of Pakistani rural women participate in the educational system. For the authors this sorry record is not necessarily the disaster one might expect. They argue that the view of women taught in the schools of an authoritarian Islamic state is not one that fosters the individual growth and intellectual freedom of female students. The authors pin their hopes on the potential of nonformal education and cite some remarkable achievements to back up their assessment.

In-ho Lee's essay introduces us to the unacknowledged political tensions of Korean society, in which women have the same access to elementary and secondary education as men and in which more than one-third of university graduates are female. Korea's inherited Confucian values require a strict separation between male and female roles, but the industrial growth that has made Korea one of the new miracle industrial states has required the recruitment of women into the industrial labor force. In this situation the critical factor for women's analysis of their situation is the curriculum, which, Lee points out, still stresses conformity to such a degree that, the higher the level of a woman's educational attainment, the more likely she is to define her interests exclusively in the home. The feminist challenge to this style of education is a new theme in current Korean education. It is a challenge that motivates women to seize and use the rights conferred on them in the 1955 constitution, and to expand their conception of women's sphere beyond the confines of the home.

Amaryllis Torres, a social worker whose life is spent encouraging female-led families in the poor areas of Manila and the rural villages of the Philippines, sees the colonial heritage as the major constraint to be removed before Filipino women can secure the kind of education that will prepare them to deal effectively with the realities of daily life. Women who must run small businesses to maintain their families do not benefit from the current curriculum designed for beauticians and secretaries, Torres argues. Their needs can only be met by forging a curriculum that takes as its point of departure the realities of life in a culture in which men regularly form several families and expect women to assume the economic responsibility for raising and educating children.

Regional Patterns: Africa

In Africa the problem of adapting externally imposed colonial educational systems to the needs of emerging nations has been complicated by extreme poverty and by inexorable population pressures on available resources. The African continent contains twenty of the world's poorest countries and exhibits the world's lowest rates of literacy.

Clearly, circumstances have favored those states that won their independence in the late 1970s and 1980s versus those that embarked on the uncharted territory of nation building in the 1960s. Thus, Zimbabwe could avoid the uncritical emulation of European models, which led Kenya to expend as much as 37 percent of its annual recurring budget expenses on education. The mobilization of rural populations for wars of national liberation could also be undertaken with ideologies that rejected Western devaluation of traditional knowledge and preserved some traditional forms of authority and leadership for women.

Nevertheless, the migration of men to paid work in the formal economy has left women everywhere on the continent responsible for 80 to 90 percent of food production, yet without adequate access to a male-staffed agricultural extension service. Not surprisingly, female food producers in Africa have been the political advocates of environmental preservation in conflict with state policies designed to develop commercial agriculture for export.

In Africa today population pressures, foreign debt, and population relocation threaten the gains made in developing national education systems over the past two decades. In countries such as Kenya these pressures have led to the development of a two- and often three-tiered educational system, to which women have broad access only at the poorest funded and most marginal level. Thus, we may speak about a widening pattern of inequality separating women and men. States such as Zimbabwe, alerted by history and by strong female leadership, have been able to drive down the unit cost of education and achieve a more equitable distribution of resources, but the question remains about whether these policies will survive the pressure of population growth.

The same tensions concerning popular versus formal education experienced in Latin America and Asia manifest themselves in Africa. The daily realities of life for rural women concern grinding physical labor to secure water, food, and shelter, realities that formal school texts focused on literacy and numeracy do not properly recognize.

Dorothy Njeuma's essay provides a broadbrush picture of the constraints and achievements of Africa's efforts to deliver education to women, stressing the positive outcomes as well as the dimensions of the problem. Kabiru Kinyanjui describes the postcolonial dilemmas of Kenya, its achievements in increasing educational access, and the persistent lack of equal science training for girls. He underscores the need for reforms that effect profound cultural and attitudinal changes. Fay Chung represents a later generation of educational leadership in Zimbabwe, acutely aware of the economic and population pressures that have undermined educational aspirations elsewhere in Africa. She notes the significance of women's political and military roles in Zimbabwe's war of liberation and the difficulties in preserving that inheritance in postwar institutions. All three essays highlight Africa's environmental predicament, women's relationship to the land, and the pressing need for agricultural education delivered to women, who bear the brunt of the environmental crisis and who are the food producers for the continent. There is no doubt that significant gains have occurred over the past forty years; yet, despite those gains, significant barriers remain to women's full educational participation.

Regional Patterns: Latin America

Remarkable progress in women's access to education has characterized the past several decades in Latin America, and yet these advances are neither secure nor have they produced greater equity for women. Despite the marked democratization of schooling, the region's educational systems are now under greater scrutiny from governments anxious to cut public expenditures and from a public increasingly dissatisfied with the system's performance. Moreover, the economic crisis is leading to higher rates of school attrition. The essays in this section describe the unsolved problems in the formal system and also experiments underway, particularly those directed at women, that are the subject of renewed interest for educational reformers.

Lourdes Arizpe puts the educational issues in the context of the Latin American debt crisis. She argues that the abrupt halt in growth that occurred in the 1980s may seriously curtail women's recent educational advances. She argues that the region faces a growing sense of cultural anomie that can only be rectified with an educational system that appreciates and preserves the traditional knowledge and cultural heritage of Latin American societies.

Susan Bourque sets the questions of women's education in the context of the political crises in Peru and Mexico. In both nations popular social movements, which include substantial numbers of newly politicized women, have emerged as potent political forces. She traces women's mobilization in part to nonformal popular education programs and in part to middle-class women's access to universities and feminism. As the economic crisis has deepened, more women are forced into the informal labor market and are facing basic problems of subsistence. Nonformal education projects tend to address women's economic needs as well as contribute to new levels of self-esteem, personal and familial, both critical factors in the need to develop survival strategies. The significance of these programs has not been lost on the political leadership of Mexico and Peru.

Hernán Fernández argues that Peruvian education, despite the enormous increase in access, is riddled with inequities. Class and gender have profound effects on the experiences of students. Fernández describes the new programs developed for adult women in nonformal education but ultimately argues that meaningful change will only come through renewed attention to the content and structure of the formal system.

A substantial part of Lima's population consists of rural female migrants who have missed the formal educational system. Living in the squatter settlements that ring the city, these women have drawn the attention of a spectrum of political actors—including political parties, Catholic and Protestant church groups, and a variety of women's organizations. Virginia Vargas describes the ideology and the nonformal education programs of one of Peru's leading feminist organizations, the Flora Tristan Women's Center.

Fúlvia Rosemberg links education, race, and gender and tackles the failure of women's education in Brazil to improve their condition in the labor market. She posits that the schools, rather than alleviating the problem, contribute to it. Schools have become educational ghettos that channel blacks and women into the lowest echelons of the labor market, exacerbating sexual and racial discrimination within Brazilian society.

For Latin America politics and education are deeply entwined, and, as these essays make clear, improvement in women's status is at least as dependent upon their ability to mobilize politically as it is on educational achievement. Nevertheless, political consciousness or its lack is closely linked to educational content.

We conclude our volume with two critiques of the standard models for assessing the impact of education. The essay by T. Paul Schultz reviews the assumptions of standard economic models and their impact on our assessment of the outcomes of women's education. Schultz identifies the theoretical problems and possibilities of assessing the returns on investment in women's education and the dynamics of intrafamily resource allocation. He proposes a model more appropriate to the nature of family systems and gender patterns in societies in which the major part of women's productive work is unpaid. His analysis provides a new framework with which policymakers can interpret and analyze the political and economic consequences of women's access to education, as described by the authors in this volume.

Jill Ker Conway examines how historians' preconceived notions and myths about education and its impact have shaped the direction of public policy. She reviews the history of women's education in the West, the demographic and economic patterns that shaped the outcomes of women's increasing educational access, and the ways in which this Western context differs from the current setting for many Third World educational systems.

The essays by Schultz and Conway emphasize the need for methodologies that truly record women's experience and assess their contributions accurately. Both authors note the tendency of scholars, whether historians, social scientists, or economists, to base their analyses on presumed relationships, often steeped in gender stereotypes. The cost of such assumptions has often been misguided policies. Both authors urge us to adopt a broader vision of education and recognize that its benefits may be demonstrated by a variety of measures not necessarily captured in the standard historical paradigms or economic accounting methods.

Despite the magnitude of the challenge and the distance between today's reality and the world envisioned by educational and feminist reformers, these remain hopeful essays. The sense of hope comes from a much more thorough understanding of the nature of the obstacles that must be overcome and a deep belief in the importance of the task. The studies, assessments, and reflection in this volume point out the critical importance of women's education, whether in a formal or nonformal system. The authors' voices make an eloquent statement about the positive benefits for individual women, families, and society, while cautioning us to recognize the mistaken assumptions that have produced misguided policies in the past.

Part 1
Asia

A Survey of Gender Issues and Educational Development in Asia

VINA MAZUMDAR

Until very recently women's movements all over the world have given primacy to education as the means for achieving equality. But hopes for equality have always been focused on women's access to education. Even in international feminist thought access has been seen as the key to improving women's situations. In developing countries women have been concerned with their relative lack of access to one of the principal engines of development, while in the developed world feminists worried about the underrepresentation or absence of women in the high-status areas of learning, especially science and technology.

In the Third World two main schools of thought about improving women's status have governed past attitudes toward education. The first assumes that access to scientific and technological education will integrate women into the process of development. The second argues for the inclusion of women in the development process through their participation as educated decision makers, teachers, planners, and administrators. Some adherents of this second school even argue for encouraging women to enter "nontraditional" fields such as agriculture, forestry, and environmental sciences, not recognizing that agriculture, forestry, and animal husbandry have long been women's most traditional spheres of activity in many parts of the world.

The failure to recognize women's past or present economic role in developing societies has only very recently been remedied. It is instructive to examine the reasons why development planners everywhere have been so slow to recognize women's real economic contributions.

Most non-Western students of development today agree that

Western-style educational programs have been one of the principal culprits in making women's work and aspirations invisible to educated people. Therefore, the critical issues for any analysis of the relation between women's status and their participation in the educational system is that of educational content, values, and structures, rather than access.

In Asia the existing educational infrastructure represents a compromise between indigenous social systems and the cultural pressures emanating from the encounter with the Western world. The shape of the compromise has been molded by the forces of worldwide industrialization and the associated Western science and technology; population growth; colonialism and the rise of anti-imperialist movements. These popular agitations have covered the spectrum from liberal democratic through secular nationalism to international socialism and, more recently, religious revivalist conservatism. Moreover, many choices affecting the pace and direction of educational change have been dictated by the acceptance of the goal of rapid economic growth and the problems of allocating scarce national resources in cases where economic growth was seen as competing with education. In order to compromise on educational aspirations, realistic analysis of gender roles was never undertaken in Asia, even as inherited gender patterns were being called into question by economic and political transformation and by the importation of Western structures of knowledge.

Most Asian political elites, after encountering Western imperialism, have accepted the ideal of gender equality, but the principle has been hard to square with the traditional value systems and social organizations on which Western imperialism was superimposed. Most Asian societies share common traditional patterns, while exhibiting major cultural differences. In all of them women have played a major role in agriculture and in all aspects of the rural economy. Social stratification along patriarchal lines was deeply entrenched among elites, and religious ideologies (Hindu, Buddhist, Confucian, Islamic, or Christian) imposed strict controls on women, thereby strengthening patriarchal authority.

In Southeast Asia, and in some tribal communities on the Indian subcontinent, women have been subjected to fewer restrictions. Their relative freedom has been the result of the major role they have played in the economic support of their families and associated patterns of kinship and marriage customs. The degree of women's freedom has also been related to traditions of community control over land and other basic resources. Where women had traditional rights to the use of communal land, their status was enhanced, while, wherever private land ownership was well established, patriarchal control of women was equally entrenched.

Southern and Southeast Asian societies experienced Western cultural imperialism not merely during the colonial era but also in the process of developing their educational systems during the postcolonial period. The development of educational systems were shaped by the models of educational transformation and the growth strategies adopted by individual countries. Regardless of whether socialism or a free-market economy was the preferred model, education was seen primarily as a vehicle of socioeconomic mobility for individuals and families, rather than as a means of developing new values or achieving social liberation.

As in the case of Japan and China (with the exception of a brief period of cultural revolution in the latter), educational systems have preserved rather than challenged the existing social hierarchies. The gender norms conveyed through formal schooling reflect the traditional beliefs of elites rather than the life experiences of the majority of women.

Another factor shaping educational policy has been the constraint of limited resources. With the exception of Malaysia, educational expenditures have declined as a percentage of gross national product (GNP) in all southern Asian countries over recent years. As resources have contracted, demand for scientific and technical manpower and expanded higher education has grown. Thus, higher education, the entry point for elites, has expanded, while the majority of women, who must enter the system at earlier stages, have remained excluded.

Western modernization as imported into Asian societies did not carry within it any concept of gender equality. The traditional roles of women had been undermined in the West by the agrarian and industrial revolutions, and European women had lost their right to serve as professionals during the sixteenth and seventeenth centuries. Western-style texts held up the Victorian wife/mother role of service as the ideal in southern and Southeast Asia. As the educational system expanded, this model reached rural and working-class groups in which women's labor was of critical economic significance. Thus, Western-style education could not serve as a vehicle for economic, social, or political development but, rather, taught rural and lower-class men and women to reject manual labor and traditional crafts and to disregard the value of agriculture. Since Western texts taught about a Western-style division of labor in which women were dependent and subordinate, access to education did not encourage gender equality.

In Pakistan, for instance, forty years of planned development has had little impact on the status of women. A recent government commission described the mass of Pakistani women bluntly as "dehumanised possessions with little control over their lives . . . dispossessed and disinherited in spite of legal safeguards, overworked and unrewarded." Pakistani scholars see the colonial education system as one "designed to produce a pool of competent clerks and administrators who were adequately acculturated and suitably impressed by Empire . . . to oppose indigenous educational systems and thus . . . diametrically opposed to the values of society."[1]

The current two-tiered system of Pakistan, stratified by language (English vs. vernacular) and by content (modernity vs. traditionality), is an outgrowth of this colonial experience. Not only have the two systems served to broaden social divisions; they have also reduced education to a certification process that does not require training in understanding one's own environment, a process that cannot convey the informed ability to act.

For rural women, in particular, the curriculum inherited from the colonial period—which fails to address agriculture, health care, sanitation, and political rights—makes schools seem unattractive and their teachings useless for daily life. For poor women in urban settings the absence of any self-employment training in formal education prevents women from developing the economic base that they need to escape from dependence. Hence, the formal system fails to attract or retain large numbers of female students, and the literacy rate for women in Pakistan hovers around 16 percent.

Any serious study of women's access to education in southern and Southeast Asia raises basic questions about the role of education in bringing about the transformation of value systems necessary to achieve a more just society. These questions concern not only women but the entire society. Alongside women's inequality is the differential between rural and urban access to resources and the congruence between social and occupational hierarchies. At present the educational system reinforces existing hierarchies and concentrates on the transmission of salable skills, since a broader education that raised questions of value could destabilize the social and political system.

Across many parts of southern and southeast Asia nation builders have relied upon fostering religious solidarity and stimulating economic growth as dual means of building strong nation-states. Thus, the forging of national identity rests upon mobilizing fundamentalist forces, with which women themselves are deeply involved. Thus, the symbolism of the return to the Islamic veil means *both* a rejection of Westernization and a recognition of women as a group capable of organizing politically. Many Western commentators fail to understand that, along with fundamentalist Islamic views of women or other antimodern efforts to return to traditional culture goes a romanticized view of that traditional culture often quite divorced from historical reality. When played off against the negative consequences of Western-style development, however, such romantic images have powerful appeal. It is easy to look to an idealized past to redress problems such as the vast deforestation produced by the lumber industry or the increased agricultural burden placed on women because of male migration to urban centers and to offer one simple method of opposing misguided development.

In India the major response to Western-style development shown by rural women has been organized opposition to strategies that undermine the rural environment. Women's groups have opposed large-scale deforestation and have criticized the introduction of new plants, such as the eucalyptus tree, beloved of the World Bank. Eucalyptus trees do not meet rural women's need for fuel, fodder, and food, and the species has a negative impact by drawing off too much moisture and destroying soil nutrients. Women have also opposed the introduction of many new crop varieties that require excessive use of chemical fertilizers and pesticides because these too damage the soil and poison the groundwater on which rural people must rely.

Women's groups have thus urged a reversal of the accepted style of learning, calling for less-educated (often illiterate) rural women to teach the rest of society about their inherited traditions for preserving the environment. Systematic efforts to transmit their traditional knowledge might, it is argued, produce the change of values needed to make education something more than the transmission of skills prized by an external market.

Certainly, Indian women have responded to the degradation of the environment by calling for radical new curricular materials for the national educational system and for the West as well. These must teach the history of peasant women's contribution to agriculture, to textile production and pottery, and to the beginnings of productive activity in the Indian subcontinent. For we do not need new agencies to educate rural women. We need education to convey a new perspective, not just in India but all over the world.

While Indian women's groups vary in their emphasis, all strands of opinion draw their inspiration from women's struggles at the grass roots. Some reformers are so disillusioned with the present role of education that they see formal education as valueless unless it is transformed by a new philosophy and vision. Others assert the feasibility of transforming the formal system by progressively changing its methodology. Such reformers see the illusion of value neutrality in educational institutions, imported from the West after World War II, as masking the role of existing educational institutions as mere skill conveyers serving the goals of existing exploitative power structures. Proponents of transformation of such a system believe that change could nonetheless be brought about if the value orientation of education were clearly acknowledged, curricula and pedagogy reformed, and teachers encouraged to serve as involved agents of social change. Reorientation of content and methods of instruction would not, in this view, mean abandoning academic objectivity and scientific rationality but, rather, merely rethinking the social goals that such intellectual skills would serve.

This critique of existing educational structures has a unique form in India, but its main theme, the inadequacy of curriculum and pedagogy in formal education, is characteristic of the international women's movement throughout the Third World. Much of this critique applies also to the formal system in the West, wherever it must come to terms with the needs of the poor and the dispossessed. Modern educational reform will owe a great deal to the international women's movement for focusing attention on this central problem of educational systems.

When all these points have been made, however, the fact remains that exclusion from the educational process, however defective the current one may be, is one of the major causes for women's inequality and lack of power. Women share this inequality and exclusion from education with some other segments of the population, and they will not escape from this socially created inequality until they have access to meaningful and effective institutions that promote equality and democratic values and that embody respect for human dignity in their daily operations.

Defective as they were, it was colonial educational institutions that paved the way for nationalist movements and provided leaders of the struggle for freedom from colonial rule with the captive audiences that enabled them to recruit and train their "freedom fighters." The very success of these nationalist revolutions has created a requirement to romanticize the "oriental" past and to do so in ways that will enhance the power of existing national elites. Women's education is caught between these conflicting pressures: on the one hand, nationalist leaders campaigned to promote the education of women, but, on the other, the patriarchal values of existing elites undermined any real commitment to changing gender roles or expanding women's opportunities.

Today we see a battle of ideologies occurring in which conflicting definitions of gender identities for women and men play a large part. Whether individuals are to remain confined to a narrow identity defined by religion, language, inherited culture, and redefined ethnicity or instead to acquire a broader identity reflecting their life experiences and expanding horizons is the issue. Women play a crucial role in this struggle for political identity, symbolizing as they do the confrontation between human and group rights, gender versus sectional justice, and universal versus culture-bound perspectives.

In this time of reassessment of education and development the international framework of scholarship generated by the women's movement has played a major role in redefining issues and bringing women together in search of a new model of education and development for the future. And, with all their limitations, Asian educational systems have prepared women to contribute on equal terms in this global debate. The cooperative spirit encouraged by this, the United Nations Decade for Women, has made it clear that creating new educational systems and development goals cannot succeed in a single country or even a single region and that there is a global community of scholars and educators whose work collectively shows the path toward creative change.

NOTE

1. Khawar Mumtaz and Farida Shaheed, Women's Action Forum, "Women's Education in Pakistan: Opportunities, Issues and Challenges" (Paper presented at the International Conference on Worldwide Education for Women, Mount Holyoke College, South Hadley, Mass., November 1987).

Women's Education in India
NEERA DESAI

Since the nineteenth century, when the first voice was raised against the inferior status of women in Indian society, social reformers have given high priority to providing girls with access to education. At that time many people thought that to educate a woman was "to put a knife in her hands," that a girl with education was destined to widowhood. In this atmosphere of ardent opposition social reformers made a fervent plea for girls' education. Although these liberal reformers recognized the value of women's education, their major concern was the gigantic task of modernizing the tradition-bound Indian social structure; it was hoped that educated women would work in complementary ways with their partners in ushering in the new society.[1] Modern educated women were to play new roles but to do so in ways that did not disturb the accepted division of labor in the home. Thus, while reformers advocated educating girls, they thought in terms of providing a grade school–level education— nothing more. They did not envisage women's education as an equal right of an equal citizen. There was no suggestion of any change in the traditional role of the woman as wife and mother. On the contrary, the reformers expected education to make women better at fulfilling those roles. Nor did the reformers visualize that women would participate in outside employment or welfare activities.

These early reformers generated a social climate in which girls' education was accepted. This contribution was very important, particularly in light of the attitude of the British rulers, who were not opposed to women's education so much as apathetic about it. Thus, the social reform movement created an atmosphere favoring women's education, yet its appeal was restricted to a few progressive regions and upper-caste groups.

Women took an active part in the mass movements associated with nationalism, particularly after the 1930s. Many women, especially those from the upper castes and upper-class urban centers, built up women's organizations that constantly emphasized the need for women's education.[2] Even though there was no fundamental change in the view of the woman's role, many women who took part came to realize that education is an asset for participating in larger political activities. In the 1930s and 1940s more women entered higher education, and quite a few took to professions such as teaching, medicine, and law.

Nonetheless, the growth of women's education affected only a small elite. In 1947, on the eve of independence, only about 8 percent of women were literate, 25 percent of the relevant age groups were in elementary classes, and barely 5 percent were in middle school. Higher-education classes contained a meager 18,675 women, about 10 percent of total enrollment.

With independence came a new chapter in the aims, though not the achievements, of women's education. The new Indian nation—full of optimism and dedicated to democratic goals—declared that women were to have equal rights of access and opportunity in education, but any account of women's education in India over the last four decades shows how inflated those aims were in light of the record of four decades of missed opportunities and lost ground.

A recent plan for Indian education states categorically that, without adequate measures for the spread of education, "the chasm of economic disabilities, regional imbalances and social injustices will widen further, resulting in the building of disintegrative tensions . . . . Human resource development has a multiplier effect on the utilization of all other resources."[3] The document reiterates the role of education as an investment in development and considers it to be the only instrument of peaceful social change. It recognizes the need for a serious, concerted commitment to increasing the spread of education in the population in general, and among women in particular. To state these policy goals is easy, but their actual implementation must be understood within their Indian context.

What Do We Mean by Equality of Education?

In a developing country such as India the obvious inequality of women and men is part of a more pervasive inequality among various sections of the population. In societies with age-old distinctions of caste and estate, in which privilege and discrimination are entrenched through custom and usage, the constitutional assertion of equality carries the promise of new life. But in developing societies the task of redressing inequality is enormous, and the job of establishing gender equality is formidable.

In developing countries equality is a long-term goal advanced upon wherever people are enfranchised but always rendered a distant goal because of shortage of resources and persistent cultural patterns. In education progress is assessed in terms of increases in access. How many more women have access to schooling today compared with yesterday? Are the attitudes that devalue a daughter's education vis-à-vis her brothers any less prevalent? Unfortunately, the answers to such questions show us that patriarchy is entrenched in India and that girls continue to be disadvantaged compared to boys.

In a developing society formal education becomes a fundamental prerequisite for improving one's status. (And, as we shall see, certain types of education are more "status giving" than others.) Better skills, a wider range of information, and more knowledge are essential for administering programs and agencies, improving productivity, and taking part in a modern democracy. If a part of society is denied access to knowledge or skills, the group that is deprived will not only fail to be part of the development process but also may eventually become a victim of development. The denial of access to education is the denial of access to status and power. This has been the history of modern education for large segments of India's female population.

Even though, on paper, formal equality has been legislated, there are many groups of women who are denied access to education. Thousands of tribal or scheduled caste girls are unable to attend school because their families depend upon them to work at home (caring for siblings or fetching water and fuel). And not all parents are willing to accept the importance of education for their daughters. One mother, a member of an untouchable caste, when asked why she did not send her girl to school, replied: "Why should I waste my time and money on sending my daughter to school where she will learn nothing of use? What does the Hindi alphabet mean to her? Too much of schooling will only give girls big ideas and then they will be beaten up by their husbands or abused by their in-laws."[4]

Over time these attitudes change little because too often the outcomes of access can be disappointing. Women who take advantage of increased educational opportunities are often met with and accept very modest career rewards. In spite of solid training in the sciences or engineering, and in spite of opportunities to work in prestigious research organizations, many women play their traditional roles alongside their occupational roles because only then are they assured of their family's cooperation and their husband's support; their career becomes more an extension of responsibility than a shift.[5] Thus, to talk about equality in women's education we must see the realities of the existing cultural context.

Research by the Committee on the Status of Women in India (CSWI) documents that institutional and cultural context. Indian women continue to be the victims of a process of marginalization—economic, social, political, and intellectual—a process that has accelerated during the postindependence period. Gender bias persists, strengthened by the operation of development policies that result in the intensified subordination of women. Development policies relying largely on technological advances have resulted in the displacement of female labor in several industries. Technology simultaneously alters forms of production from precapitalistic modes, or from small to large scale. In the cotton hand looms and woolen cottage industry and in hand block printing, for instance, there has been mass displacement of women. The tobacco units, which employ over 90 percent female labor, are responding to the collective struggle of women in the Karnataka border against the threat of mechanization.[6]

Technology today is a most crucial resource for development. Apart from displacement, access to new technology is also an important issue. Throughout the regions of agricultural modernization, until recently, women were never enrolled for training or extension or service programs, even though they are the major partners in agricultural production.

So far education per se has not generated social change. The phenomenon of the dowry, for instance, is not only not absent from the educated sections of society but is actually widely prevalent among them. The dowry system, which is a very complex institution, taking numerous forms, by and large indicates the unidirectional flow of cash, goods, and service from the bride's kin to the groom's. Modern dowry, as M. N. Srinivas observes, "presupposes a high degree of monetization in the community, increased agricultural and general prosperity and access to the organized sector."[7] Dowry has been associated with improving the social status of a family or a group. The spread of this system after independence has been an enigma to social scientists.

It was believed that, with education, the bridegrooms would not ask for dowry because it suggests the commodification of relationships. With the growing consumerism in India, however, the menace of the dowry system has not lessened but, rather, has grown both in size and extent. The more educated a bridegroom, the higher is the price to be paid to acquire him.[8]

In sum, although the goal of equality has been formally accepted in the Constitution, there are many cultural and economic obstacles to realizing this goal. The promulgation of a right does not ensure its existence. The attitudes, values, and institutions of Indian society must change in profound ways before these formal rights will have concrete social expression.

Government Policies and Action to Promote Women's Education, 1947–85

Over the years since independence the Indian government has warmly endorsed the need for improving women's access to education, an endorsement never forthcoming from the British. The government's ability to translate policy into effective action, however, has been slight. This problem has been compounded by ambiguity about the real goals of women's education.

In 1948, soon after independence, the University Education Commission, headed by S. Radhakrishnan, was established. The commission maintained that "a well-ordered home helps to make well-ordered men": "The mother who is enquiring and alert and familiar with subjects such as history and literature will be the best teacher in the world of both character and intelligence."[9] The commission further stressed that the greatest profession of women is—and will probably continue to be—that of wife and mother, thus expressing views very similar to those of nineteenth-century educational reformers.

A major step was taken in 1958, when the National Council for Women's Education concerned with primary and secondary education, was set up under the chairmanship of Ms. Durgabai Deshmukh. The National Council's main objective was to inquire into issues such as low enrollment, the dropout rate, and vocational learning. Although the council seemed to favor the prevailing view—that a woman's place is in the home—it could not ignore the country's growing need for women to perform multiple roles. Consequently, the council asserted, without any power to implement its proposals, that men should join the women in doing work within the home.[10]

The council strongly recommended that women's education should be regarded as a major and special problem for the immediate future, especially to close the gap in education between men and women. Differences in curricula for boys and girls were also the subject of debate. A committee appointed to study this issue in 1962 asserted unequivocally that the home responsibilities of girls could not be used as criteria to divide subjects on the basis of sex. The committee felt that such stereotypes did more harm than good and made the important point that the so-called psychological differences between the sexes arise not out of sex but out of social conditioning.[11] Nevertheless, over the next few years women's education did not advance substantially. In 1961 only about 13 percent of the female population was literate, while 35 percent of males could read and write. Similarly, little progress was seen in primary education; only 42 percent of girls attended primary school, and only 11 percent of girls in the relevant age group made it to middle school. Alarmed at these sorry figures, the government appointed another committee in 1964 to examine the reasons for women's low participation.

In 1964 the Indian Education Commission (known as the Kothar commission) recommended a series of steps for improving women's education: efforts should be made to overcome difficulties in providing education to women; the funds required to close the gap between men's and women's education should be provided on a priority basis; and in both the nation's center and the states special government machinery should be set up to improve the education of girls and women, bringing together officials and laypersons in planning and implementing programs.[12]

Nonetheless, the commission exhibited an unstated ambivalence toward the role of education in the lives of girls. As Malvika Karlekar remarked: "While their schooling was to be expanded, it was not clear whether this was for the individual benefit of the recipients themselves, or because they were to be responsible for full development of our human resources, the improvement of homes, and so on. At the same time, the Commission accepted women's right to work outside home, adding that there was no case for a differentiation of curricula."[13]

In 1974 the Commission on the Status of Women in India exposed the urban and middle-class bias of educational planners and bureaucrats with regard to women's roles, needs, and priorities. It also attacked the continued differentiation of curricula, the neglect of the widening gender gap, and the educational reinforcement of "traditional" sex stereotypes that reflected middle-class values.

The Ministry of Education's recent document, "Challenge to Education," has been the culmination of various official efforts at promoting women's education. After candidly appraising the situation the ministry lays the blame for slow growth on family attitudes. The report states: "As far as the participation of girls in education is concerned, it is clear that despite considerable acceleration in recent years because of deliberate measures to facilitate their participation, they are still way behind the boys. To a great extent this disparity is more the result of economic and occupational problems and cultural biases of society than the accessibility of educational facilities."[14]

Thus, government officials have absolved themselves of the responsibility for the dismal situation. In its action program, too, the ministry offered more in the way of platitudes than concrete steps for the advancement of women's education. Though the report mentions creating support services to relieve young girls of their household responsibilities, the means for funding and administering such programs are not discussed. In the absence of specific measures and strategies for implementation, the programs, like earlier policy measures, will remain mere promises.

The Status of Women's Education at Various Levels

Because of ambiguity about the goals of women's education and the inadequacy of resources in government efforts to foster women's participation, their absolute progress has been limited, and growth at different levels and in different regions has been uneven.

At independence the government aimed to provide free and compulsory education for children up to fourteen years of age by 1962. That goal is still unattained, and, more significantly, the actual number of illiterate females has increased: from 162 million in 1951 to 215 million in 1971 and 241.6 million in 1981. The march of literacy has failed to keep pace with the growth of the population, and women have been particularly disadvantaged.

In 1981 over 45 percent of girls aged six to eleven, 75 percent of the twelve-to-fourteen age group, and over 85 percent of the fifteen-to-seventeen age group were out of school. For boys the figures were 20 percent, 57 percent, and 71 percent, respectively. The main failure in progress toward universal education has been the problem of girls' enrollment.[15] Regional imbalances compound the problems. In Kerala, a state renowned for its progressive social programs, female literacy is as high as 73 percent, whereas in Rajasthan fewer than 12 percent of women are literate. This imbalance is further accentuated by the rural-versus-urban situation. According to the 1981 census, female literacy in rural areas was 17.96 percent, as opposed to 42.82 percent in urban areas.

Can we reduce this gap in the near future? It appears that, unless more drastic steps are taken to enroll and retain girls in school (including providing support services), the gap will remain and probably widen.

Further, it has not been possible to evaluate the social returns in terms of health, sanitation, or fertility that come with three or four years of schooling. In fact, many times, steps must be taken to prevent girls with only three or four years of schooling from lapsing back into illiteracy. Girls with marginal literacy may lose it through lack of use. Similarly, improving health and sanitation is not merely the results of schooling; along with an education, material conditions need to be favorable for students to apply what they have learned in school.

Table 1 illustrates the situation in primary and middle schools. In elementary, middle, and secondary education the enrollment of girls has increased, but the gap between boys and girls is widening. As the data show, over a period of two decades there has been virtually no improvement in the situation. Out of ten girls who join class 1, barely two reach class 8. The regional variations here are also striking: in some states, for instance, fewer than 30 percent of girls aged eleven to fourteen are enrolled.

The efforts of various commissions, committees, and researchers have pointed out that socioeconomic factors are responsible for the grave dropout rate. Poor families are very much dependent on the labor of children and women, and the return on education—a few years of learning—is believed to be low. Being in school means forgoing the opportunity to help in the home or to contribute to the family exchequer. The daughter of a female servant who wishes to improve her status through education will need a minimum of ten years' schooling. Waiting such a long period, with no income, is impossible for many families.

The lives of poor women are very closely linked with the forest. The collection of fuel and fodder has become the primary responsibility of poor women, and they are dependent upon raw materials

TABLE 1. Percentage of Enrollment, Comparison by Age Group

Year	Primary-Level Class 1–5			Middle-Level Class 6–8		
	Boys	Girls	Total	Boys	Girls	Total
1950–51	60.6	24.8	43.1	20.6	4.6	12.9
1960–61	82.6	41.4	62.4	33.2	11.3	22.5
1970–71	92.6	59.1	76.4	46.5	20.5	34.2
1975–76	95.7	62.9	79.3	47.9	23.3	35.6
1978–79	100.2	67.8	84.5	49.4	26.0	38.0
1979–80	100.2	65.9	83.6	52.0	27.7	48.2
1980–81	99.0	66.2	83.1	52.1	27.2	40.0
1984–85	100.1	81.5	95.2	63.1	36.8	50.3

Source: Ministry of Education, Draft 6th Five Year Plan, 1980–85

for carrying out their economic activities. Deforestation, however, has adversely affected women. They have to travel long distances to collect the fuel, food, and raw materials they need to live.

Privatization of common property resources has also led to an inequitable distribution. In this context the government has been rebuilding forest resources, described as social forestry programs. These activities have been launched to promote afforestation on nonforest lands, private farms, and village common and government revenue lands.[16]

In rural areas most girls are married by age fourteen or fifteen. Furthermore, most rural girls find their mobility curtailed when they attain puberty. For parents, the readiness to send girls to school depends upon whether certain facilities—such as single-sex schools or those with female teachers or good transportation—are available. Moreover, early marriage limits girls' access, no matter what services are supplied. The new education policy recommends the provision of support services, free midday meals, drinking water facilities, and social forestry programs; it is hoped that these services will relieve girls of the burden of daily chores and leave them free to attend school.

Sexist bias also operates in denying certain vocational courses or work experience to girls. Vocational institutions continue to teach girls tailoring, dressmaking, and secretarial skills, but many schools do not teach girls science, let alone agricultural science, encouraging them to study "domestic science" instead.

Women in Higher Education

Because higher education is the province of the urban middle class, the picture of women's participation in it is very different than for vocational schools. Although only 4.8 percent of the relevant age group is enrolled in college, the progress of women in the postindependence era is striking.

In 1950–51 women constituted over 10 percent of the total college-level enrollment; by 1984–85 that figure had risen to 38 percent. Interestingly, the ratio of women to men is higher at the postgraduate level than at the undergraduate level. And a cursory look at the enrollment in various disciplines points out that there are certain clusters in which women are more visible. As table 2 indicates, a large majority of women take education, liberal arts, and science courses. One marked change over the ten-year period is the increase in the number of women studying commerce, an indication that many of them aspire to work in the service sector.

A more alarming change is the decline in the enrollment of women in medicine. One hypothesis holds that the rise in the number of private medical colleges has meant a rise in fees and an escalation of dowry. Parents are reluctant to spend money on both education and dowry; consequently, quite a few women are discouraged from studying medicine.

M. S. Gore, while discussing social equality, mentions that when resources are limited families must often choose which of its members should be educated. Professional education is quite expensive, and this problem is uppermost. Further, there is a dilemma about whom the additional expenditure benefits, apart from the daughter herself. The parents see a daughter's education as a potential benefit—to the daughter's husband's family.[17]

Among highly educated working women the persistent priority given to family responsibility is indicated by the nature of the work they perform. Many times, as in the West, the major criteria for selecting one job over another are the regularity of hours, flexibility of attendance, and the ability to take one's own leave during the children's school holidays. In short, there has been constant emphasis on the primacy of the family in a woman's life. Thus, female doctors often prefer to work in hospitals with fixed hours or to specialize in anesthetics or pathology, disciplines with

TABLE 2. Distribution of Female Enrollment Faculty by Percentage of the Total

	1975–76	1980–81	1985–86	1986–87
Arts	36.4	37.7	40.4	41.6
Science	24.1	28.8	30.5	31.4
Commerce	6.6	15.9	19.1	19.7
Education	39.3	47.3	49.0	50.5
Engineering/Technology	2.1	3.8	5.9	6.0
Medicine	18.3	24.4	29.5	30.4
Agriculture	1.4	3.3	4.3	4.5
Veterinary Science	1.4	3.3	4.9	5.1
Law	5.0	6.9	8.1	8.3
Others	36.1	39.8	39.5	40.7
Total	24.5	27.2	29.6	30.6

Source: University Grants Commission Report for the year 1986–87, app., 30.

less erratic hours than most. Similarly, a recent study of female scientists and engineers pointed out that within the leading research institution more women are in administrative jobs.

Another important dimension of higher education for Indian women is that ordinarily it behooves a woman to be less well educated, in a position of less power, than her mate. Tensions are avoided if a successful woman is able to marry a man with a profession different from her own, thus allowing a certain ambiguity to obscure relative status.[18]

In short, it is true that, relatively speaking, more urban women today are entering the portals of learning. They are taking part in new disciplines, and they are taking jobs in prestigious institutions. Nonetheless, the basic traditional role definitions continue to determine a woman's priorities and aspirations, a factor that has implications for their attaining positions of more power or higher status.

Alternatives to the Formal System of Education

In the developing world the role of formal education as an agent of democracy and a means for upward mobility has been seriously questioned in recent decades. Because the Indian education system has been, by and large, a continuation of the one established in colonial times to suit the needs of the colonial rulers, there have been many critics of its usefulness or relevance to Indian life. The existing system serves the interests of the upper and middle classes of urban areas, who use education to achieve status and power, as a mechanism for upward social mobility, and as a means for maintaining the status quo. In terms of accessibility and content the formal system has discriminated against the rural masses and against women.

A noteworthy experiment has recently been launched: an open university. Of course, as early as 1916, Shreemati Nathibai Damodar Thackersey Women's University (SNDT) had embarked on a program to make education easier for women who could not attend classes. Today this scheme has been organized in a wider and more systematic fashion. Correspondence programs provide materials for learning, and contact with teachers is arranged. For working women or women with family responsibilities this kind of facility is a great boon.

Realizing the inadequacy of the formal educational system vis-à-vis most of the poor people in such a vast country, the Indian government has made efforts to compensate. These efforts have included adult education, social education, and continuing education programs. And since 1975 more serious attention has been given to nonformal education for women. The University Grants Commission has taken this mode of delivery seriously, and universities are encouraged to organize nonformal education centers.

But it is now clear that, for those women who live in poverty, deprivation, and powerlessness, the only effective educational strategy is to bring these women together around common issues and concerns. Dialogue and discussion are the tools needed to raise their critical consciousnesses. Existing programs do not teach women how to understand and analyze the social, political, and economic systems that govern their lives and oppress them. Nor will awareness come from merely learning the "Three Rs"—reading, writing, and arithmetic—or from being drilled in nutrition, health, and family planning. If women are to participate in India's development, the education offered to them must equip them for the task, a task that, nevertheless, must be defined on their terms. The task for women today is to evaluate critically the nation's developmental strategy. Education ought to develop the student's faculty for raising relevant questions, debating, and discussing the efficiency of the programs. Women are not merely passive recipients of a welfare package but also active participants in development. If this goal has to be achieved, it is necessary that the poor, who are targets of nonformal education, must also be equipped with the critical skills for evaluating the programs. This is empowering women for development.

The most recent documents on the new Program of Non-Formal Education (NFE) advocate popular education that is comparable in quality to that provided by formal schooling. This equality is essential; one major limitation of NFE programs is that the formal system is considered to be status giving and elitist, while the nonformal system conveys no status. Some form of evaluation and accreditation is necessary so that the formal and nonformal systems are seen as equivalent.[19] The new program also makes provisions for a new approach to learning, building up programs in which students can learn at their own pace, adding more audiovisual facilities, and encouraging participatory learning environments.

Besides the NFE programs there are activities being run by grass roots organizations that are especially concerned with developing alternative educational systems. Some of the mainstream women's organizations, while running skills and training programs for income-generating activities, simultaneously give courses designed to generate awareness about how development in India will affect women. Similarly, there are health groups, media groups, and legal literacy groups, sensitive to women's needs, that prepare kits to be used in nonformal courses. The nonformal courses are based on slides, film strips, picture booklets, posters, and songs to make the learning process informative and interesting—and, in fact, some of these materials have worked so well that they are now being used in formal education.

An extensive study in a backward part of Andrha Pradesh indicated that an integrated program of education with basic maternal and child health services resulted in a high degree of awareness and receptiveness toward modern health practices. Follow-up studies on programs for pregnant women and new mothers showed that knowledge of nutrition, health, and general development had increased considerably. Similarly, organizers of income-generating schemes for rural women in Punjab reported that some familiarity with numbers helps in simple cost accounting exercises. Education has helped self-employed women to deal with exploitative brokers and deceptive family members.[20] Moreover, their motivation for learning is great when the curriculum is linked to real-life situations that such women encounter daily.

Yet a major criticism of the adult education programs is that their curriculum reflects a middle-class worldview, and course materials rarely take into account the vital role of women in production. Many programs stress the position of women as homemakers, providing training in conventional areas that is irrelevant for the mass of women. Most women who must earn a living need information on alternative channels of employment and awareness of their rights as workers.

Reinforcement of Gender Inequality

In the process of disseminating knowledge there are various overt and covert means by which inequality can be perpetuated. In a poor country such as India many decisions are taken on the basis of cost-effectiveness rather than ideology. The establishment of coeducational institutions, for example—particularly at the primary or middle school level—is done more for the sake of economy than equality. In many rural areas the government simply does not have the funds for separate schools; consequently, most government schools are coeducational. In urban areas where separate schools exist coeducation is still preferred by most students; although, for learning vocational skills, women's polytechnics and women's industrial training institutions (ITIs) have been established.

Although these separate girls' and women's schools are equal in theory, in practice they are not up to the standard of the boys' schools. Separate curricula for boys and girls are not strongly advocated, yet in practice there is unequal exposure to knowledge and skills development. Vocational options clearly indicate, for instance, that girls flock to courses in typing, embroidery, health care, nutrition, and beauty culture; boys concentrate on auditing, accounting, machine repair, carpentry, and electronics. Many review committees have found the polytechnics and ITIs ill equipped, lacking in some cases the minimum of facilities for teaching vocation-oriented courses.[21]

Another means to inequality is sex stereotyping through textbooks. As Narendra Nath Kalia observed:

> Almost 20 years ago India's official educators promised to deliver a curriculum that would recognize and nurture the fundamental equality between men and women. The Indian Government agreed to rewrite the textbooks of independent India to prepare its young for an era of equality by inspiring each sex to develop a proper respect toward the other. . . . Indian school textbooks have continued to exude sexist bias.[22]

In his study Kalia found that not only were the majority of characters in the textbooks male but also that, in 75 percent of lessons, men emerge as dominant figures. Similarly, as Karlakar reported, a National Council of Educational Research and Training (NCERT)–sponsored study of Hindi textbooks that are widely used in the country found that the ratio of boy-centered to girl-centered stories was 21:0. Ninety-four out of 110 biographical references relate to prominent men.[23] Boys were portrayed as courageous achievers, interested in science and technology; girls and women were rarely portrayed in roles associated with economic activity or independence.

This kind of sex bias is not restricted to formal schooling but extends to the nonformal textbooks as well. Kamala Bhasin, who has been involved in an analysis of materials used in adult education programs, reviewed seven literacy primers used in north India; the main subject matter of the books proved to be housework, child care, and family planning. No lesson referred to the role of women in agriculture. Bhasin adds:

> Besides questioning dowries, frequent pregnancies and one or two other social evils, these primers question nothing else. . . . The qualities being prescribed are the age-old ones of sacrifice, self-abnegation, living for others, docility, love, softness.[24]

In 1985 the National Seminar on Education for Women's Equality recommended that "all textbooks, both by NCERT and other publishers, need to be reviewed for the elimination of gender bias and also for proper incorporation of women's perspective."[25] The suggestion has been accepted by the government of India in its Programme of Action for Education.[26] The effort at eliminating sexism does not end with providing bias-free books; the promoters must also provide training to teachers, who are likely themselves to be biased.

Women's Studies at the University

One essential for developing better curricular materials is vigorous research on the actual lives of Indian women. During the past decade female academics have become increasingly involved in research on women's issues from a feminist perspective. In 1975 the Committee on the Status of Women in India brought out very disturbing findings: a declining male/female ratio; a startling number of illiterate women; and declining political and economic participation on the part of women.[27] These and other such facts cast doubt on the meaning, in real terms, of constitutional equality for women. In 1986 the Indian Council of Social Science Research (ICSSR) initiated a sponsored program of research on women to encourage policy analysis in different sectors of development. This program launched a period of further research that has contributed substantially to our stock of knowledge, particularly as many of the studies focused on the hitherto neglected nonelite women.[28]

Apart from increasing awareness of women's marginal place in Indian society, this research has raised some basic questions regarding the organization, content, and results of higher education. Why have expanding educational opportunities made so small a dent in changing sex stereotypes? Why have women's issues so far remained invisible from research and teaching? Why are social scientists not looking at their disciplines from the women's perspective as well as the men's?

Recognizing the validity and significance of these challenges for academic and social development, the University Grants Commission has initiated several programs to incorporate women's studies into higher education. It is slowly being realized that the introduction of women's studies to the curricula of different disciplines will fulfill both academic and social goals.

This "top-down" approach has resulted in the establishment of women's centers in a dozen universities, and efforts are underway to restructure curricula from this perspective. Summer/winter institutes for orienting teachers to this new point of view have also been organized. The Programme of Action document also includes plans to incorporate women's studies into policy measures, with regard to programs in teaching, research, training, and extension.[29]

Those who wish to make innovations in the university structure still face obstacles at every step, however, because of the rigidity of the system and the male-oriented atmosphere of educational institutions. This kind of obstacle is less prevalent in research on women because by and large such research is an individual activity.

Concluding Observations

Any assessment of the status of women's education has to start with an understanding of the socioeconomic framework, cultural norms, and value system that impinge upon and influence the role expectations and behavior of Indian women. Women's equal access to education, their retention in the system, their chance to enter more prestigious and status-giving disciplines, and the objectives of women's education are all linked to the development of the Indian economy and the values attached to the role and position of women in society. These economic and cultural factors, in turn, reflect inequalities of class as well as of gender. The problems of poverty and unemployment, the limited scope of women's career choices, and the persistence of the patriarchal value system seem to pose serious obstacles to equality of education for women.

The problem of access to education in a poverty-ridden society is not strictly a women's problem. But the problem is greatest for women. The efforts of the last four decades have not successfully expanded educational opportunities for girls and women. In a society that claims to be on the path to modernization, 75 percent of women do not know how to read and write. But, unless women are educated, how can they participate in decision making? How can women contribute to India's development if they have no relevant skills? How can they assess their situation if they have no information about the options available? We cannot boast of moving toward an egalitarian society if the vast majority of women lack even a rudimentary education.

Furthermore, until some means is found to alleviate the burden of household chores for young girls from poorer families, these girls will continue to be unable to attend school. These responsibilities are the chief reason that so many young girls receive no formal education.

Along with the problem of expanding women's education, an equally serious problem is how the policymakers and the community at large view the role of women in Indian society. The nineteenth-century social reformers who lobbied so vehemently for women's education aimed merely to make women better wives and mothers. We have not moved much beyond this concept.

In Indian society marriage is virtually obligatory for a woman.

As Srinivas has mentioned, "colleges and universities provide respectable waiting places for girls who wish to get married."[30] The Council for Scientific and Industrial Research provides interesting data on the marital status of postgraduate students; the figures suggest that for women in higher education—particularly those in sophisticated professional courses—earning a degree may mean postponing or forgoing marriage. For those with a master's degree the median age of men who marry is twenty-five, and for women twenty-three; at the doctoral level the median ages are twenty-six and twenty-five, respectively. Twenty-three or twenty-five may not appear old, but within the context of Indian society, in which most women are married by eighteen or twenty, a woman may lose her chance at marriage by pursuing higher education.[31]

What is more, Indian society allocates to women the burden of caring for home and family. Thus, women who work, or women who are dedicated to a career, must do double duty. In India the family is the social, economic, and moral basis of a person's identity; working women necessarily have strong familial values. Depending on the wishes of the family, a woman can be forced to enter the work force or to withdraw from it. There is no doubt that quite a few Indian women have attained positions of power and status, but studies of female executives have also highlighted the fact that the family usually comes first; the familial role has priority. Education is supposed to help modify role models and do away with sexual stereotypes, but thus far it has not done so.

A crucial issue in women's education is the society's image of an educated woman. Men and women who value the "traditional" image of women—obedient, docile, self-effacing—tend to look with suspicion on educated women, who they fear will be ambitious, abrasive, disobedient, and questioning. The media, particularly the cinema, help to sustain this suspicion by portraying educated women as bad and selfish, while the uneducated woman is represented as full of virtue. In poor families education takes children away from their responsibilities within the family. Many poor parents fear that education will keep a girl from doing menial jobs and, thus, keep her from being an asset to the family. It has been observed that the educated daughters of factory workers would prefer to be primary teachers than to continue their mothers' occupation.

Another problem for education, for both men and women, appears at the ideational level. Often an education may impart knowledge or values that it is impossible for a person to follow in private life. It was once believed that education would prove a panacea, that egalitarian virtues would be infused along with knowledge. But a review of the events of the last four decades proves that education alone cannot inculcate progressive values. A doctor can still demand a very high dowry; an engineer may harass his wife. And well-educated women continue to perform rituals or observe fasts for the welfare of husband and children. Thus, the dichotomy between public and private life continues.

As we observed earlier, women—despite advances in higher learning—are notably absent from those programs and professions that confer real status and power in India's modernizing society. In 1980–81 only 15 percent of girls were enrolled in professional and technical colleges. Similarly, under the craftsmen's training scheme of 1977 the total number of women enrolled in engineering was 399—versus 130,296 men: 0.3 percent. Yet in the nonengineering sections women made up 44 percent of the total enrollment. In the apprenticeship training scheme there were only 47 graduate women to 5,691 graduate men and 154 women diploma holders to 8,168 men who held diplomas.[32] Women thus lose out in the first round. Since they are not adequately qualified, their chances of entering status-lending employment are slim.

All these problems raise certain fundamental issues. In a society whose economy is based on profit making, in which 50 percent of the population lives below the poverty level, is "Universalization of Education" for girls practicable? Will the new educational policies of the government—a government that is hardly touching the economic structure—realize its objectives by the year 2000?

The history of India's women's movement has shown that, whenever there is a vitally pressing demand for reform, the results are more lasting. In amending the rape laws, in improving working conditions for women, in providing access to decision-making positions or banning harmful drugs, women's groups have had to assert their rights repeatedly. The "welfare model"— waiting for the good intentions of the policymakers to trickle down to the ordinary members of society—does not work. Women have had to campaign and organize constantly to win their needed reform. In short, Indian women have learned to adopt a "struggle model" for realizing their goals of gender justice.

Similarly, in the sphere of educational equality, to implement even the limited reforms envisaged by the government's New Education Policy, women will have to press constantly and to spread knowledge and information to the vast majority of Indian women who live in abysmal ignorance. A few experiments in alternative education systems, launched at the grass roots level, make us hopeful about the future. Ultimately, women's liberation is an act of women themselves.

NOTES

1. Refer to G. A. Natesen, ed., *Gopal Krishna Gokhale's Speeches*, 1987. D. K. Karve, *Looking Back: Hindu Women's Home Association*, Hingne Pune, 1936. Ramabai Ranade, *The Miscellaneous Writings of M. G. Ranade* (Poona, 1915).

2. Chattopadhyaya Kamladevi, *The Awakening of Indian Women* (Madras: Everyman's Press, 1939); also refer to *Inner Recesses and Outer Spaces* (New Delhi: Navrang, 1986). *Our Cause: A Symposium by Indian Women*, ed. Shyamkumari Nehru (Kitabistan, Allahabad, n.d.); Neera Desai, *Women in Modern India*, 2d ed. (Bombay: Vora and Company, 1977), 2.

3. Ministry of Education, Government of India, *Challenge of Education: A Policy Perspective*, New Delhi, 1985.

4. Malvika Karlekar, "Education," in *Women and Society in India*, ed. Neera Desai and Maithreyi Krishnaraj (New Delhi: Ajanta Publications, 1987), 163; also refer to Kaur Kuldip, *Education in India, 1781–1985: Policies, Planning and Implementation*, Centre for Research in Rural and Industrial Development (New Delhi: Ajanta Publications, 1985).

5. Maithreyi Krishnaraj, "Women, Work, and Science in India," in *Women's Education in the Third World: Comparative Perspectives*, ed. Gail P. Kelly and Carolyn M. Elliot (Albany: State University of New York Press, 1982), 257.

6. Krishnaraj, "Women, Work, and Science," 48–49.

7. M. N. Srinivas, "Some Reflections on Dowry," J. P. Naik Memorial Lecture (New Delhi: Oxford University Press, 1983), 10.

8. Karuna Channa, ed., *Socialisation, Education and Women* (New Delhi: Orient Longman Ltd., 1988), 25.

9. Quoted in Karlekar, "Education," 153.

10. Karlekar, "Education," 153.

11. Karlekar, "Education," 154.

12. Quoted by Kaur Kuldip, *Education*, 254.

13. Karlekar, "Education," 155.

14. Ministry of Education, *Challenge*, 58, par. 3.58.

15. Vina Mazumdar, *Education and Women's Equality* (New Delhi: Centre for Women's Development Studies, 1985), 13.

16. Shramashakti, *Report of the National Commission on Self Employed Women and Women in the Informal Sector* (Government of India, 1988); and *National Perspective Plan (NPP) for Women, 1988–2000 A.D.: Report of the Core Group set up by the Department of Women and Child Development*, Ministry of Human Resource Development (Government of India, 1988).

17. M. S. Gore, "Education for Women's Equality" (mimeo), Fifth J. P. Naik Memorial Lecture (New Delhi: Oxford University Press, 1986), 8.

18. Gore, "Education for Women's Equality," 22; also refer to Neera Desai and Sharyu Anantram, "Review of Studies on Middle Class Women's Entry into the World of Work," in *Women, Work and Society*, ed. K. Sardamoni (Calcutta: Indian Statistical Institute, 1985).

19. Report of the National Seminar, 1985, 32; also refer to *Revised Centrally Assisted Scheme of Non-Formal Education* (New Delhi: Ministry of Education, 1987).

20. Karlekar, "Education," 174.

21. Vina Mazumdar, *Education and Women's Equality* (New Delhi: Centre for Women's Development Studies, 1985), 16; also refer to Report of the National Seminar, 22–23.

22. Narendra Nath Kalia, "Women and Sexism: Language of Indian School Textbooks," *Economic and Political Weekly* 21, no. 18 (3 May 1986).

23. Karlekar, "Education," 166.

24. Anita Dighe, "Non-Formal Education for Women," (paper presented at National Seminar on Education for Women's Equality, 1985), 6; also refer to Ila Pathak, "AWAG's Battle against the Media," *Women and Media, Analysis Alternatives and Action*, ed. Kamala Bhasin and Bina Agarwal (Geneva: ISIS International, 1984).

25. Report of the National Seminar, 1985, 23.

26. Ministry of Human Resources Development, Government of India *Programme of Action, National Policy on Education* (New Delhi: 1986), 107 (g).

27. The Committee on the Status of Women in India (CSWI) was appointed in 1971 following a resolution of the Ministry of Education and Social Welfare at the insistence of the United Nations (UN) General Assembly. The report is entitled "Towards Equality" and was published in December 1974.

28. Vina Mazumdar, *Emergence of Women's Question in India and Role of Women's Studies* (New Delhi: Centre for Women's Development Studies, 1984); also refer to Neera Desai, "Relevance of Women's Studies in India" (mimeo), 1986.

29. Ministry of Human Resources, *Programme of Action*, 107.

30. Karlekar, "Education," 172.

31. Neera Desai, "Women in Scientific Life" (mimeo), Centre for Research on Women Studies, Shreemati Nathibai Damodar Thackersey (SNDT) University, Bombay, 1984, 7.

32. Maithreyi Krishnaraj, "The Price of Gender Inequality is Technological Backwardness" (mimeo), Research Centre on Women's Studies, SNDT University, Bombay, 1986.

Healing the Wounds of Development

DEVAKI JAIN

Our education must be for resistance and our curriculum
must inform people of cultural danger.

In the global context the term *development* has been used to rank
countries as developed, developing, or underdeveloped based on
various indicators and indices. Most are economic; they measure
the output of goods and services, income, money supply, and so
on. Simultaneously, there is some concern with poverty and unequal distribution of wealth. The developed countries provide the
yardstick by which all other countries are ranked. Implicit in this
ranking is the idea that all countries should aspire to be like developed countries.

But what is it that the developed countries have achieved? Basi-
cally, they have achieved mass mechanization and industrialization, high levels of production of goods and services, super afflu-
ence in material goods, an employer-employee relationship in all
kinds of work, and high energy consumption. All are essentially
forms of economic growth. They represent one meaning of development, but only one. An alternate form of development would
be in the growth of people's capacities and strengths, of their
public involvement and their self-reliance, and of their equal
status. Why must development be equated with economic growth
and, consequently, with mass industrialization? This equation has
not helped the majority of the people in so-called developing
countries, and there is no good reason why the West should be
our model, especially since India's historic pattern has been self-

45

employment for the masses and cultural concerns very different from those of a consumer society.

New Strategies: New Organization of Work

We need to understand other options. Can we come out of poverty without damaging our ecosystems, our values, our identities? Can we avoid transforming all work into nine-to-five jobs? Can we structure our economies so that the majority of our workers remain self-employed, which is their historical and traditional form of employment? We must create our own options of progress and growth.

We must also transvalue "backwardness" so that we can better understand what we want from progress and modernization. We have to understand the functioning of traditional cultural institutions, which have helped the majority of our people participate in decisions affecting them and which are now being eroded. We have to understand the displacing effect new technologies have had on the work, the culture, and the identity of our people. We have to identify the forces that encourage the concentration of resources in the hands of a few and destroy the decentralized nature of our traditional systems. We have to develop and nurture a sense of pride in our own ways of living and our own value systems, instead of criticizing them. We have to aspire to reasonable levels of consumption that can be sustained for the whole world, rather than pursue superconsumption at the expense of others. We have to change the direction of development, even in industrialized countries.

Efforts are underway to combat poverty and injustice at the grass roots level. They are, however, still scattered. Despite massive antipoverty campaigns, we have not been able to improve the lives of our people. One reason for this is that we do not know our own people. There is a wealth of wisdom in their ways of work, their ways of communication, in the food they eat, the clothing they wear.

Julius Nyerere, former prime minister of Tanzania, observed:

Development needs to be rooted in the culture of a people, and the cultures of peoples. However slow or fast, real development will be "organic" growth not the accretion of a foreign body. It will be compat-ible with the ways of looking at the world which the society has evolved through historical experience. To the extent that this does not happen, the result will be discontent and possibly social unrest.

... Yet rejecting the concept that development is merely a matter of increasing the gross national income is not to reject development. Nor is it to say that the levels of production are irrelevant to development. Similarly, the inevitable uncertainties and social up-sets which accompany change must not be used as an excuse for not trying to make changes. The present level of existence of hundreds of millions of human beings is an insult to the very concept of humanity.[1]

As women enter education and development, they must pause and reflect—then perhaps backtrack to advance again in new ways. The equality game that we played in the past decade is not leading us into green pastures; instead, it is leading us into the swamps in which our predecessors in progress, men, are trapped. Options that are foreclosed for them, and for advanced nations, are still open to us and to all women in developing countries who are planning and participating in their own advancement. But time is short and we urgently need to clarify and elaborate our goals.

In what follows I will present some areas of thought and action for feminists concerned with education, who see its link to women's endeavors for the healthy development of our planet and its people.[2] Specifically, I will identify areas for curriculum development, which, if introduced into formal or informal educa-tion, can facilitate these endeavors. They are:

1. Providing a new theoretical and philosophical backdrop to the con-tent of education.
2. Providing information about the dangers of "old" development and mobilizing resistance to it.
3. Building curriculum suited to the local environment, culture, and economic patterns and organizing macro-educational systems that can accommodate this diversity.
4. Building women's self-worth by replacing myths with truth and building their confidence with new thoughts on the nature of women's struggles for equality.

Many of these topics have already been addressed by feminists. Now it is time to consolidate them and to make a revolutionary effort to introduce them into the delivery mechanisms of education. Below I present a case study illustrating the kind of consolidation I mean.

Lakshmi Ashram, nestled in the Himalayas at Kausani, is a residential school for girls of all ages, started by an Austrian woman, an environmentalist who was an associate of Gandhi. It has an enrollment of eighty to one hundred high school girls, a dozen teachers, and another dozen teacher trainees. The ashram has always been a focal point for the three hundred scattered hamlets and households in the surrounding mountains. The only way to get from hamlet to hamlet is on foot, over pathways that thread through the mountains.

Since the school follows the Gandhian mode of pedagogy, in which there are no divisions between childhood and adulthood, manual and intellectual work, or domestic and productive labor, all students live as they would in their homes and are aware of social and environmental issues. They wake at 5 A.M. and clean the school, cook, garden, or serve breakfast, according to the roster. They start their classes at 8 A.M. and read or work on crafts until lunch. In the afternoon they do homework, play, sing, and dance. Their creativity and respect for labor, food, and shortages are not dampened by electronic media, playing fields, or adult servers. Students have graduated from the ashram to become street vendors, nurses, and even air hostesses. Most return to live in their villages but remain agents of the ashram.

It is in the tradition of any Gandhian ashram to be a counseling shelter, a receiver. That is, the request comes to it; its members do not go out and proselytize or "provide extension services." It follows a system. If it attracts users, then it lets people "take" what they seek. Padayatra, or traveling by foot, is associated with village-to-village preaching, like the activities of Vinod Bhave.[3] But, in fact, it is a way to make oneself accessible to others in the most humble way. The "self" who is doing this for her own salvation must be a self-developed person who is fine-tuned to receive. As a receptacle, the padayatari only reverberates. She strengthens the resolve of those she encounters and teaches by precept. She demonstrates the consistency between precept and practice.

Every outside development impulse the padayatari receives is injurious, and one of her tasks is to build up her resistance to these development impulses. Education policy, for example, which positively discriminates toward members of the so-called backward classes of the lower castes, requires that the school keep records of these children so that it can get special grants-in-aid. These children are entitled to a free education. Such identity keeping, however, carries the social stigmas of the village to the classroom, which should be the child's refuge from negative discrimination. In the case of Lakshmi Ashram the school refused the grants and barred the inspector of schools from entering.

The school has evolved a curriculum suited to the environment, the ways of life, and the aspirations of the hill people. The state has refused to certify the school, however, unless it changes its textbooks, courses, and schedule. The school is striving to give its graduates the option of entering "the rest of the world." But it does not want to sacrifice appropriate education, education that does not alienate children from their environment, their creative intelligence, or their past.

This curriculum issue, for which uniformity is demanded, is especially harmful to girls, something that has been demonstrated by the work of the Institute of Education in Pune and in many other field research and action reports.[4] Certain important conclusions emerged from the Pune research project:

> The reasons for non-enrollment and drop-out of rural children, particularly girls, are mainly two: (a) the indifference or irrelevance of the educational system to the needs and difficulties of the children, and (b) cultural, social and economic constraints which have not yet been clearly noted and dealt with by educational planners and administrators.

Furthermore, the writers of the Pune report concluded,

> there was no lack of motivation among parents for sending children to school. Nor did children resist learning once the project tried to meet their convenience and basic urges for playing and learning.[5]

The report's relevance is emphasized by the conclusions of Vina Mazumdar about the drop-out rate of girls.[6] "According to 1981 figures," she has written,

> over 45 percent of girls in the 6–11 age group, over 75 percent in the 12–14 age group, and over 85 percent in the 15–17 age group were out of school, as compared to 20 percent, 57 percent, and 71 percent of boys in the respective age groups. The main problem of universalizing elementary education, is the problem of enrollment of girls. Girls constitute 80 percent of the total non-enrolled children in the age group of 6–14.

Another researcher in education, Krishna Kumar,[7] has pointed out that, "together, the curriculum, the methods of teaching, and the teacher comprise an agency constantly threatening the child's, especially the poor child's, self concept." In rural communities poor children develop many talents and abilities that are devalued by the formal education curriculum. Thus,

> the problem is not of a solely educational nature. It concerns a wider range of issues in children's lives, not just their learning behavior. . . .
>
> . . . A child centered view of education, which is required for the progress of primary schooling, just cannot catch on in a milieu where children must work to feed the family and where they die of minor illnesses.

Instead, the curriculum must treat the realities of their lives, and the school delivery system must operate in a manner that recognizes that the children work.[8]

In a socioeconomic survey of one hundred villages prepared for an economic credit plan for women the Institute of Social Studies Trust in Delhi found that April examinations coincided with coffee bean harvest time.[9] Children, both boys and girls, could not take exams during this period of peak economic demand. A request that school hours and examination periods be modified has been accepted by the government's education department. But the teachers, who want standard holidays, rejected it. In developing countries we cannot separate family, child, and workplace. This transition did occur in the West, but it is not one we want to bring about.

Moreover, schools must integrate learning with productive work, rather than separate children from a valued craft tradition. Ashrams such as Lakshmi are licensed as production units for spinning and weaving. They receive benefits, such as looms and spinning wheels as well as the underpinning of all produce from the Khadi and Village Industries Commission (KVIC), a national state-funded "commodity" board.[10] Thus, the school children learn and earn. The Khadi and the local industries have yielded, however, to pressures and mechanized carding and have poor pricing and costing practices. The school wants to opt out of the KVIC umbrella because it is hampering its efforts to make Khadi a way of life and not "primitive" production.

The wider community around the ashram is facing other crises. The ecosystem is being destroyed through mining in mountain pastures. Alcoholism is growing because of an alliance between the state's exchequer and the local politicians and merchants. Women of the villages are always resisting, in one way or another, the cutting of the trees, the mining, the extension of liquor shops, and the civic bodies that do not provide drinking water. Battles for survival, legitimacy, and peace surround and dominate their lives. They have little time for anything else; every mental and physical space around them is being wounded by one or another of these "development" impulses.

It seems, then, that the content of education for the poor, especially for poor women, has to be information that can be an "early warning system" to help them resist Western-style development, not education that will increase their participation in development. They need a curriculum that enables them to value their own culture soundly and to look critically at the West, especially at Western science and technology.

Another major preoccupation must be how to resist science and technology. Advances in biotechnology will eliminate the livelihoods of millions of farmers and damage the health of millions of women. The poor need to be given reliable information about things that threaten their livelihood and also about how they can place people who understand these impending dangers into positions of political power. Early warning systems will build up resistance. In other words, our education must be for resistance, and our curriculum must inform people of cultural danger.

I can illustrate what such an education means by describing my own path toward my current assessment of the equation between education and development in South Asia. Because of my interest in adult education programs for poor women, I had recommended that curriculum be developed so that each program (dairy, silk, or fish, etc.) would design a module for adult education manuals. I felt that this would encourage women to attend the classes and would be useful to them in their economic tasks.[11]

In another forum I proposed that information gained through research could improve understanding of women's roles and give them infrastructural support.[12] One useful illustration is a project in which milk producers were to form a cooperative. After studying that site and the project, I proposed (because of my belief that participation in decision making would be a way to integrate women into development) that the project should first bring more women into the cooperatives and also that the project develop a social infrastructure of child care, water, and fuel support to reduce household drudgery. When both these suggestions were adopted I was thrilled and felt a sense of achievement. I wrote a paper for the mid-decade United Nations (UN) Conference on Women in Copenhagen in 1980, celebrating the possibilities of integrating women in development through research and advocacy. But, with hindsight, I now believe that the project should be resisted by women.[13]

A survey of 120 households at Kaira revealed that the introduction of this collective market support system to dairy households added two hours to the twelve hours a day that women already worked. It took away the little bit of milk that had been kept for home consumption and ended the tradition of preserving milk by making butter, ghee, and whey, the latter of which was an important food. Household income had risen and become more reliable, but women had lost control of food resources. The money had been appropriated by the men of the household, the cooperative, which was led by men, and the urban consumer. Introducing cash-generating projects does not help a poor family, which relies on twelve hours of women's labor a day for its food supply.

Another popular recommendation was to make the poor, especially women, aware of development services, of modes of organization, and of management. The radical edge to this is the awareness of rights. I prepared and designed schemes for government funding, including a proposal that 1 to 2 percent of development funds should be spent on raising awareness about the programs, especially programs that credit self-employment, public works programs for wage employment, and commodity promotion programs in milk, silk, tea, and textiles.

The end result of many of these programs was to divert the poor from known options of sustainable development to highly vulnerable production and a harsher, more deprived level of living, especially for women and children. In my own evolution I have gone from recommending sectorally specific "employment-strengthening" curricula for adult women taking literacy classes to objecting to that very employment, be it in dairy farming or sericulture.

It has to be admitted that, while these worthy ideas were developed by researchers, like myself, through an "ear to the ground" approach, we were leading our "poor illiterate" sisters into the "open world." We were naive and realized too late that this great goodness, development, into which our mandate had been to integrate women, and that this great public world, which men occupy and into which we were to bring women through employment and health strategies, was dangerous, even devastating.

These experiences have shown me that we must teach ourselves and others the "macro" consequences of "micro" choices. It is such micro-experiences of project impact—not only class and gender differentiation, but also the larger perspective of macro-reverberations—that have made feminists engaged in development research step back and look at the macropolicies of development.

A rural women's group may be encouraged by a national policy or a local development project to take up the farming of mulberry trees to provide fodder for silkworms. They may plant the trees on land formerly used for food crops. The silkworms bring cash into the household, usually to its male members. In a low-resource household this change in land use reduces food for the female members. Poor women are literally made to go around the mulberry bush.[14]

Looking back the emphasis of the pioneers of the women's movement seems to have been on education. Development, however, challenges the whole foundation of education and its content. Today even specialists in the field of education have stopped looking for ways to bring more women into education. Instead of focusing on access, they are thinking again about the framework, goals, and content of education.

Even men and women from within academic institutions are questioning the actual contribution of education to social development, because it can be and often has been a means for teaching the stereotypes of an unjust society. A ministerial level conference of nonaligned and other developing nations on the role of women in development, held in Delhi in April 1985, blamed educational systems for playing a subtle and powerful role (more powerful than the media or art) in promoting this: "through myths like the supplementary nature of women's work.... In reality, there are extraordinarily few areas or circumstances where women's economic contribution could be dismissed as merely supplementary or optional or dispensable. But this myth has been very successfully practiced increasingly over the ages to keep women under subjugation politically, economically, and socially."

I suggest that building self-confidence and increasing self-worth are the pegs on which our knowledge is to hang. From the individual woman to the nation we need to legitimate ourselves economically, politically, socially, and culturally. Rethinking development requires a new body of thought, one that looks at new and existing political, economic, and social theories, theories which include women's languages, values, descriptive statements, and the principles derived from them. Once this is done the new indicators of progress will emerge.

There are many illustrations of the intelligence embedded in the cultural practices of the south, or of developing countries: the choice of crops and methods of water management in agriculture; the worship of trees, which ensures their protection in forestry; the recycling of waste; herbal medicines; attention to diet, pollution, and personal relationships between ages and genders.

Carefully edited catalogs of these cases could become manuals for those designing local projects. Imagine a project formulator—his or her head full of the usual preconceptions that the local people are ignorant, unscientific, and believe in voodoo and superstitions—opening a manual and finding references to local practices that are conserving and efficient. He or she may then design the project from that base. Imagine also the effect that this kind of documentation and approach would have on those who make up a "backward group." Their own self-worth would be enhanced.

For women it seems to me that building self-worth requires a new look at the way we order human characteristics, or, to use the old-fashioned words, our moral theory. I suggest that we are still mesmerized by male characteristics. Whether it is the women of Lakshmi Ashram or those women of Kumaon who prefer fuel trees to mineral mines or fruit trees, another view of agenda and of methods exists. This is most evident among the poor, for whom the pressure for survival deepens differences and intensifies creativity.

One ideological, or philosophical, approach that seems to be consistent with the issues, concerns, and characteristics of the women's experience in India is that of Gandhi. Gandhi concentrated on consciousness and the mind of the individual. Though his collection of do's and don'ts are often laughed at as being too austere, even perverse, they were immensely appealing to the people he addressed. They felt that they were being drawn into being better than themselves, into being mini-saints. Unity and homogeneity were built on personal ethics—not on class, gender, religion, race, or political ideology.

Gandhi, not the -ism but, rather, the perspective and the method, offers a valuable experience of how to use education to build both harmony and power in communities. It offers a way to link the individual to society. In his approach to equalizing social and economic patterns, Gandhi released less aggressive moral, cultural, and economic processes. He attempted to bridge the gaps between social divides by stressing identification with others, experiencing the experience of the "other." He played the role of women, as he saw them—as caring, moral, and courageous beings. He wanted to be called "Maa." He identified with the poor by wearing clothes like theirs and living in their homes. He lived in harijan colonies, in Muslim houses. He had great trust in human nature and in human imagination. He believed that, if one could see an injustice or a hurtful act from the side of the recipient, one would never be unjust or hurtful again.

He also sought to set up alternative styles of social relationships, not only in the ashrams, where inherited hierarchies and role allocations were replaced by new equal relationships, bonding for social action, but also in alternative economic systems based on intimate accessible production-consumption linkages. His perspective was to prevent any concentration of power in any one area—state, corporation, trade union, patriarch, temple, or church—by building a basis for autonomy within each household.

This process of identifying with oppressed groups is one of the methods used today by female social activists in Gandhi-based institutions such as Lakshmi Ashram. In some respects it removes the problem of outsider-insider, elite-mass, alienation. The women subscribe to the approach of letting each person's consciousness develop by offering a support system, often provided just by walking among the people as padayatari. They are patient. They do not push too hard to change class, caste, and gender divisions but, instead, live a life that rejects these divisions and shares with others in the faith that, step by step, society will evolve, by adjusting and readjusting toward harmony.

Naitalim, Gandhi's philosophy of education; Sarvadharma, his formula of transforming religious barriers into common worship; Sarvodayd, his method of transforming class and caste barriers into communal harmony—all are slogans today. None of them will work, however, without the "godly" men and women, or the mini-saints, that Gandhi trained. And these godly men and women cannot emerge without each one having developed consciousness of self.

I suggest that, without rethinking and specifying the philosophy, the vision, and the specific vocabularies, including the basic syllabus of education, it is not useful to draw women into education. The stance that poor women are forced to adopt, as it now stands, is one of resistance and struggle. To recycle that stance into more enriching "building" roles requires going back, or down, and not going forward. It can be done. There is much material among us. We are also rich in resources. The question is to what use we will put them.

What we have been working at articulating is a vision of the new educated woman. No matter whether she is a product of the formal or nonformal systems, she will embody important characteristics of a new educated class. She will have the necessary knowledge to assist in saving the planet from environmental degradation. She will have learned to respect difference, but she will be rooted in her region and community, ready to accept sacrifice to preserve both. And, because she has been taught through texts that describe women's real contribution to economic and political life, she will no longer be a self-sacrificing servant of patriarchy.

NOTES

1. Julius K. Nyerere, message sent to M. A. Singamma Sreenivasan Foundation roundtable on "Survival Strategies of the Poor and Traditional Wisdom: A Reflection," Rajmahal Vilas Extension, Bangalore, May 17–18, 1987. A full report on the roundtable is available from the International Institute for Environment and Development, London.

2. Tom Woodhouse, *People and Planet* (Hartland, Bideford, Devon: Green Books, 1987).

3. Vinod Bhave, disciple of Mahatma Gandhi who undertook Padayatra throughout India in the mid-1950s, to redistribute land through appeals to the consciences of those who owned land. His campaigns were known as *Bhoodan* (land gift) and *gramdan* (village gift).

4. Chitra Naik, "Making Childhood Learning Happier," *Future* (UNICEF magazine) 20 (1987).

5. See Woodhouse, *People and Planet*.

6. Vina Mazumdar, "Education and Women's Equality" (paper presented at the National Seminar on Education for Women's Equality at Vigyan Bhavan, New Delhi, 3–5 November, 1985).

7. Ibid.

8. "Development of Women and Children in Rural Areas" (DWCRA), Preparation of a Plan with Focus on Women Block Chikmagalur (Karnaraka)," (proposal submitted by the Institute of Social Studies Trust, New Delhi, September 1983).

1. Krishna Kumar, "Ending the Poverty of the Primary School," *Future* 20 (1987);

2. Kumar, "Elementary Education: The Unfinished Task," a future supplement on Early Learning in India, *Future* 11–12 (Summer–Autumn 1984);

3. Kumar, "Breaking the Illiteracy Barrier: Shifting Focus, Elusive Goal," *Future* 17 (Winter 1985–86);

4. Kumar, "Growing Up Male" (seminar);

5. Kumar, "Education for Decay," *India* magazine (May 1985);

6. Kumar, Workshop Proceedings on Some Issues in Educational Philosophy;

7. Kumar, *Raj, Samaj aur Shiksha* (State, Society, and Education) (New Delhi: Macmillan, 1978).

9. Kumar, DWCRA, "Preparation of a Plan."

10. Khadi & Village Industries Commission.

11. On adult education see the following:

1. Devaki Jain, five-year plan suggestions and final report, Task Force on Adult Education, 7.

2. National Seminar on "New Trends in Adult Education" (for women, with special references to literacy), sponsored by Indian Adult Education Association, New Delhi, 1980.

3. Workshop on Educational Programmes for Adult Women, New Delhi, 1984.

4. Rajkumari Chandrashekhar, *Aspects of Adult Education* (Madras: New Era Publication), 1982.

5. "Case Studies: Adult Education for Women" (MS, Institute of Social Studies Trust, Delhi, 1984).

See also Devaki Jain, "Women's Employment—As Related to Rural Areas" (paper presented at the Kulu Women and Development conference, Copenhagen, 1980).

12. Malini Chand Singh, *Women's Quest for Power: Five Case Studies* (New Delhi: Vikas Publishing House, 1980).

13. Gita Sen and Caren Grown, *Development Crises and Alternative Visions: Third World Women's Perspectives* (New York: Monthly Review Press, 1987).

14. "A Proposal on Household-Level Food Security," submitted by Institute of Social Studies Trust to the Food and Agricultural Organisation (F.A.O.), Nutrition Department, Rome, 1985.

Women's Education in Pakistan

FARIDA SHAHEED AND KHAWAR MUMTAZ

Introduction: A Profile of Pakistani Women

In 1992 the profile of Pakistani women is distressing. Their life expectancy is fifty-three years, two years less than Pakistani men. Three-quarters of all women are married by the time they are fifteen years old; by the age of twenty nine out of ten Pakistani women are married. On average, Pakistani women bear seven or eight live children, and their peak fertility occurs between the ages of twenty and twenty-four. Some twenty-six thousand women die from childbirth-related causes each year because of closely spaced pregnancies, unhygienic conditions in childbirth, long periods of lactation, poor nutrition, and a lack of pre- and post-natal care. Girls are three times less likely to attend primary school than boys and are far more likely to drop out of school—just one of every thirteen girls in village primary schools continues to secondary schools. Ninety-five percent of the women in rural areas (where three-quarters of the population live) are illiterate.

In villages women work fifteen to sixteen hours each day preparing food, caring for children and livestock, and working in agricultural production. Their labor is unrecognized in official statistics and largely unrewarded in the family and community. Women do not participate in financial decisions, nor do they have the influence over household production to which their labor should entitle them. If a woman works as a paid laborer, which some 2 to 7 percent do, they almost always turn their wages over to the male head of the household.

Urban women make up 28 percent of all of Pakistan's women; most belong to the working class and lead lives of great physical hardship. They carry a double burden, both working and taking care of their homes. They are the first to rise and the last to go to sleep. When there is not enough food they go hungry, and many suffer from persistent anemia and malnutrition. The cloistered women of the lower middle class are perhaps the most restricted of all Pakistani women.

The lives of middle- and upper-class women provide a stark contrast to the lives of the majority of Pakistani women. This is best illustrated in contemporary times by Benzir Bhutto, Pakistan's first female prime minister. Middle- and upper-class women hold jobs in law, journalism, architecture, and engineering, all professions that have recently opened up to women. Many are medical doctors, and many teach—a third of both professions are women. They are five times more likely to be literate than their rural sisters (32 percent can read and write), and they form a highly visible class in Pakistani society. Although the possibility of change is greatest among middle- and upper-class women, they suffer from the same social attitudes that prevail among the lower classes, attitudes that devalue them and turn them into appendages of male relatives. Even Bhutto, having inherited the mantle of political leadership from her executed father and combined it with her own courage and charisma to break some of the barriers that constrain women's participation in public life, had to submit to the customary marriage arranged by family elders to a man she had hardly ever met or knew.

In a 1985 report, the government-appointed Pakistan Commission on the Status of Women was forced to conclude that:

> The actual status of women . . . is today at the lowest ebb. Women in general are dehumanized and exercise little control over either themselves or affairs affecting their well-being. They are treated as possessions rather than as self reliant self-regulating humans. They are bought and sold, beaten and mutilated, even killed with impunity and social approval. They are dispossessed and disinherited in spite of legal safeguards. The vast majority are made to work 16 to 18 hours a day, without any payment. . . . The participation . . . of women in national life is marginal and most of them are still mute spectators of the changes taking place around them.[1]

There is little to add to this succinct appraisal. We can ask, however, why, after forty years of planned development, the situation is so bleak and to what extent education has or can help to ameliorate the lot of the Pakistani women.

By itself, education is not a sufficient (and perhaps not even necessary) condition for women's self-realization. Nevertheless, to the extent that education shapes people's perceptions and expectations, defines what is normal and what is not, and prescribes roles for members of society, it is an important institution, one that can both constrain and liberate.

Part 1: Education and Development

Education
Education should increase the intellectual and moral resources of individuals, so that they have a better understanding of their environment and, consequently, can interact in it in a more informed way. Unfortunately, the nation's social organizations may dictate other goals for the educational system. Nasreen Shah and Neelam Hussain have written that to stay in power ruling groups or classes are impelled to do more than merely control the obvious forms of state machinery. They also try to consolidate their authority by designing the ways in which a given society conceives and speaks about itself and its experiences.[2]

Colonial rulers had no desire to educate the colonized to be independent, creative thinkers who might threaten imperial power. Instead, they set up an educational system that would produce a pool of competent clerks and administrators who were adequately acculturated and suitably impressed by the empire. The formal school system was deliberately designed to oppose indigenous educational systems and, thus, was in many ways diametrically opposed to the values of Indian society. Enrollment in the colonial system was a way for the indigenous population to gain power; learning English was a necessary qualification for a job in government. As a result, an Anglo-educated elite developed, whose thinking bore the heavy imprint of colonial masters. Alienated as they were from their own environment, the members of this elite assumed a derisive attitude toward all vernacular and indigenous education, an attitude that is still in evidence today.

It is a common perception that the impact of colonialism on the colonized is confined to the dislocation of economic activities. Yet, the disruption and dislocation of social and cultural patterns may be more significant. If it was economic policies that linked colonized societies to distant (and therefore uncontrollable) market economies, it was the social and cultural dislocation (in which education played such an important role) that allowed this state of affairs to continue well past independence to the present day.

When the British first introduced their system of "modern" education to India, there was some resistance. For historical reasons this was strongest among the Muslims of north India, and there was great reluctance in these areas to send girls to school. By the turn of the century the situation had changed considerably. With the emergence of a growing nationalist sentiment, women's education began to receive some support. But, while one group of advocates believed that education should give women greater awareness and augment their human development, another group fought to establish institutions, such as the "Zenana" (women's) schools in Lahore, that would counter what they saw as the insidious undermining of values and morals caused by modern education. Consequently, even before Pakistan was created there were two opposing camps: one that believed that education could free women from their social shackles and one that intended to use education to further consolidate the constraints on women. This conflict has never been resolved, and women's education in Pakistan remains a victim of contradictory policies.

The ongoing debate about whether a separate women's university should be established is a case in point. In Pakistan the proposal is opposed by female activists, who view it as a subtle method to further marginalize women by circumscribing the type of education available to them. They fear that with a separate university women will find it increasingly difficult to be admitted to high-quality institutions (particularly in technical and professional fields), while the course offered in the women's university would be limited to "female-appropriate" subjects.

It would be unfair to suggest that only women's education is problematic. In fact, Pakistan's entire educational system is a problem-ridden morass. The educational needs of an independent state are radically different from those of a colonial power; in the former the system should "help (people) lead meaningful and productive lives as individuals and as members of society, by opening their minds to knowledge and training them to use that knowledge as citizens of a free country for its progress and development."[3] To fulfill this function the educational system inherited from the British needed to be largely dismantled and entirely reoriented. But those who came to power after independence were not equal to this task. They were too well acculturated by their own education to see the changes required by the new circumstances.

While they did increase enrollment vastly, Pakistan's new rulers maintained the dual hierarchical system, which subordinated Urdu language schools to English language schools and all traditional systems (*madrassahs, maktabs*, etc.) to modern systems. They declared education to be a universal right. English remained the official language until the 1970s, however, and English language schools continued to cater to the elite, with better-quality education and preferential opportunities in employment. Thus, the elite continued to study, conceptualize, and make policy in English, while the masses learned in Urdu translations and were, in effect, excluded from university education, which was largely conducted in English.

Today, lacking a vision to give it national direction and uprooted in its own society, Pakistan's educational system is a poor imitation of the one the colonial powers left behind. More than ever before people attend schools not to learn but, rather, to obtain the certificate or degree, which is often worth less than the paper it is written on. Instead of understanding, schools stress memorization, and students fail to gain any meaningful understanding of their own environment and a consequent informed ability to act. As a result, after forty years

only a fraction of the young get an education; the overwhelming majority of those getting an education do not learn to think for themselves nor do they acquire basic reading and writing skills; a large majority of those who graduate are unable to find employment. . . . Parents complain that their children learn nothing, teachers complain that students are not serious, and students feel they are not getting a fair deal.[4]

Development

With respect to development the picture is not much more encouraging. The theory of development that has emerged from developed countries would have us believe that a systematic increase in production of goods and services, combined with the laws of supply and demand, will eventually benefit everybody equitably. The emphasis is always on producing more. Thus, development is largely, if not exclusively, equated with macro-level, quantifiable growth—growth, that is, that can be added up and shown to exceed previously measured growth. The quantitatively measured reduction of undesired variables, such as disease and illiteracy, are used as parallel yardsticks.

The danger of this definition is that it makes an abstraction of the historical process of development, thus negating the differentiated impact experienced by various nations and sectors within a country. Furthermore, when development is measured by gross national product (GNP) and per capita income, inequalities that may have been intensified or even created in the process tend to be ignored. And the possibility that one country or sector of society may have benefited at the expense of another may be glossed over. This is not merely a question of semantics. The definition of development and the way it is measured have immediate and tangible repercussions and are a very clear demonstration of the relationship between knowledge and power.

In Pakistan and most ex-colonial states the decision-making elite adhere to this quantitative macro-level definition of development. Anxious to "catch up" with industrialized countries, these nations usually adopt a fragmented approach to development. At the macro level this fragmentation is reflected in the unequal emphasis applied to different sectors in society—social versus economic, agricultural versus industrial, rural versus urban, female versus male—and to the consequent unequal development these sectors experience. Desiring to achieve measurable success in development, postcolonial states first identify those aspects of industrialized countries that appear responsible for the latter's economic and political power (a process in which they are aided by the institutions working in those countries, such as the World Bank and the International Monetary Fund [IMF]), then emphasize them. Economic growth is normally considered most important. With respect to social services, emphasis is given to quantity and not to quality or appropriateness. For example, the number of schools, vaccinations, or sterilizations performed become the focus of attention, and little attempt is made to see the needs of the people and the country in a qualitative way. The organic links between the social and economic and the psychological and political aspects of life are at best ignored and at worst deliberately severed. Similarly, at the micro-level the totality of an individual's needs are not considered. Rather, they are fragmented, and only those needs that coincide with quantifiable and generally accepted measures of growth are included in development plans.

Part 2: Women's Education: Policies and Ideology

Access to Education—Development Plans and Women's Education
Since 1955 there have been a series of optimistic plans to improve education for women. Starting in 1955, each successive national five-year plan has recognized the need for women's education and formulated specific recommendations. The first three of these plans recommended that existing primary schools be opened to girls and that new schools be established and scholarships provided as an incentive. The fourth plan attempted to link women's education with development needs.[5] In the current plan, the sixth, there is a separate chapter that officially endorses the need to integrate women into national development. It proposes an integrated approach to improve the state of women and recommends increased health facilities, more positions for women in government, and additional vocational training and educational programs to increase women's employment opportunities. Specifically, the plan suggests that polytechnic schools and technical training and skills development centers be built, that existing vocational institutes be expanded, and that a new female paramedical staff be trained.

The results of all these plans, however, have been consistently disappointing. Exceedingly few women in Pakistan have access to formal education. Their literacy rate of 16 percent is one of the lowest in the world. Policymakers may not be neglecting women's education, but implementors certainly are. This is demonstrated in the bias against women's institutions. There are only one-third as many women's schools as there are men's schools. Only 8 percent of all professional colleges are women's schools. At the primary level girls represent just 31 percent of all students; at higher levels they make up 24 percent of the student body. In professional colleges only 18 percent of the student body is female.

The economist M. L. Qureshi points out, in his evaluation of the fifth plan, that "the disparities in enrollment of males and females have also widened between the years 1977–1978 and 1981–1983."[6] His observation is important because analysts usually compare percentage increases within gender categories and conclude that women's enrollment is increasing. Given the very poor starting level for women, this procedure magnifies small increases in absolute terms and overlooks the position of women relative to men.

There are, we believe, two distinct sets of reasons for the current situation—one springing from the general attitude adopted by policymakers toward education and the other rooted in societal perceptions of women. The attitude of policymakers and planners can best be gauged by examining allocation patterns, actual expenditures, and the priorities given to the various sectors of education. It is not possible to explore each of these areas in detail here, but examples will suffice to illustrate the prevalent trends.

Declared commitments notwithstanding, the resources actually made available for education are few, and they reflect the real priority that education receives. From 1959–60 to 1982 education's share of the GNP rose from 1 percent to just over 2 percent, and later plans to increase this percentage have failed. Meanwhile, there have been no comparable cuts in defense expenditures, which consume up to 68 percent of planned and nonplanned expenditures annually. Thus, even when planning documents express the intention of drastically reordering priorities—putting greater emphasis on primary and secondary education and consolidating higher education within existing facilities—the paucity of available resources and distorted priorities combine to render such good intentions meaningless. An examination of the expenditures during the span of the fifth plan reveals that "the actual expenditure on education and training was only 54 percent of the plan allocation . . . [and] the priority assigned to education under the plan was drastically lowered in the course of implementation."[7]

We would argue that another main reason the government's plans consistently fall short of their targets is because education is isolated from social realities. It is seen as a self-contained sector that is more or less immune to influences from other parts of Pakistan's society. For example, no account is taken of the social constraints that prevent women from going to school and that reinforce the view that education is irrelevant to women's lives. Unless such outside factors are recognized and addressed when programs on women's education are created, women's participation in schools will continue to be low. Nor can Pakistan's drop in status from UNESCO's category "b" to "c" be rectified unless the poor state of women's education is improved.

Access to Education: Ideological Constraints to Women's Education
Society's perceptions of what women are and should be determine the direction of development plans for women. A worldview binds the people of a society together and gives them a collective memory and a vision of the future. It also demarcates behavioral parameters for various groups, including relations between the sexes. In Pakistan one of the most prominent aspects of the worldview is the perception of women as economically nonproductive childbearers.

Women's mobility is controlled through the institution of purdah—female seclusion and rigid gender divisions. Generally, women are secluded and kept out of public life, which curbs their participation in economic activity and decision-making processes. In the educational system this division of the sexes has negative implications for women. First of all, it necessitates separate schools for girls and boys. While coeducation through primary school is generally acceptable in rural as well as urban areas, girls are taken out of schools when they turn ten, the reason for the high dropout rate at this level. Because resources are limited, few schools exist for older girls. To make matters worse, during the peak of the Islamization process, overzealous proponents of the Islamic system decided to discontinue even primary-level coeducation in many areas. Not surprisingly, the girls and not the boys were thrown out of schools, and no alternatives were provided.

School location is another factor that affects women's attendance rates. In areas in which a family's control over its female members, especially with regard to unrelated men, is a matter of family honor, distance between home and school can be a powerful deterrent to female attendance. The greater the distance, the less control families have over girls, and the more likely it is that girls will simply not be sent to school. Further, where women are not seen as economically productive, their education is considered both unnecessary and a possible threat to the role they are expected to play in the family. (In other words, "education ruins a girl. . . . It gives her ideas.") In the average Pakistani household education for women is a dispensable item.

Segregated schools also imply differentiated courses for boys and girls. Domestic science and home economics are considered subjects suitable for girls, while boys are educated in technical areas. As a result, women's intellectual horizons are circumscribed and their options reduced.

This survey of the outreach, scope, and quality of education does not present a very positive picture of the educational situation for Pakistan's women. Shortages of schools and teachers have combined with limited financial resources and entrenched gender biases to create a vicious, and as yet unbroken, circle. Shortfalls in finances mean that there will be fewer schools; the dominant male bias means the priority will go to education for men; and distances between schools and homes prevents women from attending schools.

The Ideological Content of Education

While faulty planning and certain social attitudes make education inaccessible to women, the quality of the education they are missing leaves much to be desired. That there is a crisis in education is recognized by all educators. Constricted by structural rigidity and limited by textual narrowness, the educational system fails to give its students confidence, develop their ability to challenge, or make them conscious of their community and give them a global perspective. Neither does it tolerate originality or creativity. Instead, it is geared to a rigid examination procedure during which, at the end of each academic year, students are expected to reproduce what they have learned rather than analyze it. There are, of course, a few exceptions, most at the lower school level. (All colleges are nationalized and therefore have less room to maneuver.) But these exceptions are few and far between and are almost entirely confined to elite urban private schools.

For girls conditions are even more limiting. Extracurricular activities for women are nonexistent. Textbooks, which are dull and clichéd at best, reflect and reinforce traditional stereotyping of women. This is not something that is peculiar to Pakistan. Writing on sexism in reading programs for children in American schools, G. Lobban noted: "The world they depicted was not only sexist; it was more sexist than present reality and in many ways totally foreign to the majority of children, who do have . . . at least some experience of cross-sex activities."[8]

In Pakistan a study examining images of men and women in school and college texts reaffirmed that women are portrayed solely in their domestic roles. They are shown cooking, cleaning, bearing and rearing children, and serving as domestic help.[9] The only occupation that women are shown working at is cleaning and picking cotton. Patriotism, religiosity, and creativity, qualities depicted as desirable for males, are not associated with females. Instead, obedience and docility are presented as desired female attributes. Similarly, attributes such as bravery, rationality, respectability, and humaneness are all associated with males, while women, especially in Urdu textbooks, are quite prominently portrayed as cunning, careless, noncooperative, and repentant.[10]

In history texts women are ignored. The few heroines mentioned are not portrayed positively. Emphasis is placed on their roles as wives, mothers, and daughters, not on their achievements. It is a fact, for example, that women actively participated in the Pakistan movement; they demonstrated and courted arrest, and it was a woman who first raised the Muslim League flag over the civil secretariat in Lahore. But the history of the movement, as taught in courses from high schools to universities, barely mentions women.

In rural areas the material in these texts is totally irrelevant to daily life, thus providing parents, who perceive women as dependent and unproductive, with an added incentive to keep their daughters at home. Parents may also want their daughters at home for the unpaid labor they provide to the family. Nor do urban families feel persuaded to send them to school, unless they see employment as part of their daughters' futures. Other needs, such as looking after younger siblings or helping with household chores, are seen as more pressing.

Part 3: Challenges, Issues, and Alternatives

In Pakistan education for women has traditionally consisted of information, skills, and training transmitted informally from mother to daughter and intended to prepare and equip young women to cope with life. Rapidly changing circumstances have rendered this system, which was based on the predictable patterns of traditional life, inadequate.

The penetration of market-based economies to the remotest parts of the country has exposed and linked women with forces outside the village. In urban areas the compulsions and dynamics of economic growth are pressuring women to participate in the affairs of the world. Today women face situations about which their mothers or grandmothers could not have dreamt. For example, the electronic, textile, and pharmaceutical industries are eager to recruit women as production workers. (Recently, a Lahore newspaper advertised job opportunities for women in the garment and pharmaceutical industries; middle to high school education was a minimum requirement.) Simultaneously, financial constraints are forcing women to seek work. While women are responding to these new realities by entering (or trying to enter) the job market, no system has developed to prepare them for their new roles.[11]

School lessons also have a subliminal, implicit content. They indirectly convey that the urban culture is superior to the rural culture, that males are superior to females, and that there are rigid male-female roles that are correct. Because education is such an important institution, the textbook, and the perceptions it transmits, become the truth. The result is immobilization, particularly of women who receive only a primary or middle-level education. The gender roles in textbooks described earlier are internalized by young girls who later often become the strongest defenders of rigid role segregation. From grade 1 onwards public school girls are taught to cover their heads and refrain from participating in sports. Instead, creativity is channeled into reciting religious hymns (*na'at*) or embroidery and cooking. It is no coincidence that in Pakistan, and many other countries, the capacity for assertiveness of the first-generation of educated women of the lower middle class compares negatively to that of the illiterate peasant or urban working-class woman. Thus, education, at least in its initial phases, alienates women from their environment, depriving them of self-confidence and initiative.

Another challenge, therefore, is to transform education into a mobilizing experience. Currently, the parallel structure of education (in English and Urdu), which was described by one observer as an intense form of apartheid, undercuts a child's confidence by negating his or her previous experiences. Instead of building on a child's existing knowledge system and teaching the ability to assimilate new information, the educational system leaves the child uncertain and insecure, incapable of taking initiative or being creative.

Despite all these shortcomings, however, there are signs that a gradual change in attitude is occurring. In a random survey of a lower- and middle-class urban district an investigator discovered that the average man considers education to be a necessity for both his sons and his daughters. Most of those interviewed were stretching meager resources to send their children to school. Some bias still existed: sons were sent to private English-language schools (which are believed to be a ticket to upward mobility), while girls were sent to cheaper government or municipal schools.[12] Given the limited infrastructure of the educational system, however, only a small percentage of those desiring an education can be accommodated. There is a pressing need for more facilities and for an alternative system that breaks out of the rigid and confining molds of the current one. There have been both governmental and nongovernmental initiatives in this direction. Governmental efforts, despite greater resources, have not been entirely successful. Localized initiatives seem to offer more hope.

Official Alternatives

A target of the most recent plan was to increase the reach of education and convert over two million illiterate Pakistanis into primary-level literates. Toward this end a scheme was launched in mid-1985 that would achieve this goal by the end of that year. Rs.320 million ($16 million) was earmarked for the project, and twenty-five thousand education centers were envisaged. Priority was given to women in general and rural women in particular. By September, however, the project had been abandoned, an admitted failure. The government is reported to have spent approximately Rs.9 million in the first six months of the drive, with disappointing results—only one-quarter of a percent growth in literacy occurred in the Sind province, for example.[13] The 3,150 literacy centers that had been constructed were closed and the services of the teachers terminated.

In October 1986 the government launched another program. By spending Rs.90 million ($2.5 million) to establish twenty-two thousand Nai Roshni (New Light) schools for primary-level dropouts between the ages of ten and fourteen, the program planned to raise the literacy rate to 50 percent over the next four years. Although its effectiveness has yet to be formally assessed, within six months Doctor Mahub-ul-Haq, who was the minister of planning, had already declared it a failure, saying that, if Pakistan reached 50 percent literacy by the year 2000, it would be an accomplishment.

Other Initiatives
In the absence of adequate efforts from government, communities with collective awareness have made attempts to solve their own problems. In Baldia, a low-income neighborhood of Karachi, a self-help community development project sponsored by UNICEF and guided by an experienced development worker, has been underway for the last five years. Although the program was initiated to improve sanitation, it has since expanded to deal with the high dropout rate in schools. A new system of home schools has been developed; in it the literate women of the neighborhood run classes in their own homes for dropouts and girls who do not go to school. Schedules are flexible, and, along with courses in reading and arithmetic, drawing and other creative subjects are taught. The teachers have formed an organization, the Home Teachers' Association, to expand their work systematically.

This experiment has grown to incorporate a few hundred

schools, and it now spans several neighborhoods, an indication of the kind of innovation and community participation that is possible. And its success, as compared with the consistent failure of government schemes, illustrates the difference that community participation and innovation can make once people's needs have been accurately identified.

Alternatives in the formal sector of education are also being discussed. In a consultation last year the Society for the Advancement of Higher Education proposed radically overhauling the system. Their suggestions included increasing the length of secondary schooling by one year and raising the requirements for a bachelor's degree from two years to three. They also suggested scrapping the examination system and replacing it with evaluations from each institution, creating more degree-granting institutions and introducing women's studies as a course.[14] This society has also developed a World Perspective Course, which discusses international issues such as disarmament, environmental affairs, the economic order, the role of women, and the role of the media, from a Pakistani perspective.

In our opinion transforming the educational system requires a two-pronged approach: one led by mainstream educators and the other led by mobilized communities. And, given the powerfully patriarchal nature of the society, special efforts on every level must be made for women. We believe that, together, these two groups will be able to take a radically different view of development and use people as a starting point, instead of statistics and figures. By shifting the definition of development from one that is purely economic to one that encompasses social and psychological factors, a more meaningful form of development will result, one in which individuals can fulfill their potential, increase their control over their environment, and participate in decisions related to growth.

The Baldia experience proves this. While it was begun to provide women with a livelihood and girls with literacy, it has coalesced into a forum for social action and change. Its members have started health training projects, in which they monitor child growth and administer injections to children. And, in response to requests from the community, the Home Teachers Association has established a women's training and production center. The association, because of its informed ability to intervene for improved social conditions, has become a valuable community asset.

Finally, despite the excitement engendered by successful alternative educational experiments, it is clear that such small-scale localized efforts cannot hope to replace, or even displace, the formal system in the country. They can, however, provide positive models for growth. Yet, to do this they must first receive public recognition and support from mainstream educators. Furthermore, any radical change in the educational system, particularly in women's education, implies a corresponding modification in society. Such a change must grow organically. Thus, the educational system and those in it will have to be open-minded, receptive to new ideas, and responsive to needs.

The time is right in Pakistan for this process to begin. Mainstream educators are painfully aware of the shortcomings of the system, and there is a substantial pool of women who are ready to go out and experiment in education.

NOTES

1. *Report on the Pakistan Commission on the Status of Women* (Islamabad: PCSW, 1985), 3.

2. Nasreen Shah and Neelam Hussain, "Scope and Methods of Education Information to Women" (paper presented in Aurat Publication and Information Service Foundation Workshop, Lahore, 1987).

3. Society for the Advancement of Higher Education, *Pakistan's Education Jungle* (Lahore, 1985), 18.

4. Society for the Advancement of Higher Education, *Pakistan's Education Jungle*, ii.

5. Prolonged civil strife in the country, followed by a war with India in 1971, disrupted the plan period, 1970–75. The period 1970–78, therefore, is a period of nonplan development. But in 1972 the government that came into power declared its commitment to women's equality in society and initiated special policy measures to open up services to women. It also established a Women's Rights Committee to examine the status of women in society and recommended measures to improve women's conditions. Increased availability of education was one of the committee's basic recommendations. The government also formulated a new education policy (1972) whereby male primary school teachers would be replaced with female teachers to boost female attendance.

6. M. L. Qureshi, *Development Planning and Women* (Islamabad: Women's Division, Government of Pakistan, n.d.), 67.

7. Qureshi, *Development Planning*, 61.

8. As quoted in Rosemary Deem, *Women and Schooling* (London, Henley, and Boston: Routledge and Kegan Paul, 1978), 25.

9. Muhammad Anwar, *Images of Male and Female Roles in School and College Textbooks* (Islamabad: Women's Division, Government of Pakistan, 1982), 64.

10. Anwar, *Images of Male and Female Roles*, 66.

11. A 1987 survey of fifteen women's training institutes in Pakistan showed that both urban and rural women willingly enroll in training programs and that there is a strong demand for skills training. Farida Shaheed, *Diversification of Women's Training and Employment in Pakistan* (Islamabad: ILO/APSDEP, 1987), 119.

12. Eqbal Ahmad (unpub. survey, Lahore, 1987).

13. Rashid Akhtar, "Mass Literacy: The Drive That Never Took Off," *Viewpoint* 12, no. 6 (18 September 1986): 21.

14. Khawar Mumtaz, "Need for Alternatives," *Viewpoint* 12, no. 21 (1 January 1987): 28.

Work, Education, and Women's Gains: The Korean Experience

In-Ho Lee

The history of Korean women's education is both an encouragement and a warning. The percentage of women in higher education is rising very rapidly. In 1983, 98 percent of all women and 99 percent of all men who completed compulsory elementary education advanced to junior high school. Now over 35 percent of women continue through college, and women make up 37 percent of the students in vocational and junior colleges.

But, while educational input for women has increased rapidly, their resulting output is somewhat problematic. Today there is an inverse relationship between a woman's level of education and her participation in the labor force, and this is because the content of education for women encourages them to accept traditional roles. We must face this issue squarely: access does not change very much unless the content of their education helps women to question traditional values.

In the long history of women's struggle to win the right to a decent life, full suffrage, access to formal education, and opportunity for gainful employment are the chief indicators of women's status in a rapidly modernizing society. When gauged by these three factors the Korean situation seems to present a bright enough picture. The women of Korea were given full political rights simultaneously with their male counterparts during the establishment of the very first republican government forty years ago. Not only has illiteracy been wiped out, but the female-male gap in the number of years spent in schools has steadily narrowed (table 1, fig. 1). In 1980, 42 percent of all students enrolled in the senior high schools were female (table 2), and 31.8 percent of those graduating from colleges and universities were women (table 3, fig. 2). In 1983 the participation rate of the women's labor force rose from 36.8 percent in 1960 to 41.6 percent in 1983 (a slight reversal in the trend occurring only in the recession years of 1970–80) (table 4, fig. 3). As more and more women acquire opportunities for better education and access to jobs traditionally reserved for men, they manifest greater assertiveness and resourcefulness.

In broad outlines the Korean case is a development "success" story. The policies adopted do not seem to depart greatly from the pattern prevailing in many other newly industrializing countries. The rapid expansion of the economy, rising educational standards, and the increasing participation of women in the job mar-

TABLE 1.   Average Years of Educational Attainment by Sex and Age

		Average	6~19 Years Old	20~29 Years Old	30~39 Years Old	40~49 Years Old	50 Years Old and Over
1960	Total	3.86	3.28	6.22	4.28	2.44	1.40
	Female	2.92	2.91	4.71	2.79	1.33	0.60
	Male	4.78	3.62	7.73	5.92	3.54	2.20
1966	Total	5.03	4.98	7.44	6.15	3.90	1.52
	Female	3.97	4.75	6.40	4.49	2.40	0.74
	Male	6.19	5.25	8.48	7.90	5.43	2.46
1970	Total	5.74	5.33	8.32	7.15	4.83	1.98
	Female	4.72	5.21	7.48	5.64	3.36	1.09
	Male	6.86	5.47	8.81	8.65	6.42	3.06
1975	Total	6.62	6.16	8.83	8.12	6.26	2.74
	Female	5.70	6.08	8.41	6.88	4.75	1.72
	Male	7.61	6.26	9.25	9.33	7.90	4.02
1980	Total	7.61	6.53	9.88	9.17	7.52	4.16
	Female	6.63	6.10	9.44	8.10	5.95	2.25
	Male	8.67	6.60	10.33	10.19	9.01	5.03

Source: Economic Planning Board (EPB), *Social Indicators in Korea* (Seoul: EPB, 1983).

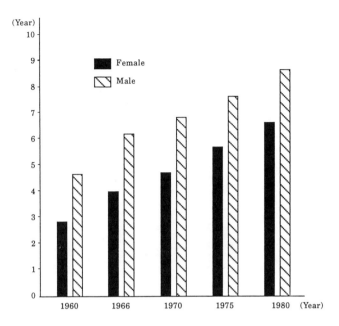

Fig. 1. Average years of educational attainment by sex. (From Economic Planning Board, *Population and Housing Census Report.*)

ket signify increasingly diversified opportunities for women to prove their human worth. Most policymakers in the country and some social scientists assume the effect of modernization and development on women as unquestionably salutary. Others, however, regard such an interpretation of the women's situation as groundless. A grand illusion, if not a willful deception, is suspected here.[1] For the vast majority of Korean women, they argue, modernization means an accelerated process of dehumanization.

The debate often is carried on at the political and ideological level, rather than on the scholarly plane. Empirical studies dealing with women's new experiences are still very scanty, while political sentiments run high. The situation is exacerbated because of the strong role assumed by the state in bringing about the rapid development of the economy and the resulting high degree of social stratification. Thirty years ago Korea was a predominantly agricultural society devastated by a war. It had to rebuild and maintain its subsistence economy on the strength of foreign aid and loans.

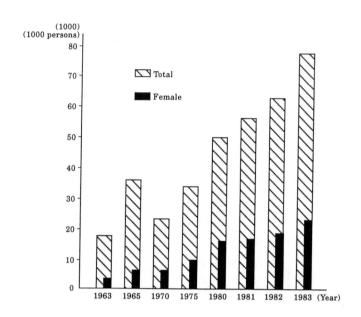

Fig. 2. Number of college graduates by sex. (From Ministry of Education, *Statistical Yearbook of Education*.)

TABLE 2. Number of Students at Each Level of School by Sex, by Person and Percentage

	Total			Elementary School			Middle School		
	Total	Female	Rate of Female	Total	Female	Rate of Female	Total	Female	Rate of Female
1963	5 582 684	2 453 424	44.0	4 421 541	2 088 401	47.2	665 760	223 375	33.6
1965	6 357 365	2 840 594	44.7	4 941 345	2 350 900	47.6	751 341	267 285	35.6
1970	7 985 876	3 588 445	44.9	5 749 301	2 754 648	47.9	1 318 808	503 002	38.1
1975	9 204 060	4 159 636	45.2	5 599 074	2 709 133	48.4	2 026 823	855 729	42.2
1980	10 568 247	4 845 791	45.9	5 658 002	2 745 382	48.5	2 471 997	1 161 351	47.0
1981	10 894 050	5 049 709	45.7	5 586 494	2 712 067	48.5	2 573 945	1 225 104	47.6
1982	11 037 830	5 110 214	45.6	5 465 248	2 652 240	48.5	2 603 433	1 247 107	47.9
1983	11 096 727	5 162 363	45.7	5 257 164	2 550 371	48.5	2 672 307	1 282 007	48.0

	High School			Junior Vocational, Junior and Teachers' College			College, University and Graduate School			Others		
	Total	Female	Rate of Female	Total	Female	Rate of Female	Total	Female	Rate of Female	Total	Female	Rate of Female
1963	364 313	113 209	31.1	18 248	5 969	32.7	107 929	20 544	19.0	4 893	1 926	39.4
1965	426 531	142 583	33.4	21 456	8 975	41.8	109 485	24 062	22.0	107 207	46 789	43.6
1970	590 382	218 938	37.1	17 097	8 904	52.1	153 054	33 448	21.9	154 234	69 505	45.1
1975	1 123 017	428 454	38.2	12 291	7 285	59.3	222 856	57 717	25.9	219 999	101 318	46.1
1980	1 696 792	722 394	42.6	161 018	47 613	29.6	436 918	96 420	22.1	143 520	72 631	50.7
1981	1 823 039	786 346	43.1	199 176	63 130	31.7	580 607	129 913	22.4	130 789	62 960	48.1
1982	1 922 221	838 247	43.6	222 683	74 013	33.2	715 333	169 271	23.7	108 912	52 301	48.0
1983	2 013 046	897 879	44.6	228 222	83 697	36.7	833 189	209 697	25.2	92 799	43 815	47.2

Source: Ministry of Education, *Statistical Yearbook of Education* (Seoul: Ministry of Education, 1963–83).

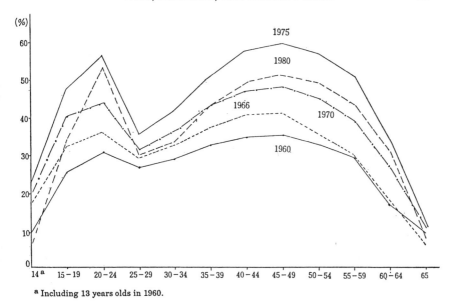

ª Including 13 years olds in 1960.

Fig. 3. Trends of labor force participation rate of women by age. (From Economic Planning Board, *Population and Housing Census Report*.)

TABLE 3. Number of College Graduates by Sex, by Person and Percentage

	College Graduates			Rate of Female College Graduates
	Total	Male	Female	
1963	17 966	14 000	3 966	22. 1
1965	36 180	30 065	6 115	16. 9
1970	23 515	17 442	6 073	25. 8
1975	33 610	23 893	9 717	28. 9
1980	49 735	33 923	15 812	31. 8
1981	55 846	39 263	16 583	29. 7
1982	62 688	44 448	18 240	29. 1
1983	77 272	54 569	22 703	29. 4

Source: Ministry of Education, *Statistical Yearbook of Education.*

The transformation of the same country into a modern industrial state within two short decades was largely the result of government policies designed to achieve maximum economic growth, even at the expense of suppressing human rights. The burdens and benefits of the phenomenal economic growth and the attendant social transformation were bound to spread unevenly. In suppressing the demand for equality and fair competition, the government made use of various excuses—the need to fight communism, to build "democracy Korean style," or even to safeguard the cause of "liberal democracy." But the most significant outcome of this policy of economic growth at any price was a widening chasm between those who benefited from the system and those who did not.

For a small minority of privileged women the Korean economic "miracle" has indeed been miraculous: a period of time during which women have been able to draw benefits of living simultaneously in the old and new Korea. A privately owned car is within their reach, and a full-time maid is also affordable. They can win a respectable job yet leave the responsibility of supporting the family to their husbands.

The vast majority of women, however, have fallen between the cracks of the past and present. The traditional extended family

TABLE 4.   Trends of Economically Active Population and Activity Rate by Sex, in 1,000 Persons

		Population 14 Years Old and Over							
			Economically Active Population			Not-Economically Active Population			Activity Rate (%)
		Total	Total	Employed	Unemployed	Total	Student	House Keeping	Others	
Female	1960[a,b]	8 054	2 156	2 022	134	5 884	—	—	—	26.8
	1966	8 506	2 680	2 538	142	5 826	367	4 993	466	31.5
	1970[b]	9 629	3 625	3 575	50	5 997	631	4 574	792	37.6
	1975	11 319	5 175	4 980	194	6 144	1 108	3 952	1 084	45.7
	1980	12 945	4 973	4 638	335	7 972	1 533	5 144	1 295	38.4
	1983[c]	14 023	5 830	5 703	128	8 193	1 702	5 559	932	41.6
Male	1960[a,b]	7 336	5 387	5 006	381	1 938	—	—	—	73.4
	1966	7 603	5 975	5 426	549	1 628	665	649	314	78.6
	1970[b]	9 313	6 753	6 578	175	1 957	986	404	567	72.5
	1975	10 507	8 176	7 702	474	2 331	1 575	81	675	77.8
	1980	11 903	8 622	8 044	578	3 281	2 172	278	831	72.4
	1983[c]	13 107	9 298	8 812	486	3 809	2 449	384	976	70.9

Source: EPB, *Population and Housing Census Report.*
  [a] Including 13 years old.
  [b] Numbers may not add up to the totals due to unknown figures.
  [c] The source of data for 1983 is *Annual Report on Economically Active Population Survey.*

system has largely ceased to function under the impact of modernization, and rapidly rising divorce and separation rates have forced many women to become the economic heads of their families. But the employment opportunities that these women have are not commensurate with either their needs or their capabilities.

Seen in this light, the overall situation for women in South Korea is not so bright, nor does it permit complacency. While the acquisition of voting rights, access to formal education, and employment opportunities may have laid the groundwork for potentially advancing women's political and economic status, it is clear that they alone do not guarantee women either a decent quality of life or a status equal to men. By examining the problems related to work and education together, we may hope to find a path out of the morass of inequality into which women seem to keep falling.

Women and Work

Traditionally, Korea was a Confucian society in which the separation of the roles of men and women was not only a functional arrangement but also had a philosophical basis. The distinction between husband's and wife's assignments outside and inside the home, respectively, was one of five basic principles that had to be observed if social harmony were to be preserved (recently this interpretation has been challenged).[2] Women's roles began to change not because of any ideological recognition that such a bifurcated view of female and male responsibilities should be changed, but out of sheer economic necessity. With the onset of industrialization it became necessary to draw upon the vast pool of inexpensive and reliable labor that Korean women could provide.

Thus, the tension between a social mind-set that regards the home as the proper sphere of activity for women and an economic reality that draws them into the world of production was bound to throw Korean women into a dilemma. Moreover, the contingency of the export-oriented Korean economy on fluctuations in the world market and the constantly shifting division of labor within the world capitalist economy make it doubly difficult for the working women of Korea to retain a sense of control over their job situations or even over their own personal lives.[3] That the number of women in the labor force increases as the economy modernizes is only to be expected. But this correlation alone says little about the gains or losses in terms of the quality of women's lives or about their relative standing vis-à-vis men.

One certain gain is that some of the worst social taboos against women have been broken. Both in terms of the absolute and the relative increase in the number of women who work outside their homes, and in terms of the variety of pursuits that are open to them, modernization has brought about unprecedented opportunities for women. Practically every kind of work is now open to women. Even deeply held prohibitions against women working in mines or on board fishing vessels have disappeared, as has the nasty reception given to bespectacled women boarding a taxi early in the morning.

Yet, despite the relaxation of certain inhibitions against women's employment outside the home, the realities women face once they enter the work force can be daunting. The first is that most working women are concentrated in unskilled, low-paying sectors of the economy (see table 5).[4] Between 1960 and 1980 the largest increase in women's labor participation rates (from 30.4 to 44.9 percent) was in agriculture, forestry, and fisheries.[5] The relative importance of these industries declined sharply during this period, however, and they registered a growth rate far below that of the economy as a whole. In manufacturing the number of working women increased from 26.7 to 36.2 percent of the labor force, an eightfold increase in absolute number from 127,235 to over one million.[6] But these women were concentrated in the expanding export economy, an industry that relied on readily available, cheap female labor.

The participation of women in the white-collar labor force has grown from 10,200 to 400,200 between 1960 and 1980, raising their participation rate from 5.6 to 33.3 percent.[7] Here too, however, most women worked as receptionists, typists, telephone operators, or in other positions requiring little or no skills. Men, by way of contrast, had a near monopoly on middle management and supervisory positions.[8] In 1981 women earned an average of 44.8 percent of what men earned, a figure that is far below the comparable percentages in developed countries and in many Third

TABLE 5. Monthly Earnings of Workers by Sex and Industry, in Won, Percent

	1975			1980			1981			1982			1983		
	(A) Female	(B) Male	A/B	(A) Female	(B) Male	A/B	(A) Female	(B) Male	A/B	(A) Female	(B) Male	A/B	(A) Female	(B) Male	A/B
Whole Industries	25 465	60 319	42.2	95 691	222 957	42.9	118 736	265 633	44.5	135 979	309 247	44.0	153 475	339 664	45.2
Agri., Forestry, Hunting & Fishery	17 206	57 767	29.8	108 766	207 706	52.4	264 235	391 766	67.4	158 451	306 235	51.7	—	—	—
Mining	30 171	56 173	53.7	106 598	216 472	49.2	115 928	269 506	43.0	140 603	294 945	47.7	150 138	321 693	46.7
Manufacturing	23 171	54 840	42.3	86 102	145 019	59.4	104 348	232 663	44.8	119 443	271 511	44.0	132 909	296 081	44.9
Electricity, Gas and Water	47 821	105 433	45.4	115 680	272 989	42.4	137 422	321 713	42.7	188 053	403 304	46.6	180 020	440 663	40.9
Construction	33 668	72 319	46.6	118 859	298 989	39.8	131 106	335 725	39.1	161 230	388 369	41.5	168 533	402 409	41.9
Wholesale, Retail Trade, Restaurants & Hotels	31 429	73 677	42.7	115 010	249 931	46.0	135 391	293 929	45.3	162 443	353 271	46.0	170 476	370 111	46.1
Transport, Storage & Communication	25 894	49 977	51.8	124 250	214 982	57.8	142 451	264 061	53.9	153 639	298 885	51.4	167 643	312 886	53.6
Financing, Insurance, Real Estate & Business Services	51 761	111 395	46.5	141 549	302 992	46.7	197 353	365 257	54.0	217 531	405 072	53.7	235 796	460 835	51.2
Social & Personal Services	48 339	73 620	65.7	175 285	307 415	57.0	227 431	377 920	60.2	260 925	442 948	58.9	298 839	499 741	59.8

Source: Ministry of Labour, Report on Occupational Wage Survey (Seoul: Ministry of Labour, 1975–83).
a Excluded from survey in 1983.

World countries as well.[9] That year most working women earned less than the minimum cost of living for a single female city dweller, as calculated by the Korean Union of Labor.[10]

A vicious cycle seems to be at work here. Men have traditionally been regarded as the economic providers for the family. When they are incapable of doing this the women who assume their responsibilities have to keep their profiles as low as possible, even at the expense of forgoing opportunities for a more lucrative employment, to keep peace in the family. This negative strategy has further limited opportunities for women's employment.

As long as this fundamentally negative attitude toward women working outside the home prevailed, even university education for women was primarily seen as a means for them to contract a more desirable marriage and only secondarily in terms of advancing one's career (which, one assumed, would be abandoned upon marriage). It is not surprising that, as recently as the mid-1970s, serious arguments against the higher education for women were advanced by people who claimed to have the interests of both women and society in mind. While uneducated, lower-class women working in factories, field, and mines in subhuman conditions won the social and governmental approbation as the motor forces behind Korea's economic growth, the attempts of college-educated women to enter the professions were, and still remain to be, met with covert and overt resistance. It was customary for major corporations to deny women the right even to submit applications.[11] In the late 1970s, when there was an acute shortage of trained manpower, some employers (usually at banks) reluctantly abandoned their policies that had barred women altogether or forced their resignation upon marriage. Currently, however, most business firms continue to bar women from all but unskilled, menial work.[12]

A fourth feature of the women's job market is its extreme sensitivity to fluctuations in the economy and a low level of job attachment on the part of women. It has already been noted that, even under stable conditions, most employers make it mandatory for women to resign when they get married. Since wages and other benefits are determined by seniority, women's low levels of job attachment mean that they earn less.[13] Even in the higher professions, in which no overt discrimination exists, women still face a lower promotion ceiling than men.

Women's attitudes toward work, however, have changed significantly in this decade, something that is to be expected in a society in which three-quarters of the population is under thirty-five years of age. A survey conducted in 1985 at Ewha University, the largest women's university in Korea and a school that has often been criticized for its finishing school atmosphere, showed that 97 percent of its graduates wanted to work. In 1970 the corresponding figure was just 53.2 percent. In the 1980 survey 79.5 percent of the respondents also said that they wished to continue work after the birth of their children.[14] But in 1985, while 66.9 percent of all male graduates found jobs, only 37.6 percent of all female graduates did. The percentage of both male and female graduates who find work has been falling since 1978; it has been falling more rapidly, however, for women.[15]

Middle-aged urban women have also been seeking work in increasing numbers as the opportunity cost of remaining a housewife has risen. The increase in the life span and the success of family planning programs has raised the number of years that a woman has free after her youngest child enters school from 22.4 in 1935 to 35.0 in 1975, providing an added impetus to the phenomenon of middle-aged women seeking second careers.[16] In addition, the accelerated pace of social change has made women who are confined to the narrow routine of household work feel hopelessly outmoded. Many fear that they might lose both their husbands and their children because of the mental distance separating them.[17]

The few but highly visible pioneering women who are successfully competing with men in the fields of journalism, law, big business, and others that were once considered to be male domains have had a galvanizing effect on the largely untapped pool of university-educated women. In a recent survey 72 percent of the women seeking jobs said that their main reason for wanting to work was self-fulfillment; only 16.9 percent cited economic constraints as their reason.[18]

What seems to be emerging is a skewed bipolarization in the employment patterns of Korean women. The vast majority of women are being forced into jobs left empty by men who have moved on to more modern and profitable areas of work, and a small but increasing minority of women with training are making inroads into technical and professional fields. This latter group has achieved success by following the male rules of the game and by seeking work closely related to their specialties; the Ewha survey also showed that positions requiring general management ability and leadership are still largely closed to women.[19] Even at this level, then, women are perceived as objects to be utilized, rather than as individuals with their own initiative. As long as university-educated women are confined to a few categories of jobs that have a shortage of trained personnel, and their lateral and vertical promotion possibilities are limited, many of the gains that they have made can be viewed as part of the modernization process and not as a real change in the male leader, female follower tradition in Korea. Women are perceived as having a lack of professional commitment, a failing that is as significant as social discrimination in their difficulties in finding employment.[20] It is especially in this connection that the problems in education for women must be reviewed.

Women and Education

By all appearances Korea's achievements in education in the last two decades have been exemplary. Women have benefited along with men. Many observers have credited the educational system as being a leading factor in generating the Korean miracle. The number of years the average Korean man spends in school has risen from 4.78 to 8.67 in this period; for women it has risen from 2.92 to 6.63 years (see table 1).

In 1983, 98 percent of all women and 99.1 percent of all men who completed elementary school advanced to junior high school; out of this group 89.1 percent of all women and 96.7 percent of all men entered senior high school. The gap still remains significant in higher education. Of senior high school students 35.8 percent of all women and 40.3 percent of all men went on to college (see table 6). Women made up 36.7 percent of the students at junior and vocational colleges, and 25.2 percent of the students at four-year colleges and graduate schools taken altogether (see table 2).

TABLE 6. Advancement Rate and Employment Rate of Graduates at Each Level of School by Sex, in Persons, Percent

		Elementary School					Middle School				
		Graduates	Entered to Higher School	Employed	Advancement Rate a	Employment Rate b	Graduates	Entered to Higher School	Employed	Advancement Rate a	Employment Rate b
1965	Female	267 389	125 533	—	47.0	—	66 493	46 103	6 314	69.3	9.5
	Male	350 165	209 856	—	59.9	—	123 233	85 016	16 037	69.0	13.0
1970	Female	369 104	208 669	70 773	56.5	19.2	116 244	79 938	5 345	69.8	4.6
	Male	430 865	319 983	53 604	74.3	12.4	196 570	139 204	9 532	70.8	4.8
1975	Female	442 029	308 301	48 625	69.7	11.0	231 083	167 171	13 217	72.3	5.7
	Male	482 699	405 778	28 332	84.1	5.9	337 565	257 446	16 164	76.3	4.8
1980	Female	426 085	400 760	14 113	94.1	3.3	335 578	271 160	18 684	80.8	5.6
	Male	448 244	436 444	6 777	97.4	1.5	406 040	355 360	10 416	87.5	2.6
1981	Female	455 346	432 791	13 545	95.0	3.0	357 039	292 922	21 813	82.0	6.1
	Male	484 092	473 617	6 234	97.8	1.3	416 382	375 967	9 395	90.3	2.3
1982	Female	440 997	427 820	—	97.0	—	387 246	318 491	--	82.2	—
	Male	467 547	460 281	—	98.4	—	433 965	394 866	—	91.0	—
1983	Female	449 613	440 820	—	98.0	—	389 717	347 238	—	89.1	—
	Male	476 146	471 693	—	99.1	—	423 439	409 610	—	96.7	—

		High School					College and University				
		Graduates	Entered to Higher School	Employed	Advancement Rate a	Employment Rate b	Graduates	Entered to Higher School	Employed	Advancement Rate a	Employment Rate b
1965	Female	36 529	12 526	8 039	34.3	22.0	9 696	663	3 342	6.8	34.5
	Male	76 247	24 852	20 830	32.6	27.3	36 036	1 826	13 859	5.1	38.5
1970	Female	51 585	14 748	11 948	28.6	23.2	11 928	647	7 391	5.4	62.0
	Male	93 477	24 325	28 015	26.0	30.0	23 975	1 515	15 847	6.3	66.1
1975	Female	102 058	25 396	28 075	24.9	27.5	14 881	701	6 622	4.7	44.5
	Male	161 311	42 659	48 730	26.4	30.2	30 261	2 072	17 672	6.8	58.4
1980	Female	193 077	44 124	63 165	22.9	32.7	20 181	2 044	10 682	10.1	52.9
	Male	274 311	83 202	64 939	30.3	23.7	39 967	5 630	24 684	14.1	61.8
1981	Female	208 135	59 084	65 344	28.4	31.4	35 514	2 531	15 877	7.1	44.7
	Male	288 865	116 181	58 603	40.2	20.3	85 257	12 857	34 887	15.1	40.9
1982	Female	235 543	75 656	70 170	32.1	29.8	44 412	2 962	20 071	6.1	45.2
	Male	310 055	129 890	58 870	41.9	19.0	90 738	11 081	41 553	12.2	45.8
1983	Female	253 336	90 737	74 501	35.8	29.4	53 723	3 714	24 387	6.9	45.4
	Male	325 787	131 299	60 340	40.3	18.5	113 824	11 956	51 708	10.5	45.4

Source: Ministry of Education, *Statistical Yearbook of Education.*
  a Rate of students advancing to higher level of schools upon graduation for each level of school.
  b Rate of students securing employment upon graduation for each level of school.
  c The source of data for 1983 is *Annual Report on Economically Active Population Survey.*

The educational input for women has grown rapidly, but the resulting output is doubtful. One indication of this is the inverse relationship that has prevailed between women's participation in the labor force and their level of education.[21]

One would expect a considerable time lag between the accumulation of educated females and the socially productive and personally fulfilling use of their education. But, even allowing for this time lag, the persistence of the inverse relationship between education and employment indicates that something has been lacking in the educational input itself. While no one with any influence in making educational policies publicly questions whether women should be given equal access to schools, there has been a failure to clearly formulate the purpose of women's education. This, in turn, has undercut the value of the education they were getting in terms of its power to bring about equality between the sexes and, ultimately, to improve the quality of women's lives.

The promise that education holds for women, the achievements it has been responsible for, and its marked failures make it a complex and fascinating subject for discussion. Essentially, there are two sets of problems. The first has to do with the general character of national educational policy and administration. The second pertains more specifically to the absence of women's influence in the upper administration echelons in which educational policies are formulated and implemented.

Educational administration in Korea is characterized by an extreme degree of bureaucratic centralization, a low degree of autonomy for the Ministry of Education, and a lack of serious concern for the humanistic purposes of education. Korea's Education Charter upholds the national ideal of producing well-rounded individuals dedicated to the principles of liberty, truth, and justice. But the charter has served as little more than a wall decoration. As is often the case in fast developing countries, the fine but essential distinction between educating human beings and producing useful labor has blurred in the minds of national policymakers.

The ministry's primary aim has been to meet the political requirements of the day—that is, to inculcate a strongly nationalistic ideology and inject the knowledge and skills required for economic development. Allocating scarce educational resources, designing admissions quotas for schools and universities, formulating curriculum objectives, writing textbooks, and authorizing teaching appointments were all controlled by the ministry, and all reflect these priorities. As the need to meet the ever-expanding manpower requirements of the economy grew to overshadow all other considerations, the ministry gave shallow consideration to the moral and social consequences of education. As long as students got good grades and passed the university entrance examinations, both the schools and the parents were content. Indeed, as antigovernment demonstrations became an endemic feature of the universities, critical thinking in schools fell into disfavor and the love of learning for its own sake became an anachronism.

Insofar as education for men is concerned, there was at least a close correspondence between the narrow conception of education as manpower training, the educational programs offered, and the actual channeling of educated resources; for women even this was missing. In 1974, when women's participation in the labor force was nearing an all-time high of 45.7 percent, girls in high school were still required to take a course in home economics with the officially stated purpose of inculcating "womanly virtues uniquely Korean which will enable them to be dutiful in their family and thereby contribute to national development."[22] Boys, in contrast, are required to take practical courses in agriculture or commerce. Single-sex education is still the norm in high schools. In this area, too, bureaucratic inertia has combined with traditional biases to perpetuate a situation that is inherently discriminatory against women. Almost invariably, the academic regime in girls' high schools is less rigorous than in boys' schools. Even coeducational schools, typically situated in rural areas, admit both sexes not out of active endorsement of coeducation but, rather, for want of facilities.[23] Other factors also work against female students' pursuit of higher education, including the attitude of teachers and low expectations among parents. In a recent opinion poll conducted by a major daily newspaper most parents wanted their sons to become doctors or professors. They listed desirable occupations for their daughters, however, as those of schoolteachers or drugstore pharmacists.[24]

The ministry's outmoded conception of education for women and the bureaucratic inertia, especially as it related to women, was compounded by the near total absence of women in the higher echelons of the administration. In Korea, and most other nations, there has been an increase in the number of female teachers, but there are fewer at higher levels. In 1983, 41.3 percent of all elementary school teachers were women, but just 102 out of the 6490 principals were women—1.6 percent of the total. That year women made up just 19.3 percent of all high school teachers and 17.1 percent of all college and university teachers. And of all the schools in the country including women's institutions just 2.5 percent were headed by women (see table 7).[25]

Within the ministry itself women are even rarer. There has been only one female minister, and she served for just five months.[26] In the Seoul City Educational District there is one woman among the seven section chiefs. Twenty-two of the 192 junior supervisors are women, six of twenty-nine junior research officers are women, and there are no women at all in the senior ranks of either category.[27]

Until recently women constituted a negligible minority at leading prestigious coeducational universities. In some areas of specialization there are still practically no women at all. There is a striking contrast, for example, in the relative distribution of major fields. The largest proportion of men are in engineering courses (31.5 percent), while just 2.8 percent of women students are in this field. Teacher's colleges absorb the largest proportion of college women (27.7 percent), followed by the humanities (24.8 percent) and the natural sciences (15.1%) (see fig. 4). There has also been a pattern of reaction against women's rapid progress. When women constituted a majority in some areas quotas were instituted. When, for example, the proportionate enrollment of women in music departments exceeded 50 percent, the Ministry of Education quickly instituted a rule limiting the number of women to half of the total. A similar restriction also occurred in the low-grade civil service examination, which suddenly began to attract a large number of women hoping to enter government service.

Most college women now desire to work after graduation, but neither employers nor job placement services in the universities have responded to their desires. Nor does the education that women receive prepare them adequately for jobs. Characteristically, institutions interested in economic development such as the KDI (Korean Development Institute) show a greater interest in cultivating and channeling women's resources than those institutions concerned with education and social well-being.[28]

The Ministry of Education does offer supplementary programs such as the Open University or the College on the Air. Various training programs are offered by other government and non-government or industrial concerns to meet the increasing need for people with professional training and broader general knowledge. But in these programs, too, the ratio of women students falls as the level of marketable professional skills offered by the courses rises.[29]

Educational programs designed to develop women's consciousness are the hardest of all to come by. It is early as yet to predict the long-term consequences of women's studies courses, which appeared in Korea in the late 1970s in response to pressure by women's groups. The Korean Association of Women's Studies was launched four years ago and has a membership of over two hundred female scholars, indicating that there is a widespread demand for institutionalized women's studies programs. But, predictably, such courses are offered at just a few of the leading women's universities and in some private coeducational ones. Only one women's university offers an independent graduate studies program in this field. Needless to say, no women's studies are found in curricula below the college level.

A final point to be made concerning education and women in Korea is the significance of contact with the outside world. Modern public education for women was begun by an American mis-

TABLE 7. Percentage of Female Teachers by Level of School, in Persons, Percent

	Elementary School			Middle School			High School			College and University		
	(A) Total	(B) Female	B/A (%)	(A) Total	(B) Female	B/A (%)	(A) Total	(B) Female	B/A (%)	(A) Total	(B) Female	B/A (%)
1 9 7 0	101 095	29 428	29.1	31 207	5 805	18.6	19 854	1 784	9.0	8 667	1 094	12.6
1 9 7 5	108 126	36 440	33.7	46 917	11 755	25.1	35 755	3 747	10.5	11 031	1 601	14.5
1 9 8 0	119 064	43 792	36.8	54 858	18 010	32.8	50 948	8 729	17.1	20 510	3 222	15.7
1 9 8 1	122 727	47 230	38.5	57 838	19 513	33.7	55 347	9 747	17.6	23 904	3 842	16.1
1 9 8 2	124 572	49 720	40.0	60 178	21 136	35.1	59 160	10 942	18.5	27 049	4 531	16.8
1 9 8 3	126 163	52 124	41.3	63 350	23 025	36.3	63 109	12 173	19.3	29 383	5 036	17.1

Source: Ministry of Education, Statistical Yearbook of Education.
a Including junior vocational college, junior college, and junior teachers' college.

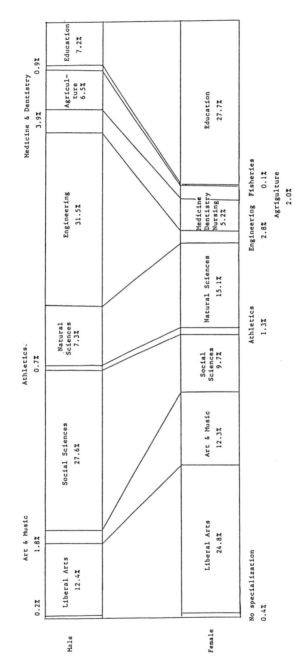

Fig. 4. Distribution of students by fields of specialization. (From *Statistical Yearbook of Education* [Seoul: Ministry of Education, 1983].)

sionary, Mary F. Scranton, who conducted a class for one girl in 1886 and established the Ewha Women's College in 1910. The first Korean woman to achieve international recognition and to be accepted by Korean men as an equal was Helen Kim, the child of a former slave, who was rescued and educated by a Christian missionary and who later became Ewha's first Korean president.

The first few generations of women who became teachers in institutions of higher learning had usually spent some time either living or studying abroad—in Japan or the United States before 1945 and in the United States or Europe after 1945.[30] Although Japanese culture was not noted for its recognition of women's independence, the Korean women who studied there enjoyed the advantage of breaking away from their parents and of being exposed to the outside world. Those women who went to the United States in the turbulent years of the Korean republic received both an education that would not otherwise have been accessible to them and a wholly new set of social perceptions. The cultural differences between Korea and the United States and Europe in those days were enormous, and the West was a source of inspiration and education for women.

Even today Korea's reliance on foreign universities to educate its best minds has not diminished to the extent that its growing economic strength might lead one to believe. For women this moral and intellectual dependence is even greater because the successful example of women's movements in the West adds fuel to their determination to use education as a social tool to improve the situation of Korean women.

Feminism and the concept of equality between the sexes, in education and every other pursuit, remain essentially foreign concepts to the Korean psyche even to this day. Many men and women are still steeped in the patriarchal traditions of male dominance. For this reason the appearance of equality is often taken for equality itself. Until the Korean women's movement becomes fully indigenous social prejudice against women will remain. Consciousness raising is thus the order of the day. But, as has been demonstrated, formal education cannot be relied upon as the best means to achieve this. Women's consciousness has to be awakened in spite of the system, not through it. In the end women should become increasingly politicized as they develop a social consciousness that reckons with the issue of power as well as of values.

Women and Power

The notion of sexual politics is even less familiar (or acceptable) to most Koreans than that of equality between the sexes. Even the most militant advocates of equality for women were, until quite recently, hesitant to formulate the relationship between the sexes in terms of power politics. The internationalization of powerlessness on the part of Korean women has such a long history and has developed such deep roots in the psyche of women that many expected the removal of discrimination would be a result not of conscious actions of women but, rather, of the magnanimity of men. That women in Korea won full political rights before any significant movement for women's suffrage was in place perpetuated that illusion.[31]

As is often the case with gifts, though, the constitutional provision for equality between the sexes, effected in 1948, turned out to be of limited value. Civil laws that relate to property, inheritance, and family relations remained highly discriminatory. After years of efforts by women to revise the laws a few minor concessions were won in 1977.[32] These revisions, however, in no way reflect the breakdown of the old land-based extended family systems, nor do they recognize that both women and men must move to seek better employment opportunities and, in the process, damage the stability of the family. Even if women are allowed to hold property in their names, their claim to ownership is discouraged by heavy inheritance and gift taxes. The laws ignore the fact that women who work as unpaid assistants in family businesses or hire themselves out as domestic servants rarely have legal proof of their earnings.[33]

When division of property becomes necessary because of divorce or the death of a spouse, the husband and his family always get the benefit of the doubt. Male heirs are entitled to inherit twice the share of unmarried females and four times the share of married female heirs. After divorce a Korean woman loses all her legal ties to her children. If she remarries, the children of the man she remarries become her legal heirs.[34]

In the past, when the extended family and village community had a high degree of economic power and moral authority, the sudden breakup of a family, or a husband's desertion of his wife and children, was unthinkable. But today it is not, and few Korean women realize how little legal support they will get if they lose their husband's favor. Working wives may finance daily expenses and encourage their husbands to invest in property in his name, in order to obviate the accusation of excessive independence that is often leveled at professional women by their in-laws. Should their husbands die or leave them, however, they may be left with nothing. Unmarried young women are also victims of the enormous gap that separates social reality from the archaic legal system and lingering prejudices of the old patriarchal tradition of male primacy. For instance, many young women invest their earnings in the education of their brothers or in joint family property. But when they marry out of the family they find that they have little or no claim to the benefits their investment may bring. The lesson that emerges from these cases is clear: education and the opportunity to work outside the home may be used against women when political consciousness has not kept pace with changing social realities.[35]

One of the most notable efforts at reform in this area was the establishment three decades ago of the Legal Aid Center for Family Relations by Lee Tai Young, South Korea's first female lawyer. Throughout its organizational history the center has maintained two main objectives: to provide free counseling about legal alternatives to women in lower-income situations and lobbying for legislative reforms of family laws whose basis in traditional customs heavily discriminates against women in such areas as divorce, child custody, and property inheritance. At the source of these discriminatory practices is the head of the household system, whose male bias (only a man can legally be named the head of the household) perpetuates the secondary status of women, through law. While ongoing initiates for instituting legal reforms in this direction have confronted perennial obstacles thus far vis-à-vis the prevailing conservatism of the National Assembly, the center has, in the meanwhile, stepped up its preventive efforts by extending its general education program about the effects of family laws on individuals.

The accumulation of women's experience of oppression eventually created a climate in Korea that was receptive to feminism. In the formal sense the history of women's liberation in Korea begins with the mid-nineteenth-century Donghak (Eastern Learning) movement leader Choe Jewoo's call for an end to the shameful oppression of women. In terms of a highly self-conscious effort on the part of women themselves to redefine the social world in women's terms, and to bring about the necessary changes, the women's movement may be said to have just begun. Its pace of development, however, has been as rapid as Korea's modernization.

The social activism of women in Korea was born out of the need to mobilize women effectively in a desperate struggle to maintain national integrity in the face of foreign encroachment at the end of the nineteenth century. An early feminist organization, the "Association of Women's Friends," in 1899 staged a sit-in demonstration in front of the Toksu Palace, demanding the abolishment of concubinage. That, however, was an exception; most of the energy was directed toward establishing educational opportunities for young women. The few most brave of the early female leaders joined men as underground auxiliaries in the struggle to fight for independence after 1910, when the country was annexed to Japan. Otherwise, women's groups took the form of social clubs or church-sponsored groups such as the Buddhist Women's Association (1920) and the Korean Young Women's Christian Association (YWCA) (1922). Nationalist, rather than feminist, concerns dominated the direction of leadership of the women's movements during the Japanese period, and the same predominance of political concern over feminist or humanitarian motives continued even after the liberation of the country in 1945. Women's organizations characteristically bore such names as the Association of Patriotic Women and the Korean Mothers' Association.

By contrast, the contemporary women's movement, which appeared on the scene in the early to mid-1970s, came from imported academic feminism and a political context of grass roots demands to secure basic human rights for women and, ultimately, for all human beings.[36] This movement sought to see the world through women's eyes, in order to obtain a more balanced perspective on life and social relations. Since 1985 a number of women's groups with specialized focuses have appeared on the intellectual horizon, and one can directly trace their organizational development and epistemological outlook to the key influence of a few individual female scholars, who were notably successful in pioneering a feminist praxis in the early 1970s through social science methodologies. In recent years one has the establishment of groups such as Yosung Minuhoe (Women for Democracy) and Another Culture, which emphasize consciousness raising about women's concerns through direct community involvement and the publishing of female-authored texts. It is significant that the younger women in these groups, often educated abroad in Europe and the United States, where they were exposed to an intellectualized women's movement, consciously identify themselves as "feminists," a label often avoided by early socially active women because of its Western cultural bias.

At the very least the new women's movement seeks to remove all formal impediments to equality between the sexes in Korea and to fight specific cases in which women's rights have been violated. It believes in utilizing every morally permissible (if not always legally recognized) means to do this. The ruling Democratic Justice party twice reneged on promises to revise discriminatory laws relating to the family and property. In 1983 the government did acknowledge the dependence of the national economy on women by installing a Special Commission on Women under the chairmanship of the prime minister and establishing the Women's Development Institute. But, as the more critical women's groups were quick to point out, the government was more interested in mobilizing women to serve the agenda of national development than in helping them to realize their human potential as individuals.

The Special Commission is ineffectual, and the Women's Development Institute is little more than a research organization, still invested with little policy-formulating responsibility. Yet its existence as a government-supported institution should not be dismissed lightly, as its regularly published journals and reports have laid the groundwork, at the very least, in setting new standards for research on Korean women. The institute, since its founding, has also absorbed a significant number of women with advanced degrees who had been looking for an outlet to pursue their theoretical interest in women's issues. The government-sponsored institute is unlikely, however, to become the focus of a new women's movement that critically questions the political foundations upon which inequities against are perpetuated.

It has already been noted that feminism in Korea, as distinct from women's organizations, was initially an imported phenomenon that is only slowly catching on with the general public. It was given a boost in 1975, during the International Year of Women. But even then the ideas of liberation fell on largely arid ground. Feminism was perceived as a luxury for a few well-educated, prominent women. The introduction of women's studies programs was probably the crowning achievement of this first generation of upper-middle-class feminists.

The women's movement entered a new era, however, when a handful of young feminists, trained by this earlier generation, delivered their message of liberation in a climate of rapid industrialization and urbanization. Feminism for young radical intellectuals and the masses of urban and rural working women who came into contact with them was no longer a luxury—it had become a means of survival. The new women's movement was officially born in 1984 when several groups coalesced into the Committee to Ensure Women's Survival and began to protest specific instances in which women's rights had been violated. The protests involved direct physical action—sit-down strikes and confrontations with the police—and they proved to be quite effective in drawing public attention to the women's cause and in galvanizing mass support.

The committee, which reorganized itself into the Union of Women's Groups in the spring of 1987, scored some major victories. Mandatory early retirement for women was declared unlawful, and a broadcasting company employee who had been abused by her male colleagues to the point that she resigned, was reinstated, and relocated. The campaign to protest the brutalization of a college woman by the police, which the committee initiated, became a landmark case in the national struggle for democracy. In each of these instances Korean women have shown themselves to be a political force to contend with in this country and one that men must recognize.

Close ties with other human rights groups is a hallmark of the new women's movement. Before the 29 June 1987 Declaration for Democratization human rights groups tended to look upon the women's movement as one area in which the fight for democracy could be waged without incurring the government's wrath. As a result, they supported it from behind the scenes. Feminism and marxism converged to build a theoretical basis for analyzing the exploited status of women laborers. The Left-oriented feminists have identified the juxtaposition of the patriarchal social structure with an economy dependent on the world capitalist market as the root cause of the oppression of the Korean working woman. Along these lines some have argued that—given the Korean woman's triple oppression—nothing short of the reunification of the two Koreas will succeed in bringing about equality between the sexes and true human liberation.[37]

From the standpoint of women the influence of marxism in an undeveloped, untested movement should be a cause for some concern. Marxism has a long history among the young men and women of Korea, and its ideology, emphasizing the importance of an anticapitalist, anti-imperialist struggle, is accepted as an article of faith by many. By contrast, feminism is a relatively young movement, which has not yet worked out a theoretical basis of its own that is suitable to the Korean situation. Some argue that the Korean women's movement should free itself from the influence of Western feminism, which is rooted in a culture that oppresses the weak.[38] The real danger here is that the less academically inclined of the new women's groups may believe that a gender perspective can be safely set aside in favor of a class perspective. If that should happen just as the national struggle for democracy is entering the phase of a genuine mass movement, the cause of women in Korea will ironically have succeeded only in circling back on itself.

Conclusion

Economic growth and social development in Korea over the last two decades have brought about dramatic rises in the educational status of women and their employment opportunities. There has not necessarily been a corresponding improvement, however, in the quality of their lives. The Korean experience clearly shows that, when economic objectives are pursued without regard to their social and human consequences, and when the national educational administration chooses to remain oblivious to the moral implications of expanding educational opportunities in a rapidly changing society, then changes that might benefit women will not occur.

Formal education has had little to do with educating women to understand their position as an oppressed nonminority. Feminism, imported from abroad, acted as a catalyst, but Korean women became receptive to feminist messages only when they were swept under the wave of modernization. The new women's movement in Korea has close ties to the human rights movement in general and has benefited from its efforts. At the same time feminism, as yet a young movement in Korea, faces the danger of being engulfed by the nascent radical labor movement and losing its specificity in relation to issues of gender.

In rapidly developing countries such as Korea changes that occur gradually in other societies are telescoped together. Unless those concerned with education are closely attuned to the rapid changes taking place both at home and abroad, and unless they constantly reexamine their values in the light of ongoing developments, education itself may forfeit its claim to serve as the guiding light of humanity.

NOTES

1. See, for example, Dug-soo Son and Mi-kyung Lee, *My Mother's Name Is Worry: A Preliminary Report of the Study on Poor Women in Korea* (Seoul: Christian Institute for the Study of Justice and Development, 1983).

2. See Sook-ja Kang, "A Study for the Formulation of an Ideology for Korean Women's Movement," *Women's Studies* (Korean Women's Development Institute) 5, no. 1 (1987): 122–27.

3. Suk-yul Huh, "Study of Labor-force Participation of Korean Women—I," *Chungbuk University Journal*, no. 30 (1984): 3–5.

4. Hyung Cho, "Women's Work in the Unofficial Sector," in *Women and Work*, ed. Korean Women's Institute (Seoul: Ewha University, 1985); Sun-young Kim, *Trend Analysis and Projection of Female Labor Force Participation in Korea* (Seoul: Korean Women's Development Institute, 1984); Hee-jun Tak, "Korean Women and Utilization of the Human Resources," *Women's Studies* 4, no. 3 (1986); Huh, "Study of Labor-force Participation."

5. Kim, *Trend Analysis*, 74.

6. Huh, "Study of Labor-force Participation," 78; Kim, *Trend Analysis*, 79.

7. Huh, "Study of Labor-force Participation," 7.

8. Kim, *Trend Analysis*, 54.

9. In-young Shin, "Organized Labor and Women in Korea," in *Korean Women and Work*, ed. Korean Women's Institute (Seoul: Ewha University, 1985), 182.

10. Shin, "Organized Labor," 175.

11. Kyung-nan Choo, "Education and Utilization of Female Labor Force in Korea," Korean Educational Development Institute, 1982, 66–67.

12. Editorial, *Dong-a Dong Daily*, 22 September 1987.

13. Tak, "Korean Women," 81.

14. Sei-wha Chung and Pil-wha Chang, "Struggles for Increasing Employment Opportunities for Women University Graduates in Korea," *Women's Studies Review* 2 (December 1985), 237–39.

15. Chung and Chang, "Struggles," 224.

16. Kim, *Trend Analysis*, 55.

17. Joo-hee Kim, "Confusion in Consciousness and Reference Group," *Korean Middle Class Women and the Culture Lag* (Seoul: Korean National Commission for UNESCO, 1985), 84–85.

18. Chung and Chang, "Struggles," 237.

19. Chung and Chang, "Struggles," 225–26.

20. Chung and Chang, "Struggles," 231; editorial, *Dong-a Dong Daily*, 22 September 1987.

21. Choo, "Education and Utilization," 48; Kim, *Trend Analysis*, 23.

22. Ministry Order no. 35, Ministry of Education, 1974.

23. Korean Women's Development Institute, *Women's Handbook* (Seoul: Korean Women's Development Institute, 1985), 80.

24. *Joong-Ang Daily*, 22 September 1987.

25. *Women's Handbook*, 82–83.

26. Hu-jung Yoon, "Korean Women and Participation in Public Policy-making," *Women's Studies* 4, no. 3 (1986): 41.

27. *Women's Handbook*, 84.

28. See bibliography in Chung and Chang, "Struggles," 270–71.

29. *Women's Handbook*, 86.

30. Yong-oak Park, *Women's Movement in Modern Korea* (Seoul: Academy of Korean Studies, 1984).

31. Sook-ja Kang, "A Study for the Formulation of an Ideology for Korean Women's Movement," *Women's Studies* 5, no. 1 (1987): 140.

32. In-ho Lee, "Social Change and Revision of Laws Related to the Family," *Voices of Modern Korean Women* (Seoul: Sammin Publishing, 1986), 194–95.

33. Cho, "Women's Work," 142–43.

34. Lee, "Social Change," 193.

35. Eun-hee Chi, "Industrialization of Korea and Women's Labor: A Theoretical Study," in *Korean Women and Work*, ed. Korean Women's Institute (Seoul: Ewha University, 1985), 37–43.

36. Hae-jong Cho, "Changing and Overcoming the Patriarchal System," *Women's Studies in Korea*, no. 2 (1986): 195–96.

37. Kang, "Study for the Formulation of an Ideology," 143.

38. Kang, "Study for the Formulation of an Ideology," 143–45.

Women's Education as an Instrument for Change: The Case of the Philippines

Amaryllis Tiglao Torres

To most Filipinos education represents hope for the future. The farmer in the countryside spends a lifetime working the soil to earn enough money for his children's schooling. The young factory worker scrimps on personal expenses and works a second shift so that she can send money home for her siblings' education. The housewife takes in laundry and sewing or hawks native delicacies, while her child sells newspapers on street corners to buy school supplies. The average Filipino man, who earns approximately three dollars a day, believes that education can elevate him from poverty to prosperity and from a life of menial drudgery to one of challenging employment. And to the average Filipino woman, or "Filipina," education is perceived to be the key to a better life. Why is education so highly valued? Is it truly the key to a better life in the Philippines?

Women's Education in the Philippines

American Public School Education: A Turning Point for Women

Women's educational status changed in many ways with the advent of the twentieth century. Following the triumph of the United States in the Philippine-American War shortly before the turn of the century, the colonial government introduced the ideals of the American public educational system to the Philippines. These were quite different from the Spanish colonial policies that had been in effect. Admission policies were liberalized, enabling men and women from all classes to go to school. Night schools were opened for working students. Women were accepted by schools of higher learning.[1]

These changes were to liberate Filipinas.[2] A closer look at education during the early years of the century, however, complicates this view. Immediately after the capitulation of Manila in 1898 a U.S. army officer organized schools in the city, inviting other soldiers to exchange their guns for books.[3] Thus, the first teachers in the public schools were American soldiers and Filipinos previously trained as "maestros" and "maestras" (male and female teachers). The Filipinos "responded to the schools with astonishing alacrity."[4] In 1900 night schools opened, in addition to elementary and high schools, and were well attended. By 1903 half of the towns in the islands had American teachers. In 1904, 400 Filipino teachers of both sexes had been trained, and 227,600 children were in school. At least five coeducational institutions, including the University of the Philippines, were established, and institutions exclusively for women were also formed, all of which are still in operation.[5]

Higher education for Filipinas helped them break out of the roles imposed by four hundred years of Spanish colonialism. Under the Spaniards the average Filipina was semiliterate; she could read prayers and write simple letters. Moreover, she was expected to be content with her lot. The advent of public school education gave women the means to look beyond their homes, prayers, and church. Eventually, they saw the gross inequality in Philippine political life and began a successful struggle for political suffrage.

Quite apart from these positive effects on women, it is equally important to understand the context of educational policies during the American period. Many of the philosophical underpinnings of education at that time still apply today.

The Colonial Context of Philippine Education during the American Period

The decision of the American government to educate the Filipino masses was not an act of magnanimity. Education was correctly perceived to be the most effective way to pacify the nation. The network of public schools established throughout the islands helped the American colonial government achieve the following ends: (1) the development of a new generation of Filipinos educated on the economic and political values of American society; (2) the suppression of independence and nationalism, which had previously been ignited by the Philippine revolution; and (3) influence over the minds of educated men and women (including educators, entrepreneurs, bureaucrats, and politicians), through the adoption of English as the medium of instruction, which introduced them to Anglo-American ideals.[6]

As a result of these policies, the twentieth-century Filipino became the caricature of the "brown American." Through America's hold on Filipino ideas and ideals the Philippines was transformed into the "strongest ally of the United States in Asia," and most of its people aspired for "the American way of life."

Consequently, Filipinos became producers for American-controlled firms. They also became consumers of its products. Industrial and agricultural development in the Philippines was geared toward benefiting the United States, and preferential trade and property agreements were made with the United States. In politics American-educated technocrats and bureaucrats applied the visions of the West to the problems of the Philippines, often inappropriately. Filipinos became convinced of the Communist threat, and the resulting hysteria facilitated the ratification of a long-term U.S. military bases agreement, which has recently been canceled.

The Americanized character of Philippine education affected the thinking and aspirations of educated Filipino men and women alike. It also had an impact on the nature of economic, political, and sociocultural life in the islands. Gender roles and relationships were likewise affected.

Gender Ideology in the First Period of Feminism

Even while public school education opened the eyes of Filipino women to worldly affairs, it did not sufficiently intrude on the value of male *machismo* nurtured during the Spanish period. In fact, the educational system under the new colonizers served to reinforce gender-role differentiation. Discrimination was obvious not only in the home but also in the workplace.

The sanctity of the family was upheld by formal training, and women were inbred with the idea that they (not men) play the pivotal role in the home. Education for homemaking became formalized as "home economics," and education for women was deemed important to the extent that they could use their knowledge to impart societal values to sons and daughters. Nevertheless, major decisions remained the prerogative of men. The male was supreme even in the home, and the female assumed a subordinate albeit caretaker position.

Feminists during this period also subscribed to a traditional division of labor, even as they espoused political equality through suffrage. They admonished Filipinas to give their homes and children as much attention as they would to the women's cause, reminding them that their responsibilities in society principally involved the family.[7]

Gender stereotypes are likewise evident in the occupational patterns among women during the early years of this century. Although a few completed courses in medicine, law, dentistry, optometry, and business, most women studied teaching, nursing, and pharmacology. Although equal opportunities for both sexes existed in higher education, society propelled most women into traditionally feminine professions, those that called for caring and nurturing others.

In the budding industries of the period the majority of women worked in cigar and cigarette factories and in the garment industry. While cigarette manufacturing may have been considered a novel enterprise, women had long participated in harvesting and rolling tobacco. Factory work merely streamlined the procedure according to industrial standards. Sewing, similarly, was a traditional skill, usually associated with women's domestic tasks. Thus, work in these enterprises capitalized on the existing repertoire of Filipina's skills and fit them to new jobs.

Besides these jobs in the manufacturing sector, women continued to work as retailers, hawkers, and microentrepreneurs. New positions included work as cashiers, clerks, secretaries, and saleswomen—all of which are classified as service-sector jobs. The majority of these paid inferior wages in comparison to jobs held by men.

The educational trends that were apparent during the early part of the present century indicate that:

1. public school education based on the American model opened the way for women's increased participation in education, politics and industry;

2. alongside this development a traditional gender division of labor was reinforced by formal education and occupational opportunities; and

3. the educational system helped entrench pro-American ideas among the educated classes, with far-reaching effects on Philippine society.

Contemporary Educational Profile of Women

In the three generations that have passed since the start of the century the educational profile of the Filipina has changed in some, but not all, areas. Moreover, the Filipine pattern of female achievement reverses trends found throughout much of the developing world.

While overall literacy rates rose from 72 percent in 1960 to 83.3 percent in 1980, the literacy rates of males have remained slightly higher than those of the females. In 1980 male literacy was estimated to be 84 percent, while female literacy was 83 percent. Younger Filipinos (between fifteen and nineteen years of age) of both sexes, however, have higher literacy rates. Furthermore, women in this age group are slightly more literate than men, 97.1 percent and 89.9 percent literacy rates for urban and rural-based females, respectively, versus 96.8 percent and 88 percent literacy for males. Therefore, younger Filipinos and Filipinas are more literate than their older compatriots, and young girls tend to be more literate than boys.

Most Filipinos finish elementary school (more than 56 percent). About one-fourth of them complete secondary school, and less than 10 percent finish a tertiary course. More students drop out of high school than out of elementary school, and, of the dropouts, more are boys: 3.3 percent of all males as compared with 2.3 percent of all females dropped out of elementary school in 1982–83, while 9 percent of all males and 6 percent of all females left high school. Boys also had higher failure rates.[8]

Of the very few students who enter college the majority are women. Fifty-four percent of the students enrolled in tertiary courses in 1977–78 were women. They also made up 64 percent of the student body in graduate schools, and 65 percent of those students pursuing postgraduate degrees.[9] In contrast, more men enrolled in public vocational schools and studied agriculture, fisheries, and trades (approximately 60 percent across all courses). Women tend to dominate certain kinds of courses. In 1977–78 most studied food and nutrition (99 percent), medical science, including nursing (87 percent), and commerce (67 percent). Fewer women studied liberal arts and sciences (47 percent), music and fine arts (27 percent), engineering (14 percent), law and foreign service (9 percent), and maritime education (0.9 percent).

This profile is not unlike that observed in earlier years. Women are still heavily involved in work involving nurturing, caring, and trading. This attitude reflects the continuing importance of their roles as homemakers. Traditional sex stereotypes are also evident in women's choices of vocational courses. Lucita Lazo reports that in 1976 most women in vocational programs chose courses related to the garment industry, embroidery, secretarial work, food and nutrition, and food preservation and processing. Men, on the other hand, enrolled in instructional techniques/supervisory courses, electricity, agriculture, and automotives/TV-radio mechanics.[10]

By 1980 some courses offered by the National Manpower and Youth Council (NMYC) had attracted a few women. These included skills training courses in welding, electricity, drafting, and silk screening.[11] Nonetheless, the biggest female enrollment continued to be in those programs that tapped traditional skills. Only about 30 percent of all female students studied agriculture, and only 9 percent enrolled in industrial skills training programs.

In nonformal educational programs sexual stereotyping is also evident. In 1982 the Ministry of Education, Culture, and Sports reported that, out of the more than 1,250,000 young people who completed its nonformal education courses, two-thirds, or some 938,000, were women. This high proportion is linked to the kinds of courses offered: dressmaking, tailoring, cosmetology, culinary arts, handicrafts, embroidery, and typing. Functional literacy classes also attracted more women than men, because it is widely believed that men are more reluctant to admit their illiteracy.

Gender Profile of Educational and Occupational Opportunities

The educational profile of the Filipina is more meaningful when it is examined within the context of the labor market: What skills and qualifications are in demand, and how have women fared in the job market? To begin with, more than half of all unpaid family workers in 1983 were female (54 percent). By way of contrast, more than two-thirds of self-employed workers and salary/wage workers were male.[12] This comparison accurately reflects the marginal status of women in the labor market. Their work goes largely uncompensated, be it in the home or as partners of men on farms, in small businesses, or in the informal sector.

It is not surprising, therefore, that the labor force participation rates (LFPR) of women in 1983 lagged behind those of men. Across all age groups the employment rates for women were also lower than those for men during the same year.[13]

Differences in the LFPRs among women were linked to their educational attainments. Women who completed college had the highest LFPR (85.6 percent), and 8.5 percent were unemployed. Those who finished elementary school had an LFPR of 46 percent, and only 7 percent were unemployed, and female high school graduates had an LFPR of 39 percent, but 15 percent were unemployed. Female undergraduates had an LFPR of 32.5 percent and a relatively high unemployment rate of 17.2 percent. Women without any education at all fared best in the labor market: their unemployment rate was only 4.8 percent.[14]

While these figures imply that jobs are available for either highly educated women or for women with little or no education, the labor market for high school graduates and college undergraduates was actually relatively low in 1983. This may have been because many garment and textile manufacturing establishments, which usually hire women with some education, closed during this period.

Since women usually seek training in female-oriented courses, they most often find employment in occupations that require gender-stereotyped skills. In 1983 women worked in the wholesale and retail trades (66 percent), as professional/technical workers (63 percent), service workers (61 percent), and clerical workers (50.3 percent).[15] Administrative positions and executive and managerial work are dominated by men (75 percent), as are occupations in agriculture, production, and transportation.

Several conclusions can be drawn from this review. To begin with, there is no apparent bias against women participating in the Philippine educational system. They may even be at a small advantage. There are, however, sex preferences for particular training programs in both the formal and nonformal educational sectors. Women's career choices veer toward fields that capitalize on their homemaking talents. The educational system has reinforced this tendency by offering courses geared toward these talents. Even secretarial courses are gender stereotyped because, in many cases, a female secretary works for a male boss.

Furthermore, the number of women who are educated does not correspond to the number who have jobs. If it did, the number of women classified as "unpaid family workers" would be minimal. Moreover, the relatively high employment rates of poorly educated women and the low numbers of women with at least a high school education indicate that the demands of the labor market are independent of educational attainment.

Sociopolitical Forces Influencing Women's Educational Profile
Developments in the Philippine educational system have largely been influenced by the same political and economic circumstances present during the colonial period. The continued use of English as the medium of formal instruction, accompanied by the adoption of textbooks from the West, perpetuated the "Americanization" of schooled Filipinos. Thus, science, literature, and social science curricula and materials have been patterned after those of the American universities in which our educators obtained higher education.

Second, neocolonial control of the Philippine economy in the post-World War II period led to policies geared at the development of skills necessary for servicing American-controlled big business. In the mid-1960s and 1970s this meant meeting the needs for servicing the labor, financial, and managerial requirements of transnationals.

Third, the political scenario, especially during the period of the cold war, propagated the idea that the American democratic system was unquestionably moral and humane and that it could do no harm where the Philippines was concerned. To have thought otherwise was deemed subversive, and most students went through school equating nationalist sentiments with treason.

Education under the martial law government of Ferdinand Marcos (from 1972 to 1986) continued to serve neocolonial interests. By this time the economy had shifted away from being merely the producer of raw materials for industrial products to being an industrial subordinate in "the global labor partition" through export-oriented light industrialization. In turn, the educational system became "a factory producing individuals with the ideology and technical skills needed by the giant corporations and whose consumption habits are attuned to their products."[16]

The features of the educational program deemed appropriate to support the economic policy of this period were designed by the World Bank. In its analysis it was suggested that priority education in the Philippines should be oriented toward producing trained manpower needed to promote economic development and should concentrate on vocational, technical, and secondary education.[17] The industrialization envisioned for the country would not necessitate the use of modern technologies nor of highly specialized human resources. Rather, semiskilled and unskilled labor were going to be more marketable. This thrust provides the explanation for the puzzling profile of LFPR among women of different educational attainments. The women earmarked for absorption by the economy were those who had little or no education, rather than those with advanced training and specialized skills.

Congruent with these plans, vocational and technical courses mushroomed in the late 1970s. Emphasis on short-term training courses, which drew women into the garment trade, embroidery, and handicrafts, was not accidental: among the principal exports of the country were garments, embroidered materials, and cottage industry products. At the same time the government's program to export labor had become successful, and replacements for skilled workers were badly needed.[18] By 1981 the NMYC had adapted an aggressive program to enroll young people into its courses. Instead of offering programs that would bring dropouts into the formal educational system, however, the Marcos government chose to give nondegree vocational training to these disadvantaged youths.

Apart from light manufacturing concerns, the government also emphasized the development of the service sector in two ways: through the expansion of international tourism and by encouraging overseas contract employment. The emphasis on tourism had a tremendous impact on the status and image of the Filipina. The hotel boom in the late 1970s led to the institution of collegiate courses on hotel and restaurant management, and college-trained men and women became front-desk managers, food and beverage managers, and entertainment managers. On the other hand, the influx of foreigners "out for a good time" (in a country where dollars are worth a fortune) enticed a growing army of impoverished and poorly educated Filipinas to seek employment in bars—as hospitality girls, nude dancers, and prostitutes.[19]

Filipinas were also lured to foreign lands.[20] Nurses and midwives lined up at recruitment offices to seek placements in North America or Europe. Teachers, secretaries, high school graduates, and other poorly paid women exchanged their professional tools for aprons and brooms and became domestic servants in Hong Kong, Singapore, Europe, and elsewhere. Lissome young women danced and sang their way through Japan and the Middle East, hoping to earn money for home and also to "catch a husband." In the process many also lost their dignity.

Effects of Educational Trends on Gender
While the Filipina has to some extent profited from the educational trends of the past decades, her status and standard of living were not elevated in the process. Although they may have jobs, Filipino women are among the lowest paid workers in manufacturing, principally because their jobs are considered to be semiskilled in nature. As domestic contract workers, women earn mere pittances on a piecework basis. Worse, domestic outwork provides no avenue for labor organizing, and, hence, pay raises and better work conditions are difficult to achieve.[21] The situation of female entertainers and prostitutes is even more pathetic. While they may earn a great deal ($10 to $150 for sex services), they also endure frightful risks, including the threat of rape, abuse, AIDS, and other sexually transmitted diseases.[22]

Filipina wives measure their self-worth by their husband's approbation. Femininity is equated with correct manners, which enhance interpersonal relationships, while masculinity is associated with strength and integrity. Working wives are generally frowned upon, both by men and unemployed women. Women enter the labor force because of economic necessity and not for self-fulfill rment. In addition, the Filipina unquestioningly carries her "double burden"; it is unthinkable that she should neglect her home and children for her responsibilities at work. Such perspectives probably make it easier for women to accept the iniquitous conditions of domestic outwork, because such work allows them to remain at home. These perspectives also motivate women to obtain further skills in food and nutrition, food processing, and the like: if the skills are not applied to trades, at least they will be beneficial to the family.

Thus far, then, it appears that education in the Philippines has not been a truly liberating force for women. Past and present circumstances have largely sidestepped the Filipina's aspirations for social mobility, dignity in work, and self-fulfillment through education.[23] The essential question—how can education be transformed to enhance the status of Filipino women?—has still to be answered.

An Alternative Education Strategy for Women

A Framework for Feminist Education

Since both societal influences and traditional perceptions of gender roles have been identified as retarding factors for the awakening of the Filipina's latent potentials, an effective feminist educational strategy should deal directly with these obstructing forces. The philosophy of Philippine education must be examined and redefined. Education must become a force that builds the nation by promoting nationalist aspirations, scientific thinking, and popular participation.

To translate such a philosophy into action, curricula, syllabi, and textbooks at all levels should emphasize the necessity of progressive and self-sufficient economic and political institutions. Education should transmit concepts, perspectives, and skills that respond to the needs of people for good-paying and self-fulfilling jobs, for democratic processes, and for peace and security in their daily lives.

School curricula should accurately portray the contributions women have made to national progress. For instance, the Filipina's contributions to agriculture, as farm worker and helpmate of the men, as well as her work in industry have been trivialized. Textbooks should fully describe how women, both as participants in the labor force and as homemakers, have contributed to national economic figures. The motives and outcomes of work in factories, bars, and even overseas should also be portrayed, so that students understand the sacrifices made by women on behalf of their families and recognize how oppressive the outcome of such "obligations" can be.

Schools should also teach students that the stereotype of the passive and unproductive Filipina applies, when it does, only to the privileged classes. Throughout history the poverty-stricken Filipina has been hard working and enterprising.[24] She has managed affairs at home along with producing food and income by raising livestock, tending vegetable gardens, selling food, weaving, embroidering, and trading wares; or by working as a laundrywoman or a domestic helper. Furthermore, she has always been a critical force in the household economy, always expected to make "ends meet."

Efforts to redefine womanhood must extend to the mass media, because present life-styles make these institutions potent educational instruments. Instead of portraying Filipinas as beautiful and sensual objects, stories and scripts should emphasize the contributions women have made to their families, communities, and nation. Women should be depicted as intelligent, decisive, and circumspect human beings—not as the passive, incompetent, and neurotic housewife of the soap operas.[25]

Despite their essentially palliative nature, adult education programs are still sorely needed by Filipino women, especially after the dismal failure of past educational programs. Functional literacy programs, technology training, and management training for small businesses should replace courses on cosmetology and embroidery. Literacy programs can also serve to reorient women's values and to awaken their latent potential. Many women never look beyond their families in molding their futures. Surely, they have as much right as men to define their goals as individuals—not just as wives, mothers, or daughters.

Conclusions

Education should be redirected toward goals that will make the Filipina blossom. Since many of the problems faced by women are rooted in exploitative global relationships, it should be both nationalistic and nonsexist. Dialogues between educators and women from various walks of life should continue, so that women's education remains relevant to the lives they lead.

Reformed nonsexist education will not only improve women's situation; it will redound to the development of Philippine society as well. First, alternative educational strategies will give life to the Philippine government's commitment to enhance equal opportunities for men and women in the country. As has been seen, education in the past has not benefited women in terms of occupational advantages as much as it has for men. Even relations in the domicile have been characterized by women's subordination to men. It is hoped that nonsexist education will change the perspectives of the whole society toward nondiscriminatory practices.

Second, the participatory character of the educational approach proposed here makes it easier for government to reach out to the citizenry, so that steps can be quickly taken in response to problems. The rapprochement slowly being builtup between women in government and those in various women's groups will facilitate the development of linkages with the grass roots that will, it is hoped, reach across the whole community.

Third, mobilizing women's participation in the economic life of the nation through skills training courses (especially nontraditional ones) will help hasten economic recovery. Present plans call for labor-intensive industrial developments, and women may very well account for half of this labor force. All they need at the moment are skills and technological knowledge.

Fourth, nonsexist education that stresses nation building through self-reliant economic, political, and cultural approaches will help future generations of Filipino women and men to build partnerships for the forward movement of Philippine society— partnerships focused on the concerns of the local people rather than tailor fit for the dominant forces in the global economy.

Given these conditions, there is no reason why the Filipina cannot emerge as a strong, decisive, and self-fulfilling citizen who can hold up her head to the world with dignity and grace. Such changes also portend the blossoming of a new quality of relationship between men and women in this nation.

NOTES

1. John Foreman, *The Philippine Islands* (New York: Scribner, 1906; reprint, Manila: Cacho Hermanos, 1985).

2. Ma. Paz Mendoza-Guazon, *The Development and Progress of the Filipino Women* (Manila: Bureau of Printing, 1928); Encarnacion Alzona, *The Filipino Woman: Her Social, Economic and Political Status, 1565–1937*, foreword by Alexander B. Ruthven (Manila: Benipayo Press, 1934), 146; Carmen Guerrero Nakpil, "The Filipino Women," *Philippine Quarterly* 1, no. 4 (March 1952): 8–10.

3. Mendoza-Guazon, *Development and Progress*.

4. Foreman, *Philippine Islands*, 608.

5. Mendoza-Guazon, *Development and Progress*.

6. Renato Constantino, *The Miseducation of the Filipino* (Quezon City: Foundation for Nationalist Studies, 1982).

7. Mendoza-Guazon, *Development and Progress*.

8. National Commission on the Role of Filipino Women (NCRFW), *Filipino Women in Education* (Manila: Government of the Philippines, 1985).

9. NCRFW, *Filipino Women in Education*.

10. Lucita Lazo, *Work and Training Opportunities for Women in the Philippines* (Manila: ILO Asia and Pacific Skill Development Program, 1984).

11. NCRFW, *Filipino Women in Education*.

12. NCRFW, *Filipino Women: Facts and Figures* (Manila: Government of the Philippines, 1985).

13. NCRFW, *Filipino Women: Facts and Figures*.

14. NCRFW, *Filipino Women in Education*.

15. NCRFW, *Filipino Women: Facts and Figures*.

16. Vivencio R. Jose, *Mortgaging the Future: The World Bank and IMF in the Philippines* (Quezon City: Foundation for Nationalist Studies, 1983), 135.

17. As cited in Jose, *Mortgaging the Future*, 131.

18. Jose, *Mortgaging the Future*; Rosario del Rosario, *Life on the Assembly Line: An Alternative Philippine Report on Women Industrial Workers*, PWRC Pamphlet Series no. 1, July 1985.

19. Pennie Azarcon de la Cruz, *Filipinas for Sale: An Alternative Philippine Report on Women and Tourism*, PWRC Pamphlet Series no. 1, July 1985.

20. Wilhelmina Orozco, *Economic Refugees, Voyage of the Commoditized: An Alternative Philippine Report on Migrant Women Workers*, PWRC Pamphlet Series no. 1, July 1985, 19.

21. Rosario del Rosario, *Life on the Assembly Line*.

22. Wilhelmina Orozco, *Economic Refugees*, 19.

23. Amaryllis T. Torres, "The Filipino Worker in a Transforming Society: Social and Psychological Perspectives" (Ph.D. diss., University of the Philippines, 1981).

24. C. B. Szanton, "Women and Men in Iloilo, Philippines: 1903–1970," in *Women in Southeast Asia,* ed. Peeny Van Esterik, Northern Illinois University, Monograph Series on Southeast Asia, Occasional Paper no. 9, 1982.

25. Rina David and Pennie Azarcon de la Cruz, *Towards Our Own Image: An Alternative Philippine Report on Women and Media,* PWRC Pamphlet Series no. 1, July 1985.

Part 2
Africa

An Overview of Women's Education in Africa

Dorothy L. Njeuma

Illiteracy among women in Africa stands at more than 70 percent on the average and more than 90 percent in rural areas; the drop-out rate for girls is higher than it is for boys, especially at the secondary level; and girls are underrepresented in crucial fields of studies, especially in mathematics, the sciences, and technology, areas that are critical to their full participation in the development process.[1]

Generally, the majority of women in Africa live in rural areas, where they constitute the bulk of the population. With the advent of industrialization men have moved to urban areas in search of work and have sometimes even migrated to other countries in search of better-paying jobs. Rural women are engaged primarily in the production of food.

In principle, women in Africa are not thought of as heads of households, especially since most African households are not only patriarchal and patrilocal but also, in many parts of the continent, polygynous. It is assumed that, as girls are dependent on their fathers, women are dependent on their households, carrying the burden alone of caring and providing for their children.

But the phenomenon of migration of men from rural into urban areas and also into neighboring countries leaves many women to look after themselves and their children, especially in the rural areas. It is reported that in Zambia, Lesotho, and parts of Senegal and Burkina Faso migration of men has left about 50 percent of women responsible for managing their households and for farming.[2] Even in polygynous unions in which the husband is physically present, women still bear the responsibility of the care, upbringing, and education of the children.

The Education of Women

Tremendous strides have been made in educating women and girls in Africa, especially since the 1960s. At that time the newly independent nations of the continent realized that development could only come about through the education of their citizens, both male and female. The overall enrollment of girls in primary school increased from 26 percent in 1960 to 69 percent in 1984. From negligible numbers in 1960 the enrollment of girls in secondary schools throughout Africa reached 13 percent of total students in 1984.

Throughout the continent girls are attending tertiary-level classes in significant numbers. Although Africa's rate of general adult literacy is still the lowest in the world, among African women the literacy rate increased from 16 percent in 1970 to 35 percent in 1985.

The Problems

Although considerable progress has been made in educating women and girls in Africa in recent years, it has come at considerable cost. In some cases, up to one-quarter of national budgets has been allocated for primary education alone, often to the detriment of other sectors of the economy.[3] In Cameroon the state has consistently invested up to one-fifth of its budget on education. Primary schools have sprung up everywhere, even in the most remote villages. Secondary schools have been built in almost every region of the country. The effect has been to bring schools nearer to the children. Similar policies have been embarked upon in other countries, including Zimbabwe.[4] Everywhere there has been a growing awareness, not only on the part of governments but also on the part of parents, of how important education, for both boys and girls, is for national and individual development. If parents were reluctant to send their daughters to school because of cost or distance, these difficulties have gradually diminished. The result is that, at least at the primary level of formal education, the gap in the enrollment ratio between girls and boys has narrowed very significantly.

But even with expenditures at these levels there are clearly factors that reduce women's participation and serve to make the transition from primary to secondary education especially difficult for girls. In Cameroon, for instance, it is natural for only a third of those girls entering primary school to continue to the secondary level. Of those who enter secondary school only one-fifth remain in the senior years of high school. This pattern is similar across the continent and is in marked contrast to the experiences of boys, some 40 percent of whom finish high school. Obviously, such differentials perpetuated over time will serve to enhance gender inequalities and limit the role women can play in African society outside the rural sector.

The problems that still plague the education of women in Africa can be summarized as follows:

—very low literacy among women, especially in rural areas;
—underrepresentation of girls and women at all stages of the formal system of education (this problem worsens as one moves up the education ladder);
—greater repeat and attrition rates among girls, especially at the secondary level;
—specialization of girls and women in certain areas of study (humanities, teaching, etc.);
—very low representation of women and girls in mathematics, physical sciences, and technical studies.

Each of these phenomena are complex and any attempt at an analysis of their causes at best can be only partial. Nevertheless, the following factors are among the most significant.

Poverty

The single most important factor that contributes to the high rate of illiteracy among Africa's women is poverty. As has been underlined above, illiteracy among African women is highest and the education level of girls lowest in the countries that count among the poorest and least developed. In these countries the overall rates of school attendance and of adult literacy are very low. Of the thirty poorest countries in the world, twenty are in Africa.[5]

To provide universal education requires that schools, teachers, and equipment are available to all children, boys and girls. In spite of the fact that some African countries are spending up to one-third of their budgets on education, they have not succeeded in providing even primary education for all of their children. With the economic crisis of the 1970s, which continued and worsened in the 1980s and 1990s, African governments have been forced to make serious cutbacks on public spending and social services. This creates enormous problems for educational systems at a time when, with increased population growth, there are more children for whom education should be provided. The education of all children has become a growing concern, and in this situation it is difficult to pay special attention to the education of girls and women as a group apart from boys and men.

Division of Labor
The social structure of African societies also creates impediments to the education of women. Labor has come to be divided along lines of gender, which society considers to be acceptable. African societies expect women to be responsible for growing food crops, fetching water and fuelwood, raising children, and doing domestic work. Society and women would not find it acceptable if men should take on these responsibilities. These tasks are not only burdensome but they also make heavy demands on women's time. Women are so overworked that they can hardly find time for education.[6] Also, in many African societies, girls are often required to help their mothers look after younger children and with household chores and farm work. This means that girls have less time to spend on schoolwork and sometimes have to drop out of school entirely.

Social Patterns and Attitudes
In many African societies the expectations of parents for their daughters are not as high as those for their sons. Education is not considered to be as crucial for girls as it is for boys. Until a girl is married her natal family wants her unpaid labor in agriculture and in the home. If school attendance interferes with this significant contribution to the household economy, girls will drop out of school. When a choice has to be made for economic reasons between educating a son or a daughter, preference is given to the son. Parents see in the son the perpetuation of the family name, whereas a daughter will invariably be married off into some other

family. The education of girls is therefore seen as a less worthwhile investment.

There is also considerable reluctance on the part of parents to send daughters to school if they will be forced to live away from home in uncertain circumstances. Because secondary schools tend to be located in distant places, this attitude contributes to the low enrollment of girls at this level. Related to this is the wariness of parents to send teenage daughters to school, where they interact with boys and male teachers.[7] The systematic rape of girls in a Kenyan boarding school vividly underscores the concerns of parents.[8]

In many African societies girls are still married off early. This custom, in addition to the labor value of girls in the family economy and teenage pregnancies, accounts for the high dropout rate of girls, especially at the secondary school level. Frequent pregnancies and childbearing are also high among African women, which seriously impedes women's availability for educational pursuits. Preoccupations about marriage on the part of women and girls may also sometimes limit their educational attainment and determine the type of studies they undertake. Although African women sometimes feel that education improves their chances of getting a "better" husband and therefore of living a more comfortable life, they are also wary of being too educated or of entering fields of study that may limit their choice of a husband.[9] While many African men prefer to marry women who can obtain salaried employment and contribute to the household budget, very few will marry women who are more educated than themselves. Many men also prefer to marry women whose jobs leave them time to attend to children and the household—hence, their preference for nurses and teachers as wives.

The School System, Curricula, and Methods
The school system itself, curricula, and teaching methods have contributed to the shortcomings in the education of girls. Girls' schools tend to be less well staffed and less well equipped than boys' schools. Nevertheless, it may be argued that the performance of girls at the secondary level tends to be better in single-sex segregated schools than in mixed schools. Some evidence from Kenya and Cameroon suggests that girls do better in all-girls'

schools because the competition is keener, and sexist behavior and discrimination occur less.

In technical schools reserved for girls the curriculum covers mainly home economics and commercial and secretarial studies. Technical schools for boys have a much broader curriculum, which includes carpentry, welding, mechanical drawing, plumbing, electricity, mechanics, electronics, leatherwork, pottery, etc. This disparity contributes to the notion that certain types of studies and therefore certain jobs are reserved for men and that others are reserved for women. Paradoxically, the hotel and tailoring industries are dominated by men, and a substantial number of domestic servants in Africa are men.

The stereotyping of roles in textbooks, in teaching methods, and in the attitudes of teachers limits the achievement of girls. Girls come to accept certain fields of study as being "soft" and therefore "more feminine." Mathematics, physics, and technical subjects are considered to be "hard" and therefore more suitable for boys than for girls.

Employment
The degree to which employment possibilities limit the education of women and girls in Africa is not clear. There is no evidence of discrimination against the employment of qualified women and girls. If it is true that the majority of women in salaried employment are teachers, nurses, and secretaries, this is a reflection of the career options they choose. Women's obligations as wives and mothers prevent them from taking on certain types of work and also account for the reluctance of employers to hire women in these salaried positions. Such responsibilities also seem to reduce the efficiency of women in certain types of employment. Official working hours are not flexible enough to cater to the double load—domestic and professional duties—of many working women. This factor also impedes women's progress in highly demanding careers. It also appears that stricter guidelines are applied to women when it comes to promotions. Although women are now found at significant levels of responsibility in many African countries (and this has been increasingly the case since 1975), they often have to be of exceptional ability to be recognized.

African governments have become increasingly aware of the

need to promote the participation of women in their overall development efforts. A good number of countries have taken concrete steps to enhance the status of women and to provide better opportunities for the education of women and girls. It is toward this goal that there now exist separate ministries charged with women's affairs in some African nations. Measures are being taken through extension work and the development of appropriate technologies to lighten the burden of women's work, especially in rural areas. In some countries, such as Burkina Faso, early marriages are now prohibited by law.

In order to curtail the damage done to the education of girls by pregnancy some countries, such as Cameroon, now allow girls who become pregnant to return to school after they deliver. In some instances, too, laws exist to prohibit the abuse of minors. And, in addition to the efforts made to educate both boys and girls, more educational opportunities are now available to girls specifically. For instance, in many places technical schools are no longer segregated, so girls have the chance to receive instruction in a wider range of subjects than before. Careers in organizations such as the army and the police, which were hitherto the reserve of men, are now open to women. In the area of employment women receive the same pay as men for equal work. They are entitled to paid maternity leaves of fourteen weeks and are allowed an hour off work each day until their babies are fifteen months old.

Possible Lines of Action

In order to resolve the many problems that still hinder the education of women and girls in Africa certain lines of action need to be followed. First and foremost, the poverty of African countries needs to be tackled squarely. Poverty breeds illiteracy, and literacy among women and girls will rise if the general literacy rate is improved. This implies the provision of better and increased facilities for formal and nonformal education, which in turn requires more funds than are presently available. Governments will also have to decide, in the face of the growing economic crisis, how best to allocate and utilize meager and dwindling resources.

The problem of poverty is closely related to that of population.

The population of Africa is young and expanding rapidly. More than 53 percent of Cameroon's population is under twenty years of age. So far most African governments have been reluctant even to consider policies to limit population growth. Obviously, family planning cannot be dictated; the need for it has to be felt, then implemented, by families themselves. It can, however, be encouraged. It is clear that deteriorating economies cannot cope with increasing populations, for which better services should be provided. A correlation has been drawn between fertility and the level of education: women who are better educated tend to have fewer children.[10] A general improvement in the level of literacy of women (and of men) in Africa should lead to greater acceptance of family planning programs. This also implies that the burden of women's work in Africa should be lightened sufficiently to allow women time to participate in literacy programs. In order to achieve this men will have to share some of the tasks that are now performed by women.

The majority of parents in Africa today are aware of the benefits to be derived from educating their children. They want their children—sons as well as daughters—to live better than they do, and they see education as fundamental in bringing this about. If in the past parents saw potential profit only in the education of sons, it is becoming increasingly evident that the education of daughters is also important. For one thing girls tend to be more conscious than boys of the need to cater to aging parents. Governments, too, are becoming increasingly aware of the contributions that women, who after all make up at least half of their populations, can make to the global development effort.

NOTES

I wish to express gratitude to Carew Treffgarre of the University of London Institute of Education for assistance with suggestions and access to some of the documentation used in this essay as well as to Elizabeth Fitzgerald and Patricia Wright of the Medical Research Council Cell Biophysics Unit at King's College London for their help in typing it.

1. UNESCO, *Statistical Yearbook* and *1975–1985: Ten Years Toward Equality— UNESCO's Programme for the Advancement of Women* (Paris: UNESCO, 1985).

2. UNICEF, *Within Human Reach: A Future for Africa's Children* (New York and Geneva: UNICEF, 1985).

3. UNICEF, *Within Human Reach;* and World Bank, *Accelerated Development in Sub-Saharan Africa: An Agenda for Action* (Washington, D.C.: World Bank, 1981).

4. Fay Chung, "The Situation in Zimbabwe" (Paper presented at the Mount Holyoke Workshop to prepare for the conference on the Worldwide Education of Women, Nairobi, January, 1987).

5. World Bank, *Accelerated Development; Sub-Saharan Africa: Progress Report on Development Prospects and Programs* (Washington, D.C.: World Bank, 1983); and Organization of African Unity, Lagos Plan of Action for the Economic Development of Africa, 1980–2000, *Organization of African Unity,* 2d rev. ed. (Geneva: International Institute of Labour Studies, 1982).

6. The obstacles that lack of time places in the way of the education of women in Africa have been brought out by Brenda Gail McSweeney and Marion Freedman, "Lack of Time as an Obstacle to Women's Education: The Case of Upper Volta," in *Women's Education in the Third World: Comparative Perspectives,* ed. Gail P. Kelly and Carolyn Elliot (Albany: State University of New York Press, 1982), in their study of women in Burkina Faso.

7. See also Marie Thourson Jones, "Educating Girls in Tunisia: Issues Generated by the Drive for Universal Enrollment," in Kelly and Elliot, *Women's Education in the Third World.*

8. See the reports in the *New York Times* dealing with the rape of 71 schoolgirls and the death of 19 students at the St. Kitzo's coed boarding school near Meru: Jane Perlez, "Kenyans do some soul-searching after the rape of 71 schoolgirls," *New York Times,* July 19, 1992; and "Boys at Kenya school rape girls, killing 19," *New York Times,* July 15, 1991.

9. See Jeremy D. Finn, Janet Reis, and Loretta Dulberg, "Sex Differences in Educational Attainment: A Process," in Kelly and Elliot, *Women's Education in the Third World.*

10. Susan H. Cochrane, "Education and Fertility: An Expanded Examination of the Evidence," in Kelly and Elliot, *Women's Education in the Third World;* and Audrey C. Smock, *Women's Education in Developing Countries: Opportunities and Outcomes* (New York, Praeger Special Studies, 1981).

Enhancing Women's Participation in the Science-Based Curriculum: The Case of Kenya

Kabiru Kinyanjui

Since Kenya declared its political independence in 1963 the country has undergone many changes that have profoundly affected the character of its economy, population, social structure, and education as well as the situation of women. Modern Kenya has evolved from a colonial economy dominated by a powerful minority settler community to a nation with a mixed economy. Agriculture is predominantly in the hands of African smallholder producers, while the industrial and commercial sectors are still controlled by Asian and foreign capital.

The Colonial Legacy

The colonial division of labor was accompanied by racial inequality in the allocation of political power and economic and educational resources. Racial inequality was so pronounced in the colony that it tended to mask other forms of inequalities, such as those relating to region, class, and gender. The conflicts that dominated the life of the colony occurred between the colonized majority on the one hand and the settler minorities on the other.

Reforms designated to appease majority unrest started in 1954 and continued through the first fifteen years of independence. These produced a political, economic, and social system that is predominantly controlled by an African elite in alliance with international capital. They ensured smooth transition and continuity of capitalist development, thus entrenching a system that on the one hand marginalized the anticapitalist forces and on the other hand created a favorable climate for international capital. These trends are powerfully exemplified in the evolution of post colonial agriculture and education.

Agrarian Change

Land reform, begun in 1954, changed land tenure in the former African areas, or "reserves," established settlements for the landless, and allowed rich Africans to own land in the formerly all-white highlands. Individual ownership of land became an established form of land tenure in the high-potential agricultural areas, which make up about 20 percent of Kenya's land. Most of this land is registered in the names of men.

These land measures have been accompanied by the promotion of commodity production by small-scale producers. Production of coffee, tea, pyrethrum, sugarcane, dairy cattle, and horticulture crops has been introduced in areas in which land reform has occurred. Government agencies have provided credit support and technical services.

Land owned by British settlers was acquired by the government and used for the resettlement of landless Africans. The government bought about a million acres, with which it created new rural districts, a process made possible by the infusion of international capital from Britain, West Germany, and the World Bank. The new settlements received technical and financial support to enable the smallholders to enter into the cash economy. In addition, many groups in central Kenya organized themselves into land-buying cooperatives, which acquired more land for their members.

In 1981 the government decided to disband all land-buying cooperatives and companies because of their corruption and mismanagement. This has led to further fragmentation of the former large-scale farms. The remaining large-scale farms were acquired by individuals or remained in the hands of international corporations and continue to produce tea, coffee, and horticultural crops.

In rural Kenya the production of commodities for export and for the domestic market is predominantly in the hands of small producers. In 1985 small-scale farmers produced 54 percent of market production, as compared to about 40 percent in 1965.

Small producers also account for the production of food for domestic consumption, for which no value is recorded.

With these changes agricultural cooperatives have emerged as major forces in economic and agricultural development. Cooperatives have invested their surplus capital in both rural and urban areas, and they have provided farmers with farm inputs, transport, and, above all, marketing of agricultural commodities produced by peasants. There were about 1,370 farm cooperatives in 1980 and 1,557 in 1985.

Recent research in Kenya has documented the enormous contribution women have made in the implementation of such agricultural policies as the introduction of cash crops (coffee, tea, pyrethrum), dairy cattle, and improved seeds (maize and horticultural crops) as well as in the success of agricultural cooperatives.[1] Until the end of the 1970s the contribution of women was not well documented or acknowledged. Women only gained the right to purchase land in 1985, but few can afford it, and few inherit it. Most women still have only user rights. In most cases women's access to the land was and is allocated by husbands and fathers.

Although women are the main producers of cash food crops, their membership in cooperatives has been limited to a small proportion of the total membership, which suggests that women do not have control over the incomes from their farm production. In 1975 women accounted for only 16.0 percent of the membership of the 887,000 cooperatives in Kenya. By 1984 women's membership had increased to 30.2 percent, but the credit facilities and extension services have not, as yet, been restructured to rid them of their traditional bias against women.[2]

In planning the provision of services, technology, and education recognition of the role of women in agriculture is crucial if agricultural producers are to intensify their production and to take control of the production and distribution of their products. Formal and informal education is important not only to help farmers enhance production and adopt innovative methods but also for the empowerment of women in all sectors of life. Science education for women is very important for the continued increase in food production and family welfare.

An improved standard of living in Kenya during the two decades after independence has produced measures such as land reform, the introduction of agricultural innovations and technical services, and increased health services, all through investments in rural infrastructure. These changes have occurred, however, in the context of a rapidly increasing population.

In 1963 Kenya had a population of about 8.6 million. By 1969 the population had increased to 10.9 million and by 1979 to 16.1 million. Currently, Kenya's population is estimated to be 21.0 million. Kenya's annual rate of population growth is now estimated to be 4 percent, the highest in the world. Despite the family planning measures that the country has adopted, this rate of population increase is expected to continue well into the next century. This rapid population growth results from high levels of fertility and a decline in mortality and also from the improved economic, health, and educational levels of the population, especially for residents of rural areas.

The relationship of economic and agricultural development to population growth, the expansion of education, and the emerging sexual division of labor is complex. Changes in land tenure, the introduction of cash crops, improved seeds, and better methods of farming have resulted in increased incomes, food production, and employment opportunities in rural areas. These, in their turn, have altered the traditional social structure; the division of labor between men and women and between age groups. One consequence of change is that women have taken up more of their families' economic responsibilities, a change with both positive and negative outcomes. First, the overall increase in rural incomes and food production has led to increased food consumption and better nutrition. This increase, coupled with access to health facilities and general education, has reduced infant mortality and increased fertility levels. Increased fertility has, in turn, increased the demand for food, income, education, and employment and has produced land scarcity. For many the standard of living will fall as a consequence of these factors. The change in consumption patterns has put further pressure on existing land and brought about various forms of environmental degradation, fragmentation, and encroachment on marginal lands.

Second, families now tend to invest more in education as a means of widening their opportunities. Educated children, it is hoped, will leave the densely populated farm land and enter formal employment, thereby increasing their income. The opportunities that existed for educated personnel in the 1960s fueled tremendous faith in education, a faith unshaken by either the increase in unemployment among the educated or the rising costs of schooling. Prompted by this faith in education, more girls are attending primary school, especially in the rich agricultural districts of Kenya.[3]

Third, despite the achievements and progress made in Kenya since independence, poverty remains a painful reality for many rural and urban households. In rural areas lack of access to land, employment, education, and water and in health, agricultural, technical, and credit services has left many households and individuals without adequate income or food.[4] Increased population growth has accentuated the problems of the rural landless, the poor small-scale peasant farmers, and the pastoralists, who have lost their livestock to drought. In this situation women, with limited access to land and cash crop incomes, carry heavier burdens in raising and educating their children. Consequently, girls from these families have fewer opportunities to attend primary schools, and when they do they are likely to drop out before they complete the first cycle. Hence, the existing social differentiation is reflected in the access of girls to all levels of education.

Fourth, most men are absent from their family farms for considerable periods of time while they look for work. As a result, most rural households are led by women, and decisions about farming and other matters are left in their hands. Therefore, the production of cash crops and food is often the responsibility of women, although they are not necessarily the registered owners of the land on which production is carried out. For farm matters women are the decision makers, and it is safe to assume that decisions about the education of children are increasingly falling into their hands as well. This may also be true among the households of the rural poor.

The outcome of this new role for women is the increased enrollment of girls in the first two grades of the primary level. In 1984 and 1985 girls accounted for about 49 percent of the total enrollment in these grades nationwide, and in some districts the enrollment of girls in these grades was equal to or more than that of boys. The proportion of girls to boys declines, however, in the higher grades of the primary-level cycle.

With rising population, coupled with the rising costs of education, the challenge in the next decade will be how to maintain the educational gains of the past twenty-four years and at the same time promote educational opportunities for disadvantaged groups in the system.

Educational Developments since Independence

Since independence the changes occurring in education have paralleled those in the land system and agriculture. The racial system of education in colonial Kenya was disbanded in 1964 to create a unified national system. At the same time the content of school curricula at all levels of education was revised to incorporate materials about Kenya and the rest of Africa. Subjects such as new math, business education, industrial education, and agriculture were introduced in secondary schools. Local teachers and administrators were trained and given full responsibility for teaching the new curricula and administering the new and expanding school system.

With the dismantling of the colonial system of education the country adopted a system that divided schooling into seven years of primary education, four years of secondary education, two years of higher school, and three or four years of university. This structure has now been changed to an "8-4-4" system of education (eight years of primary school, four years of secondary school, and four years of university). The system has been implemented at the primary level and secondary level, and was operational at the university level in 1990.

The most remarkable change in education during this period, however, is the quantitative expansion that has occurred at all levels of the system. Table 1 shows how enrollment at each level has expanded from 1963 to 1984. Primary school enrollment reached 4.4 million in 1984, compared to 892,000 in 1963. The same pattern is observed at the secondary level, where enrollment reached more than 500,000 in 1984, compared to 30,000 in 1963. At the university level there were 370 undergraduates in 1963, compared to 7,120 in 1984. Of them 30 percent were women, most of whom were enrolled in the faculties of arts and education.

This expansion is also reflected in resources from the national budget that are allocated for education. In the 1963–64 financial year the country spent 19 percent of its recurrent expenditure on education. The allocation increased to 27 percent in the 1973–74 financial year and reached about 34 percent in the 1984–85 financial year.

In this expansion the proportion of primary school students who are girls increased from 34.0 percent in 1963 to 44.0 percent in 1973 and to 49.0 percent in 1984. The annual rate of increase for girls entering primary schools between 1963 and 1984 was 9.7 percent. At the secondary school level the proportion of girls enrolled increased from 32.0 percent in 1963 to 33.0 percent in 1973 to 41.0 percent in 1984. The annual growth rate for enrollment of girls from 1963 to 1984 was about 15.5 percent, compared to 13.4 for boys. These data show that girls have gained more than boys from the educational expansion since independence. There are still, however, serious regional and class inequalities in women's access to and participation in education.[5] The basic thrust of any argument in this essay is that, despite the remarkable increase in the number of girls who enter the formal educational system, too few are adequately prepared in the sciences. This can only have a

TABLE 1.   The Growth of Education, 1963–84

Level		1964	1973	1984	Annual Growth Rate
Primary	Male	587,000	1,025,000	2,269,000	6.4
	Female	305,000	791,000	2,111,000	9.7
	Total	892,000	1,816,000	4,380,000	7.9
Secondary	Male	21,000	117,000	302,000	13.4
	Female	10,000	58,000	209,000	15.5
	Total	31,000	175,000	511,000	14.4
University (undergraduates)		1963–64	1973–74	1984–85	
	Total	370	4,450	7,120	15.1

Source: Annual Reports of the Ministry of Education (Nairobi: Government Printer, 1964–84).

negative impact on Kenya's ability to develop and use its human resources, especially in the critical area of agriculture. Furthermore, the curricular reforms instituted by the government intended to create a larger pool of scientifically literate citizens have had the opposite impact on women. In fact, they appear to have limited women's participation rates in scientific fields.

Secondary School Opportunities for Girls

While enrollment for girls at secondary schools has increased to about 40 percent of the total number of pupils at this level, these figures are misleading when we analyze the types of schools attended, the curricula offered, the quality of education available, and, in the final analysis, the outcome of the secondary school experience.

The types of schools girls attend ultimately affect the quality and type of curriculum they are offered. Table 2 shows the proportion of girls enrolled in different types of secondary schools in Kenya in 1984 and 1985. In the first category are the maintained secondary schools, which are highly subsidized by the government. These are considered to be the best public secondary schools in the country. They vary widely, however, in terms of teachers, facilities for teaching science, libraries, and other resources.[6] In 1984, 34 percent of the students attending this type of school were girls. This proportion remained almost the same in 1985.

In the second category of schools are the "assisted" schools. These are usually community-initiated (*harambee*) schools, which are assisted by the government by provision of teachers and in some instances science laboratories. The facilities in these schools are on the whole of average quality, as compared to maintained schools, and students tend to get average rankings in the Kenya Certificate of Education (KCE). In 1985, 24 percent of all girls enrolled in schools in Kenya attended this type of school, although they accounted for 44 percent of the enrollment in secondary schools in general.

The third category of secondary schools is composed of what might be termed "unaided" schools. These are the community-based self-help (*harambee*) schools and those that are privately owned for profit. School fees are usually higher than those in the maintained schools, yet physical facilities and learning materials (textbooks, libraries, and laboratories) are inferior, if available at all. The teachers are poorly qualified and motivated. In 1985 a third of the girls enrolled in secondary schools were in these schools, and 44 percent of the students enrolled in unaided schools were girls.

The girls who do have access to secondary education in Kenya are most likely to attend assisted schools and unaided schools, a trend that has been observed over the past ten years.[7] In 1984, 62 percent of female secondary students attended these types of schools, and in 1985 the figure dropped to 57 percent. These figures show that the burden of financing education for girls is increasingly being shifted to parents.

Since most of the girls attending secondary schools are enrolled in unaided *harambees* or private schools, they are learning in schools hardly adequate for this level. For instance, most of these schools do not offer science subjects, a fact that will be observed later in an analysis of girls' performance in the examinations taken at the end of the secondary cycle.

The quality and breadth of curriculum offered at each secondary school is largely dependent on the financial resources available to the school (from the government, if it is a maintained or assisted school) and what the parents can afford for fees and self-help donations. In a private or a harambee school the primary source of financing is parental donations and those from the com-

TABLE 2.   Enrollment in Different Types of Secondary Schools, by Sex, 1984 and 1985

| Type of school | Percentage of Total Enrollment | | Proportion of Girls | | | |
| | | | 1984 | | 1985 | |
	1984	1985	Male	Female	Male	Female
Government maintained	45	48	66	34	64	36
Government assisted	22	21	52	48	56	44
Unaided (harambee and private)	33	31	56	44	62	38
Whole country	100.0	100.0	60	40	62	38
	(297,000)	(270,000)[a]				

Source: Kenya, *Economic Survey, 1986* (Nairobi: Government Printer).
[a]The low enrollment in 1985 is because there was no Form 1 class in all schools in 1985, due to changes to the 8-4-4 system.

munity. Financial resources often determine the quality of both teaching staff and facilities. While wealthy schools can afford to offer a variety of subjects and extracurricular activities, thereby enormously enriching the learning experience of their pupils, poor schools must often limit their offering to the basic requirements, avoiding subjects that are expensive to teach. This situation mostly affects girls and, in general, pupils who come from poor households.[8] The Kenya Certificate of Education Examination results of 1985 and 1986 show that girls tend to concentrate on subjects that are inexpensive to teach, leaving out science subjects.

Opportunities for a broad, high-quality curriculum in Kenya are increasingly limited to a small number of maintained secondary schools and high-cost private schools in which males predominate. Recent research has indicated that teachers and parents have experienced a great deal of strain in their attempts to implement the new curriculum.[9] It is increasingly observed that pupils and teachers have to work extra hours at night, weekends, and during the holidays to keep up with the new curriculum. The implementation of the new curriculum has also meant that schools have had to discard textbooks they used previously, and parents who acquired books for their other children now cannot hand them down. Schools must not only buy new books for the new curriculum, but they must put up new physical facilities as well. B. M. Makau has indicated that the sums involved in this process are colossal and questions whether the country can afford the expenditure.[10]

In addition, there are serious equity issues that need to be given attention. The new curriculum tends to exacerbate regional, class, and gender inequalities in the provision of physical facilities and learning materials. Many schools will not be able to implement the new curriculum because of lack of physical facilities and textbooks. The general science courses that assisted and unaided schools once offered will be abolished in 1989. Yet these schools will not be able to build and equip the laboratories necessary to teach the new science courses.

While a few maintained secondary schools will attempt to provide the facilities and materials required, most of them will not be in a position to do so. In the final analysis it is the children from poor and middle-income households who will be most adversely affected by the new curriculum. Most of the girls in Kenya who pursue secondary educations fall into this category.

In Kenya girls perform very badly in science subjects.[11] The new curriculum reduces the time (from seventeen periods to twelve) spent on mathematics, physical sciences, and biological sciences. This reduction means that those who were not doing well in science subjects now will have to work harder to keep up.

Girls who start secondary education are more likely to leave before graduation than boys.[12] This phenomenon is perhaps more serious at the primary school level. While pregnancy and lack of financial support account for most of the dropout rate at the secondary school level, there is also the likelihood that the curriculum offered, the materials to which the girls are exposed, and the attitudes of the teachers may contribute to the dropout rate. Moreover, it has become painfully apparent that girls face sexual harassment and violence in some boarding school situations. A fundamental change in gender relations and attitudes will be necessary before girls' secondary experience promotes their full potential.

An analysis by Anna Obura of textbooks for teaching agriculture at the primary school level indicates the erroneous image of the Kenyan farmer being conveyed to girls.[13] The farmer in the textbooks is always a male, which contradicts the reality we described earlier. Obura argues that, "in failing to portray women in real roles, the textbooks deprive school girls of role models, falsify the picture of the real world for teachers and pupils alike, and conditions boys to expect men in these roles, which is not conducive to facilitating the social change envisaged by the national education objectives."[14] Ruth Kagia has pointed out how the images of women as subservient to men are perpetuated in the society to the extent that they penetrate and pervade the educational materials.[15]

Secondary schools portray women and their role in society in an unfavorable light, and girls learning from such materials are likely to have their attitudes and aspirations distorted to such an extent that they will leave school early or keep themselves out of science-based and practical subjects. Those who remain in the sciences often perform poorly in examinations. Eventually, this leads girls to choose careers that are low paying and lacking in prestige and that do not require competence in science subjects.

Consequences of Secondary School Curriculum
and Performance

Less than a third of the girls who take mathematics, biology,
chemistry, physical sciences, and physics at the secondary school
level qualify for access to higher education and training institutions, which require high grades in science subjects for entry. As
a result, most of the girls who complete secondary school are not
eligible for entry into high-level careers in science-based professions and technology.[16] This situation is evident in postsecondary
technical training institutions and *harambee* institutes of technology, in which female enrollment in 1985 was only 25 percent. If
secretarial and home sciences courses were not taught at some of
these institutions, the proportion of females would be even lower.

More than three-quarters of the girls who sat for math exams
in KCEs in 1985 and 1986 failed. This trend is likely to be exacerbated with the introduction of the 8-4-4 curriculum, because facilities and textbooks will not be available for the broad-based prevo-
cational curriculum. As a result, women will continue to have
limited access to higher education, the science-based professions,
and the commercial and industrial sectors. Anne Njenga emphasizes the need for more women to join such careers as agriculture,
veterinary science, and engineering, to make an impact and at the
same time to "act as models of young girls."[17] While the number
of women entering professional courses at universities is lamenta-
bly low, the performance of girls in science subjects at the secondary school level will make it difficult for a sizable number of
women to enter into these professions.

In short, the current secondary school curriculum offers only a
limited number of girls the opportunity to study science. Girls
attend government-maintained schools, which have laboratory facilities and relatively well-trained teachers in much lower proportion than boys. Second, the girls who do take mathematics and
science subjects do not perform well in examinations, which jeop-
ardizes their chances of moving into institutions of higher education or training and in turn affects dramatically their ability to
compete in the labor market. In this way the country is losing a
significant proportion of its human resources, especially in technical and scientific fields, where there is an acute shortage. The

curriculum changes that are being introduced as part of the 8-4-4 system are likely to exacerbate the problems discussed above. There is a great need to monitor closely the effects the new curriculum has on the performance of girls in mathematics and science subjects and its implications for women's access to higher education and science-based professions and technical fields.

Conclusion

A firm foundation for the education of women at the secondary, tertiary, and university levels, and their access to professions and positions of influence, is based on the rate and quality of the participation of girls at the primary school level. It is crucial, therefore, that we pay special attention to the factors that hinder girls' initial access to schooling and then to the type and quality of primary schooling offered. The quality, effectiveness, and diversity of the curriculum provided depends on the experience, training, and motivation of teachers and on the physical facilities (classrooms, laboratories, libraries, etc.), textbooks, and other learning materials available. While the establishment of an effective and efficient learning environment is crucial in the early stages of childhood, the continuity of this process is important in enhancing the acquisition of knowledge, skills, and behavior at all stages of the education system.

While the quality and level of participation of girls at the primary school level depends to a large extent on such parental factors as educational background, income, and expectations for their female children, we need to emphasize how these characteristics are intertwined with societal factors, such as the level and rate of economic development, the status of women, income distribution, regional and class inequalities, and the level of scientific and technological achievement. In Kenya the resources that have been available to the rural households, as a result of agrarian and land reform, have influenced the development of education at all levels. The dominant contribution women have made in agriculture and food production has to a large extent fueled the demand for the education of girls.[18] Since independence the education of girls at all levels has been growing faster than that of boys. The high rate of population growth in Kenya has provided an added challenge to development in all sectors of the society. The interaction of all of these societal forces has influenced the participation of girls in education. As Kenya moves to an 8-4-4 system of education, the challenge will be to maintain the gains of the past two decades, while improving the quality, effectiveness, and efficiency of the educational system. Science education for girls needs particular attention.

Not only does proficiency in science grant women greater access to employment opportunities, but women must also possess scientific and technological knowledge and skills if increased productivity in agriculture and improvements in health and family planning are to be realized. Added to this are the gains to be derived from women who are scientifically literate in the socialization of children.

Kenya is one of the few African countries in which internal and external conflicts have not disrupted development efforts. The benefits of this continuity can be seen in the agricultural sector, particularly in food production. The dynamic role that women play in the agricultural sector in Africa is now well recognized, but for this process to accelerate there must be calculated interventions in fields of land law, education and training in science and technology, and access to financial and credit facilities.

The gains that women have made in Africa in the past two and a half decades of independence are seriously threatened by the conflicts that have persistently diverted meager resources from development to the military. This has affected all regions of Africa, especially countries in the southern part of the continent. Women and children have been the primary victims of these conflicts.[19] Another major threat to women is the economic crisis in Africa, which is manifested by environmental degradation, food deficits, high population growth, deteriorating terms of trade for agricultural commodities, and the rising burden of external debt. These problems are leading to the impoverishment of many Africans. Poverty, which stems from both external and internal factors impinging on African development, is going to continue to be the major obstacle to the advancement of the education of girls on the continent.

Although Kenya has fared reasonably well in the development of education, any continued progress in this field will nevertheless depend on the careful and efficient utilization of available resources and opportunities. To enhance educational opportunities for girls in Kenya the managers and administrators of schools must utilize the available human and financial resources effectively. Paradoxically, curricular reforms have impeded women's access to scientific training. Schools and policymakers must face up to the challenges outlined in this essay. Textbooks must be rewritten and girls must gain access to science equipment, laboratories, and other basic facilities. The cultural attitudes and behaviors that limit women's educational experience must also be addressed and educational opportunity allocated in such a way that effective learning and teaching is possible.

NOTES

1. Wanjiku Mukabi Kabira and Wangui Njau, "Barriers to Rural Women's Contribution to Economic Development: Kiambu District—A Case Study" (Mimeo, University of Nairobi, 1985); International Labor Organization (ILO), Jobs and Skills Programme for Africa (JASPA), *Women Employment Patterns, Discrimination and Promotion of Equality in Africa: The Case of Kenya* (Addis Ababa: JASPA Publications, 1986); Eddah Gachukia, Wanjiku Mukabi Kabira, and Wangui Njau, "Women's Contribution to Economic Development: A Study of Agricultural and Pastoral Women in Kenya" (Mimeo, University of Nairobi, 1986); and C. Safilios-Rothchild and Edward K. Mburugu, "Men and Women's Agricultural Production and Income in Rural Kenya" (Paper presented at a seminar on "Agricultural Development, Population and the Status of Women," Nyeri, Kenya, 2–3 September 1987).

2. Parker MacDonald Shipton, "Land Credit and Crop Transition in Kenya: The Luo Response to Directed Development in Nyanza Province" (Ph.D. diss., University of Cambridge, London, 1985).

3. Kabiru Kinyanjui, "Education and Inequality in Kenya: Some Research Experience and Issues," Institute of Development Studies, University of Nairobi, Working Paper no. 373, 1981.

4. ILO, *Employment, Incomes and Equality: A Strategy for Increasing Productive Employment in Kenya* (Geneva: ILO, 1972); Central Bureau of Statistics (CBS) (Kenya Government) and UNICEF, "Situation Analysis of Children and Women in Kenya" (Nairobi: Government Printer, 1984), secs. 1–4.

5. Angelique Hangerud, "Household Dynamics and Rural Political Economy among Embu Farmers in Kenya Highlands" (Ph.D. diss., Northwestern University, Evanston, 1984); and Maureen A. Lewis, *Girls Education in Kenya: Performance and Prospects* (Washington, D.C.: Urban Institute, 1986).

6. Kabiru Kinyanjui, "Distribution of Educational Resources and Opportuni-

ties in Kenya," Institute for Development Studies, University of Nairobi, Discussion Paper no. 208, 1974.

7. CBS and UNICEF, "Situation Analysis."

8. CBS and UNICEF, "Situation Analysis"; B. M. Makau, "Improving Teacher Effectiveness in the Schools of Kenya: Approaches to Quality Learning through Cost-Saving Professional Management," Institute for Development Studies, University of Nairobi, Discussion Paper no. 281, 1986.

9. B. M. Makau, "Educational Planning and Development and Its Implications for Self-Employment," Institute for Development Studies, University of Nairobi, Working Paper no. 433, 1985.

10. B. M. Makau, "Management and Financing of Secondary Education in Kenya: The Effectiveness of Policy at the School Level," Research Report for the International Development Research Centre, Nairobi, 1987.

11. G. S. Eshiwami, *Report of the National Seminar on Women's Access to Higher Education in Kenya,* Bureau of Educational Research, Kenyatta University, Nairobi, September 1983.

12. Ruth Kagia, "Education and the Roles of Women in Kenya" (Mimeo, Nairobi, 1985).

13. Anna Obura, "Learning the Gender Bias Early: Primary School Textbooks," *CERES FAO Review* (1986).

14. Obura, "Learning the Gender Bias Early."

15. Kagia, "Education."

16. JASPA, *Women Employment Patterns;* Kagia, "Education"; and Anne W. Njenga, "Career Patterns and Prospects among Women and Men Agriculturalists and Engineers," Report prepared for Kenya Education Research Awards, Bureau of Educational Research, Kenyatta University, Nairobi, November 1986.

17. Njenga, "Career Patterns."

18. Hangerud, "Household Dynamics."

19. United Nations Children's Fund, *Children on the Frontline: The Impact of Apartheid, Destabilization, and Warfare on Children in Southern and South Africa* (New York: UNICEF House, 1987).

Educational Expansion, Cost Considerations, and Curriculum Development in Zimbabwe

FAY CHUNG

Historical Background

Zimbabwe gained its independence in April 1980, long after most other African nations had done so, following a ten-year guerrilla war. In elections supervised by the British the Patriotic Front, (an alliance of the guerrilla armies of Robert Mugabe's Zimbabwe African National Union [ZANU] and Joshua Nkomo's Zimbabwe African People's Union [ZAPU]) won almost all of the seats in Parliament reserved for blacks. Former Prime Minister Ian Smith's Rhodesian Front, which represented what was left of the colonial settler regime and which later changed its name to the Conservative Alliance of Zimbabwe, won the twenty seats reserved for whites. A second election in 1985 had virtually the same results.

At independence the government faced the daunting problems of reconciling the country's various racial and political groups and their independent armies and rebuilding an economic and social infrastructure that had been torn apart by war. Moreover, after a century of colonial and settler rule the sectors of education, health, employment, commerce, industry, and agriculture were seriously underdeveloped. The social structure of Zimbabwe incorporated the extremes of the First World and the Third World. The privileged sector of the population was composed mostly of whites, who lived in cities and towns and on white lands, while blacks were for the most part impoverished and lived in underdeveloped regions variously known as "reserves" and "communal areas."

Politically, the new government espoused the policy of "reconciliation," which meant in practice that former adversaries found themselves working side by side in the army and public service sector. The new regime did not hold trials for war crimes, and, indeed, Ian Smith became the leader of the vociferously critical opposition in parliament.

The government referred to its economic policy as "Growth with Equity," which in reality meant allowing the white- and multinational-dominated capitalist sector to continue virtually unrestrained, while protecting workers' rights by negotiating minimum wages and providing such essential social services as health and education at reasonable costs. Government has also followed a policy of buying shares in what it regards as key industries. Since independence the government has made the greatest strides in the area of social services, particularly in the provision of water, health services, and education to previously neglected rural areas.

The Situation of Women

Traditionally, Zimbabwe had a male-dominated patriarchal system, although women have been a dominant political cum religious force. The gender divisions in precolonial society were between economic power on the one hand and political/spiritual power on the other. Men, as fathers and husbands, enjoyed virtually complete control over wealth, with the women's labor power being of advantage to her guardian rather than to herself. Women were able, however, to exercise spiritual cum political power in that they were free to exercise authority as spiritual leaders as well as healers. Traditional religious beliefs enabled ancestral spirits to bestow spiritual and visionary powers on both men and women. Such religious leaders, known as spirit mediums, played a key role in legitimizing the political leaders of society. A leader who is rejected as morally and spiritually unfit by religious leaders has little chance of gaining power.

In the area of medicine women were held to be equally capable of possessing and exercising healing powers, healing being based not only on the use of medicinal herbs but also on spiritual rectitude. For example, the most prominent political/religious leader in the resistance campaign against colonialism in the 1890s was a woman,

Ambuya Nehanda. She is also believed to have played a leading role in the resistance movement up to the time of independence in 1980.[1] Zimbabwe's efforts at nation building and expanding educational networks have therefore taken place in a society in which women's traditional knowledge retains respect and power.

The precolonial marriage system depended upon the transfer of wealth, mainly in the form of cattle. Under this bride-price system, known either as *lobola* or *roora*, the husband's family gave a number of cattle to the wife's family during the period of marriage negotiation, which would usually last several years. The transfer of wealth from the husband's family to the wife's family meant that the wife's productive and reproductive capacities now legally belonged to her husband's family and not to herself or her family. Once the negotiations were completed divorce was practically impossible, since the wealth was distributed in such a way that to undo it would mean seriously disrupting the social fabric. For instance, the wife's brother's marriage may have entailed giving the cattle that the family had received from the groom's family to the family of the brother's bride, so a divorce could disrupt the distribution of wealth throughout the entire community. Although at times this system of bride price has been degraded to the practice of selling a daughter to the highest bidder, it survived the colonial period and it is still considered to be a sound basis for marriage contracts.

One of the reasons for the survival of the bride price has been the African conception of marriage as a social alliance between two large and extended family groups and the belief that such alliances contribute significantly to social harmony and social cohesion. Marriages are not contracted by individuals for their individual gratification but, rather, by individuals as representatives of strong social groups. Women serve as representatives as effectively as men and are not taught, as in the West, to see themselves as merged within the identity of their spouse.

It is the father's sister, known as *tete*, who is given the responsibility of judging the suitability of potential spouses and for advising the young on sexual and marital relationships. In this capacity the father's sister can exercise considerable social power in negotiating and cementing those alliances that are considered to be advantageous to the family.

Since an educated girl will fetch a much higher bride price than an uneducated one, and an educated woman is more likely to marry into a family of higher status, parents in Zimbabwe have seen to it that their daughters are well educated. This situation is reflected in the enrollment statistics at different levels of schooling (see table 1). Girls account for almost half of the students in elementary schools, while young women account for 40.7 percent of the students in secondary schools, 32.2 percent of the students in teachers' colleges, and 23.8 percent of the students in university.

Several factors account for the drop in enrollment at the secondary and tertiary levels. Among them are poverty, since only primary education is free in Zimbabwe; the fact that girls from lower-income families by custom tend to stay away from school during menstruation, and the curriculum and quality of the teaching is so poor that a menstruating girl who misses a week of school each month is unable to catch up; social and family demands, such as the need for help around the home or an extra income; and early marriage.[2] An experiment is currently being carried out to provide better but affordable protection during menstruation to lower-income girls so that they will be able to attend school more regularly.[3]

While the precolonial concept of the role of women is still strong in Zimbabwe, it has been seriously challenged over the past century. For one thing the colonization of Zimbabwe led to the development of a migrant labor system, which forced men to leave the agricultural sector to seek work in the industrialized "white" economic sector. The laws of the time forbade such workers to bring their wives and families to live with them in the cities. The agricultural economy was still expected to subsidize the in-

TABLE 1. Enrollments by Gender 1986

	Boys	%	Girls	%	Total
Primary schools	1,157,065	51.2	1,103,302	48.8	2,260,367
Secondary schools	323,799	59.3	222,042	40.7	545,841
Teacher's colleges	3,325	67.8	1,579	32.2	4,904
Universities	4,486	76.2	1,400	23.8	5,886
Total	1,488,675	52.8	1,328,323	47.2	2,816,998

Source: Ministry of Education Statistics, First Term 1986 (Harare, Zimbabwe, 1986, Mimeo); and University of Zimbabwe Statistics, (Harare, Zimbabwe, 1986, Mimeo).

dustrial economy, as industrial workers and their families relied on peasant production for most of their food and clothing. In the absence of men, women became dominant forces in agriculture, especially when they were de facto family heads.

Women still play a leading role in agriculture today, although the expanded agricultural extension services catering to peasants has remained a male-dominated area. Some progress has been made in that 247 of the 3,404 staff employed in Agritex, the national agricultural extension service, are women (7 percent).[4] This situation is expected to improve with the inclusion of female students in agricultural colleges. At present 26.2 percent of the students in agricultural colleges are women.[5]

Women's Roles in the Independence Struggle

The protracted war for independence affected women's position considerably. Many girls and women, including large numbers from the peasantry, were drawn into full participation in the war as fighters and as carriers of food supplies and materials of war and also in other areas such as medicine, political work, and education. Many of these women, often not highly educated, became accustomed to exercising authority as commanders over both men and women and as administrators over semiliberated and liberated districts, where they wielded considerable administrative and political power.

The rise of women to positions of authority during the liberation struggle was largely due to the nature of the war, which depended for its success on unstinting support from the local community. The freedom fighters had to live among the people and to depend on them entirely both for food and for security. Disaffection among any segment of society would lead to betrayal, to the death of the fighters, and the destruction of the society as a whole by the colonial forces. Means had to be found to maintain the highest degree of unity and commitment.

A system to secure widespread support was devised based partly on traditional religious beliefs and mores, partly on a more modern analysis of social ills known as "national grievances," and partly on an administrative system, which vested authority in military commanders, be they women or men.

Traditional religion, with its emphasis on a righteous war of liberation, played a critical role in winning peasant support for the war of liberation. The fighters were believed to enjoy the support of the highest spiritual powers. As the living representatives of ancient spirits waging a just war against colonial oppressors, the fighters had to maintain a very high code of sexual and moral conduct, as epitomized by the revolutionary song "Kune Nzira Dze-masoja" or the rules governing fighters. These rules outlined very clearly the forms of behavior expected of a fighter, particularly regarding relationships with the people. Infringement of these rules was believed to lead to death caused by the withdrawal of spiritual support from the ancestral spirits.[6]

National grievances consisted of a list of wrongs that the fighters sought to redress, such as the land issue, unemployment, and the lack of educational opportunities for blacks. It was, however, the successful administrative system consisting of political and judicial leadership, security, and health and education services that led to the ultimate success of the fighters. And this administrative system functioned with both male and female leaders and officers.

The inclusion of women in the political leadership came about not only because of more advanced political thinking within the liberation movement but also out of sheer necessity. Women aroused less suspicion and were able to move long distances carrying critical war supplies without being apprehended. It was therefore essential to give women political and military training and leadership in order to enable them to carry out these functions effectively. Moreover, a large number of the rural population were old men and women, known for their conservatism. It was quite impossible to win the war without the support of these peasants.

Female guerrillas played a key role in winning the support of the peasantry, particularly of the village elders and of the women. The participation of women as commanders and members of military units not only boosted the morale of the women but also created the popular adage that, "if women can fight, then all of us can fight." This helped to create a suitable psychological state in which every member of the rural community, including old men, women, and children, willingly contributed to the success of the liberation effort.

The use of women in the new roles of military commanders or as part of health and educational units attached to military groups made a great impact on the peasant population, whose children were being swept into the guerrilla movement by the tens of thousands. Traditional religious leaders gave their full support to these unusual developments, thus facilitating the inclusion of illiterate, semiliterate, as well as educated girls into the ranks of the guerrillas. Leadership roles were based on military ability and courage and not on academic qualifications. This led to a situation in which the women who rose to the top included both illiterate peasant women and highly articulate high school or university students.

The successful conclusion of the war in 1980 produced a reversion to tradition. For example, peasant populations that had accepted female guerrillas wearing military uniforms, including trousers, suddenly found it completely unacceptable for their returning daughters to wear trousers. The return of unmarried female guerrillas with babies born during the war in base camps in Mozambique created another social trauma for which the population was unprepared. During the course of the war sexual abstinence and purity were seen as the mark of the guerrilla. The rules of conduct among the guerrillas allowed them to have sexual relations in base camps and with other guerrillas but strictly forbade combatants from having any affairs with the local population, popularly known as *povo* (Portuguese for "people"). Moreover, combatants were never placed in their own home areas, so the peasants had never actually seen their own daughters in these new roles.

Nevertheless, a decade of social, political, and military turmoil had left indelible marks on all. Despite the strong pull of tradition, it was no longer possible to return to the prewar social order. The introduction of a system of elected local and national leadership to replace the chieftaincies gave play to new political and social forces. The integration of the former guerrillas into key institutions, such as local government and health, ensured that some of the gains made during the war became institutionalized.

The program of modernization after independence as seen in the very ambitious health and educational programs made it more difficult for traditional ways of life to continue untouched. Village women were able to gain prestigious and responsible positions as village health workers. Traditional midwives were recognized and their skills upgraded through courses in modern medicine. Perhaps most significantly, the large majority of girls in all rural areas were now able to go to school.

Finally, the influence of Western culture, through urbanization, advertising, films and television, and school curricula, has been very powerful in Zimbabwe. A small but powerful group of highly educated professional women is becoming increasingly assertive about women's rights. Since independence women have gained many rights through such newly enacted laws as the Legal Age of Majority Act, which frees a woman from the feudal tutelage and control of her father, particularly in the choice of marriage partner; the Matrimonial Causes Act, which protects a widow's right to her property after the death of her husband, in contrast to the colonial system, which left women with little property other than their personal clothing and cooking utensils; and the Sex Disqualification Act, which forbids sex discrimination, particularly in terms of employment.[7] The Ministry of Community Development and Women's Affairs, which researches and institutes programs to redress discrimination against women, is largely responsible for these substantial legal protections.

Despite these improvements in the position of women, centuries of custom and practice and the impact of a colonial heritage prevail in Zimbabwe, and there are few women in decision-making positions. Of the country's eight governors none are women; of twenty-four ministers only two are women. Overall, only 13 percent of those employed in the country's developed economic sector are women,[8] although a slightly higher percentage of women hold professional and skilled-labor positions (see table 2).

The Educational Challenge

At independence Zimbabwe faced a daunting educational challenge. With a per capita gross domestic product (GDP) of only Z$365.78 (U.S. $229.95 at the 1979 conversion rate)[9] and a population of 7.1 million, more than half of which was below the age of fifteen, the new government was under great pressure to live up to its election promise of free primary education and accessible, but not free, secondary education for all. Within a short period the

TABLE 2. Skill and Gender Distribution of Employees, 1984

	Professional			Skilled			Semiskilled			Unskilled			In Training			Total		
	Male	Female	Total	Male	Female	Total	Male	Female	Total	Male	Female	Total	Male	Female	Total	Male	Female	Total
Number	21,178	7,408	28,586	44,761	13,319	58,080	121,630	12,900	134,530	229,933	29,637	259,570	9,858	2,152	12,010	427,359	65,436	492,795
% by Gender	74.1	25.9	100.0	77.1	22.9	100.0	90.4	9.6	100.0	88.6	11.4	100.0	82.1	17.9	100.0	86.7	13.3	100.0
% by Skill	4.3	1.5	5.8	9.1	2.7	11.8	24.7	2.6	27.3	46.7	6.0	52.7	2.0	0.4	2.4	—	—	—

Source: Department of Research and Planning, Annual Review of Manpower, 1984 (Harare, Zimbabwe: Ministry of Labour, Manpower Planning and Social Welfare, 1984), 77.

government has done a remarkable job of meeting this challenge. Between 1979 and 1986 the number of schools increased by 116.2 percent, and overall school enrollment has jumped 216.8 percent (see table 3). Many over-age Zimbabweans who missed the chance to attend school during the war years are now entering primary school. About 80.0 percent of students who graduate from primary school go on to secondary school. Zimbabwe has been more successful in the development of its education system than many other African nations (see table 4).

The government has carried out a number of innovative policies that have made this successful democratization of educational opportunities possible. The first step was to harness popular support for the school expansion program. Capital investment became the responsibility of the local communities, particularly of parents, while the government supplied only a modest subsidy, technical support, and quality supervision. Government covered the main recurrent expenditures, however, which consisted of teachers' salaries and the cost of educational materials. Local inputs have included a form of self-taxation for school-building funds; the making of bricks; and the contribution of free labor. Parents have shouldered some of the recurrent costs by funding more facilities, teachers, and educational materials than were provided for in the government quota. In general, parents in Zimbabwe have been very enthusiastic about supporting government educational initiatives. Total parental input is estimated to have been between Z $72.5 million (U.S. $43.5 million) and Z $362.5 million (U.S. $217.5 million) from 1981 to 1986.[10]

Richer communities can provide for themselves more lavishly than impoverished communities under this system of self-reliance. The United Nations' International Children's Fund (UNICEF) and the Swedish International Development Agency (SIDA) have supported a program to supplement the efforts of parents in the most deprived areas of Zimbabwe. A government program known as Construction in Disadvantaged Areas also serves poorer communities. As a result, the minority of communities in which little would be achieved through community contribution are benefiting from new educational opportunities as well.

A number of other African countries, including Kenya and more recently Tanzania, have undertaken similar community-

TABLE 3. Comparison of Schools and Enrollments, 1979 and 1986

	1979		1986		% Increase 1979–86	
	No. of Schools	Enrollment	No. of Schools	Enrollment	Schools	Enrollment
Primary	2,401	819,586	4,297	2,260,367	79.0	175.8
Secondary	177	66,215	1,276	545,841	720.9	724.3
Total	2,578	885,801	5,573	2,806,208	116.2	216.8

Source: Annual Report of the Secretary for Education for 1979, as presented to Parliament, Salisbury, Rhodesia, 1979; Ministry of Education Statistics, First Term 1986 (Harare, Zimbabwe, 1986, Mimeo).

TABLE 4. School Enrollment Ratios as a Percentage of Age Group in Selected Southern African Countries

Country	Year	Gender	First Level as % of Age Group	Second Level as % of Age Group	First and Second Levels as % of Age Group
Botswana	1985	MF	104	29	76
		M	98	27	72
		F	109	31	80
Kenya	1985	MF	94	20	71
		M	97	25	75
		F	91	16	67
Lesotho	1983	MF	111	21	78
		M	97	17	67
		F	126	26	89
Malawi	1984	MF	62	4	45
		M	71	6	52
		F	53	2	38
Mozambique	1983	MF	83	6	37
		M	94	8	43
		F	71	4	31
Swaziland	1984	MF	111	44	87
		M	112	44	87
		F	110	43	86
Tanzania	1985	MF	72	3	45
Zambia	1983	MF	101	18	71
		M	106	23	76
		F	86	13	66
Zimbabwe	1985	MF	131	39	94
		M	135	46	100
		F	127	31	89

Source: Educational Statistics, Latest Year Available, UNESCO Current Surveys and Research in Statistics, January 1987.
Note: M = male; F = female.

based expansion programs, which account for a significant proportion of those countries' investment in education.[11] There is, however, a major difference between the Kenyan *harambee* program and the Zimbabwean one based on self-reliance. The *harambee* program is more or less a separate educational subsector that receives little government input, while the Zimbabwean program receives considerable government support for building subsidies and recurrent costs and is a major component of the nation's education system.

In 1981 the Ministry of Education began to map existing school facilities and compare them to the distribution of Zimbabwe's population, laying the groundwork for a plan that will provide primary and secondary schools in previously neglected areas. Under the provisions of the plan day (nonboarding) primary schools will serve a five-kilometer radius and day secondary schools an eleven-kilometer radius, and five to eight primary schools will feed into each secondary school.

Although, traditionally, boarding schools have been preferred to day schools in Zimbabwe, the new emphasis on the provision of day schools rather than boarding schools has cut the unit cost of education dramatically. In Zimbabwe the capital costs of a boarding school are seven times that of a similar size day school, and recurrent unit costs for boarders are three to four times those of day students. The policy of developing educational facilities at lower cost, close to the children's houses, has definitely contributed to allowing more girls to attend primary and secondary schools than ever before. Nevertheless, there appears to be a deterioration in the relative percentage of women at the teacher training level.

Education officials have been faced with the challenge of lowering the unit cost of education without lowering teachers' salaries. Indeed, teachers' salaries in Zimbabwe are relatively higher than elsewhere in Africa, due to the decision in 1981 to put female teachers' and black teachers' salaries on a par with those of white teachers. To meet this challenge, and to guarantee a quality education for all, the government instituted the Zimbabwe Integrated National Teacher Education Course (ZINTEC) in 1981. ZINTEC has been highly successful in terms of both quality and cost effectiveness. In the final analysis the cost of training a teacher under the ZINTEC program is 46.2 percent of the cost of conventional training, or Z$4,308.24 (U.S. $2,584.94) compared to Z$1,990.60 (U.S. $1,194.36).[12]

The program combines two sixteen-week intensive residential periods of study with continuing long-distance education over a four-year period. The continuing education consists of thirty-six self-study modules, weekend courses, and one holiday course a year. Each group of thirty to forty-eight students works under the direction of a district field tutor. Students also break into groups of three to four weekly study groups. In many rural primary schools all of the teachers in the school attend these weekly study groups. The new program did not have a significant impact on the ratio of female to male students.

In addition to the study program, each year ZINTEC students must undertake a community service project, such as adult literacy or tree planting programs. These community service projects also bring students closer to the residents of their communities. An indication of just how popular ZINTEC trainees are has been the recurrent request from local communities to appoint ZINTEC trainees as school heads.

To provide adequate, relevant printed texts to all school children, in 1983 the Zimbabwe Ministry of Education instituted a program to publish essential primary and secondary school texts at low cost by using inexpensive newsprint and covers as well as inexpensive typesetting and printing.[13] This program, which cost about Z$1 million (about U.S. $600,000) a year, provided schools annually with some three to five million free textbooks and readers, representing some two hundred titles, from 1983 to 1986. Some Z$2.1 million (U.S. $1.26 million) of the total cost came from a United States Agency for International Development (USAID) grant. The program is extremely important, as there is a serious lack of library books and supplementary reading materials in Zimbabwe's 5,573 schools. Most schools do not even have a library. Also, in 1985 the Ministry of Education embarked upon the six-year Reading Improvement Programme, geared to improve reading instruction at the primary and secondary levels.

The new curricular materials focused on a number of important themes related directly or indirectly to national aspirations. These themes included the need for a more scientific and technological approach to problems; the use of locally based and locally relevant examples; linking education to higher productivity; controlling and improving the environment; providing more positive images of girls and women; providing opportunities for study and discussion of important modern issues such as family planning; and, last but not least, looking seriously at the question of socialism, which is the declared national policy.

When the government adopted the policy of making secondary education widely available it faced two serious problems: the shortage of qualified secondary school teachers and the high foreign exchange cost of importing the large quantities of science and technical equipment necessary to carry out the government's policy of providing the national educational system with a strong scientific and technological base. The government tackled the first problem by recruiting underqualified teachers and supporting them with a publications program and regular in-service curriculum courses. Between 150 and 180 such courses are held each year, and they reach some ten thousand teachers.

The ZimSci Programme, instituted in 1981 and based on research done at the University of Zimbabwe's Science Education Unit, provides low-cost science equipment, most of it made locally, at one-thirtieth of the cost of foreign-made equipment. This equipment is accompanied by do-it-yourself experimental instructions and small quantities of chemicals. A number of evaluations have found that the program is successful and professionally sound.[14] Following the successful example of ZimSci, a technical kits program was initiated in 1985 to provide materials for such practical subjects as agriculture, building, woodworking, metalworking, technical drawing, and home economics. Unfortunately, the success of the program has been hindered by the fact that it could not rely on underqualified teachers as the science program did, and there is presently a shortage of qualified technical teachers in Zimbabwe. This shortage will be overcome within the next five years, however, as a result of the ambitious training of more than five hundred technical teachers a year. One-third of the technical graduates are women.[15]

A similar materials program has been supplying primary and secondary schools with wall maps of the world, of Africa, and of

Zimbabwe as well as globes and junior atlases, at an average cost of Z$314 (U.S. $188.41) per school. The project is funded by the Swedish International Development Agency (SIDA).

The Zimbabwe Foundation for Education with Production (ZIMFEP) is a nongovernmental organization that is responsible for running eight schools for homeless children who have returned from neighboring countries since the end of the war. These large boarding schools, each with about one thousand pupils, were put up by students and local villagers. Government and donors have provided the funds for the structures, which have been built at only one-third of the commercial costs. The schools have not only achieved a notable degree of success in rehabilitating their students, but they are also producing large quantities of agricultural goods. Income from the school farms can be more than Z$100,000 (U.S. $60,000) a year,[16] and soon agriculture and industrial projects may make the schools self-sufficient.

The future success of education in Zimbabwe may very well rest on the pioneering work of the Zimbabwe Integrated Secondary School Education (ZISSE) program, which combines conventional teaching methods with long-distance education and supervised study under a teacher's aide known as a "mentor." A preliminary evaluation of this program, begun in 1985, indicates that there is no measurable difference between the scholastic achievement of students in the experimental groups and those in conventional schools and that the experimental groups do noticeably better than study groups that use only distance education and mentors.

Conclusion

Despite the major achievements in education it has made over the past seven years, Zimbabwe is likely to face increasing pressures to lower the unit cost of education and at the same time to improve the quality of teaching and materials. The country, however, must also invest a greater percentage of its gross national product in agriculture and industry in order to provide jobs for the growing number of school graduates, which in turn is steadily increasing, despite attempts to promote family planning.[17] Also, the geopolitical situation, worsening as tensions mount in neighboring South Africa, demands an ever-higher expenditure for defense and a curtailment of economic advances.

Lowering the unit cost of education of Zimbabwe will depend not only on the provision of low-cost educational materials and on steps to make schooling more productive but also on other measures that lower teaching costs. Since it is quite impossible to lower teachers' salaries, one approach would be to use paraprofessionals, such as teacher's aides, and the child-teach-child approach, which has been so successfully pioneered in a number of pilot projects. Thus, while Zimbabwe has equalized the pay of male and female teachers, the current pressure of numbers on the school system suggests the likelihood of new status roles emerging for teacher's aides and for teachers. It is as yet unclear what gender patterns will emerge in these auxiliary roles. Perhaps the role of women will be more influenced by the fact that female teachers are gaining a base in technical and agricultural education—that is, in the fields most germane to women's daily lives.

It is important also to note that Zimbabwe's success in expanding elementary and secondary education has not undermined the importance of women's traditional knowledge in medicine or as spiritual/political leaders. In part, this is because of the power earned and the political education received by women of all levels of education by their participation in the guerrilla struggle for national independence. Because of that political education, a strong feminist leadership continues to push the national government on policy issues of importance to women and to insist on the value of women's traditional knowledge alongside the new technical skills imported from the West.

NOTES

1. David Law, *Guns and Rain, Guerrillas and Spirit Mediums in Zimbabwe* (Harare: Zimbabwe Publishing House, 1985).

2. Evaluation Unit, *An Evaluation Report on Primary School Dropouts in Zimbabwe, 1978–84* (Harare: Ministry of Education Planning Division, 1986).

3. Jacaranda Sannap Project, P.O. Box A 700, Avondale, Harare, Zimbabwe.

4. Figures from Agritex, Harare, June 1988.

5. In 1988, 254 women were enrolled in agricultural colleges, out of a total of 970 students. Figures from Agritex, Harare, June 1988.

6. "Rules of Conduct for Soldiers" (Kune Nzira Dzemasoja) is translated here:

I

There is a code of conduct for fighters
By which they must live
Abide by all the rules
As much as you can.
CHORUS
We should not take by force
Anything from the people
We should also return
Anything that we will have taken.

II

We should not be promiscuous
In our war of liberation.
We should not harass
Prisoners of war.

III

We should pay properly
For whatever we buy.
We should also return
Anything that we have taken and used.

7. *Zimbabwe Report on the United Nations Decade for Women* (Harare: Ministry of Community Development and Women's Affairs, 1985).

8. Department of Research and Planning, *Annual Review of Manpower, 1984,* Ministry of Labor, Manpower Planning and Social Welfare.

9. Monthly Digest of Statistics, October 1982, Central Statistical Office, Harare, 3, 10. The exchange rate in 1979 was about Z $9.63 to U.S. $1.00 as compared to Z $1.60 to U.S. $1.00 in 1987.

10. The lower estimate is based on the average annual building fee of Z $25 (U.S. $15) per family, it being estimated that most families have about five children at school at any time. The higher estimate is based on an annual fee of Z $25 (U.S. $15) per pupil. Because the building fee is levied at the local level by parents themselves, there are procedural variations. Enrollments (in millions) for the period 1981–86 are as follows:

1981:	1.82
1982:	2.16
1983:	2.36
1984:	2.57
1985:	2.73
1986:	2.81
	(14.46)

(From Central Statistical Office, (Harare; and Ministry of Education Statistics, First Term 1986).

11. See Jotham Ombisi Olembo, "Financing Education in Kenya," *Prospects* 16, no. 3 (1986): 369–75.

12. The cost calculation is based on data published in the Ministry of Education, Vote 18, Codes and Allocations, 1986–87; and Ministry of Education, Statistics on Enrollments and Staffing in Teachers' Colleges, First Term 1987. The breakdown is as follows:

Conventional Colleges
Unit boarding and materials cost over
4 years =   Z $1,559.04
Lecturer cost per student at average
lecturer =   Z $2,749.20
                                             (Z $4,308.24)

ZINTEC Colleges
Unit boarding and materials cost over
4 years =   Z $ 616.20
Lecturer cost per student at average
lecturer salary of Z $13,746 over 4
years =   Z $1,374.60
                                             (Z $1,990.60)

13. See Ministry of Education, *Report of the School Fees Committee*, November 1983, 98, app. 7, "Report on the Supply of Textbooks to Schools," which indicated that there was a dire shortage of textbooks in schools.

14. See V. Lake, Zimbabwe Secondary School Science Project (ZimSci) Evaluation Progress Reports 1, 2, and 3, Ministry of Education, 1981–82; E. P. Brown, ZimSci Evaluation Progress Report 4, Ministry of Education, 1983; S. T. Bajah, ZimSci Evaluation Report, Ibadan Institute of Education, 1983; Evaluation Unit, "An Evaluation Report of the ZimSci Project," Planning Division, Ministry of Education, 1984.

15. Evaluation Unit, "A Report on the Evaluation of the Technical Subjects Kits Project," Planning Division, Ministry of Education, February 1987.

16. Zimbabwe Foundation for Education, Production Report on Agriculture for 1986, Harare.

17. The school population has increased as follows:

Year	Enrollment in Millions	% Increase per Annum
1979	0.89	—
1980	1.31	47.2
1981	1.83	39.7
1982	2.16	18.0
1983	2.36	9.3
1984	2.57	8.9
1985	2.73	6.2
1986	2.81	2.9

Source: Central Statistics Office, Harare; and Ministry of Education Statistics, First Term 1986.

Part 3
Latin America

An Overview of Women's Education in Latin America and the Caribbean

LOURDES ARIZPE

There is no doubt that education in Latin America and the Caribbean has been a major instrument for development. It has created the pressure toward democratization and enhanced political participation; it has successfully contributed to demographic transition; it has fostered vigorous artistic and literary production; and it has helped improve the quality of life generally.

In recent years, however, it has been caught in the web of the contradictions of uneven development. An ever-increasing number of university graduates from Latin America and the Caribbean are now migrating to the United States as a predictable outcome of the distortions created by the debt crisis. During the 1980s the transfer of funds from the poor and middle-income countries in the region helped to create seventeen million jobs in the United States. The attractiveness of those jobs has siphoned off large numbers of educated Latin Americans. In Mexico the salaries of professionals and academics lost 57 percent of their buying power between 1982 and 1988. The exodus of scientists, doctors, engineers, already a loss for developing the economy, will be a setback for the university educational cohort.

Simply put, the higher aspirations of an educated population are clashing with hard economic and political realities. The rich and educated, emulating the life-style of their U.S. and European counterparts, have become jittery exporters of their personal capital to banks in the United States and Europe. The educated middle classes, locked into a downward economic spiral, are emigrating and are expressing their protest politically.

It is in this bleak scenario for the 1990s in Latin America and the Caribbean that women's participation in education in the region must be carefully assessed. In drawing up such an assessment, there is no doubt that the principle still holds that education and learning are among the major instruments for women's advancement.

Education: A Constellation of Functions

Educational systems are tied to ideal images of society, and these images often provide the guidelines for specific educational policies.[1] At present both the content of these ideal images, that is, the kinds of knowledge that these policies propose, as well as the function of education in modern society are being carefully scrutinized from women's perspectives.

Recent studies by feminist scholars have argued that there has been an inherent sexist bias in the philosophy of Western education.[2] From the perspective of these critics the model of an educated person, citizen, scholar, or professional expert has been falsely based on a masculine pattern of feeling and behavior that has required women to adopt male models. Not only is the content of education biased, but the formal curriculum usually ignores areas of nonformal knowledge in which women are experts as well. Such areas pertain to local, ethnic, and traditional systems of knowledge that are vital in adapting technology to local social conditions.

The assumption has always been that knowledge and expertise go hand in hand with industrialization and political democracy; each reinforces the other. In the Third World there has been no such linear path. As a consequence, the educational system has become distorted. Many Latin American educational reformers ask how educational systems can be reorganized to take account of the distinct political and economic experience of Latin Americans. How can educational systems meet the needs of women as well as men and celebrate and preserve a broader definition of knowledge?

The answer to these questions will partly depend on how women participate in the formal educational system, as pupils, teachers, and decision makers in establishing educational policy.

In Latin America and the Caribbean the present impasse in education is all the more dramatic because of the extraordinary advances that women have made in most countries during this century. Primary school enrollment is practically equal for girls and boys, female illiteracy has dropped steadily, and the percentage of women going into higher education also increased markedly. What no one expected was the abrupt halt of the 1980s.

The 1980s

After three decades of continuous, albeit, uneven, economic growth development in Latin America and the Caribbean drew to a bewildering standstill in the 1980s. The combined effects of the transfer of resources through interest payments on the debt and the historically unprecedented low prices of agricultural commodities led to a decrease of per capita income in most countries of the region. In 1987 the World Bank reported on the effects of these factors combined with the impact of structural adjustment policies in the region as follows: high unemployment and underemployment, growth of the informal sector, declining real wages, and the first signs of worsening social indicators in some countries. The report states, for example, that in Mexico "not a single job was created (on a net basis) from 1981 to 1984, while the labor force increased from 22.7 million in 1981 to 24.7 million in 1984";[3] in Costa Rica wage declines were sharpest in basic services (43 percent) in agriculture (35 percent) and in industry (33 percent); Chilean unemployment has been the worst in the region, at 19.6 percent in 1982 and 13 percent in the last quarter of 1985.[4]

A more recent report by the Economic Commission for Latin America (ECLA) begins by stating that in 1988 the economic crisis in Latin America and the Caribbean took a dramatic turn for the worse. The per capita product decreased for the first time since 1981–83 and was equivalent only to the 1978 figure, inflation more than doubled to an unprecedented 470 percent, and real wages fell in a majority of countries.[5] Eduardo Garcia of ECLA has made it clear that, with respect to educational policies, Latin America and the Caribbean have lost not one but *two* decades. That is, they are back to where they were in the 1960s.[6]

Because income distribution is so unequal in most countries of the region, however, the economic crisis has not affected all social groups in the same way. In many countries the debt was acquired by groups in government and in the private sector and often used for their own benefit, yet the repayment of the debt falls on the shoulders of the whole population and, thus, is paid for disproportionately by the poor. The hardest hit have been the most vulnerable groups, that is, the women and children of the lowest income groups.[7] Infant mortality is on the rise in many countries, nutritional levels have fallen, and health and educational services have been cut back. As social indicators worsen, the World Bank warns that "what remains hidden are the effects of the collapse of investment and the resulting physical deterioration of hospitals and schools."[8] The report warns that, "unless action is taken soon to arrest deterioration, losses may prove to be pervasive and *difficult to reverse.*"[9] Once a malnourished child—and female children are frequently more malnourished than male children—suffers damage in her or his ability to learn, no amount of capital, handouts, or development will ever reverse the personal and national loss.

All this will have direct consequences on women's participation in education. It is in this context that recommendations to redirect educational subsidies away from university education and in favor of primary education must be evaluated. This recommendation brings into relief the poignancy of the choices that women in developing countries will face in the coming decades. If funds for education will be scarce, should women strive for continued support and expanded access to higher education for a limited number of women or for greater extension of basic services to include all women, especially those in rural Indian communities?

Approaching this issue as an either- or question must be avoided at all costs; it would pit advocates of one good cause against those in favor of the other. Resources can be extended to cover both educational needs if the restrictions of the international financial and trade system are redirected to more equal exchange between industrialized and developed countries and if national resources are better distributed and used to improve productivity, eradicate corruption and inefficiency, and stem capital flight. Education can be a vital instrument in bringing about such changes, and women, with all levels of education, are needed to push for such reforms. How, then, are women situated at present in the educational system of Latin America and the Caribbean?

Expanding Women's Access

The region has taken many years to rid itself of the colonial social structure that barred women from schools and universities. At the intellectual level it still has not been entirely successful in eradicating the Scholastic heritage, which taught through rote learning and, subtly and insidiously, discouraged analytic intellectual activity generally and women's intellectual endeavors particularly. As far back as the seventeenth century, the great poet Sor Juana Ines de la Cruz was forced to put down her pen as accusations about her "masculine bent of mind," "intellectual arrogance," and "enquiries beyond the faith" were used by the church hierarchy to silence her.

The same accusations, in more modern form, are used against women's intellectual efforts and are still clearly reflected in educational statistics and in intellectual production. The academic hierarchy, national and regional, is almost exclusively male.

In all countries of the region, with the sole exception of Uruguay, more women than men are illiterate. Table 1 shows the three broad categories of illiteracy among countries: those with less than 10 percent; those with 15 to 30 percent; and those with more than 35 percent. Significantly among the latter category Bolivia, Ecuador and Guatemala all have a high proportion of Indian population. Fully one-half to one-third of the women from indigenous groups in these countries cannot read or write, highlighting the attention that must be given to educational policies and programs targeted to Indian women.

At the primary school level equal numbers of girls and boys attend schools. The problem for women is not at the level of basic education, though, as has been pointed out, this may begin to be reversed by the economic depression. The exclusion of women begins with the high dropout rate at the end of primary school and the low entry at the secondary level. This decline is highest for rural women, but it is also a problem in the urban areas.

A low percentage of students, both men and women, go on to universities, with only three countries in the region having more

TABLE 1. Illiteracy, Age 15 and Over, by Urban and Rural Areas and by Sex in Twenty Latin American Countries

Country	Year	Category	Illiterate Population Total (N)	Percentage of Total Population Total	Male	Female
Argentina	1971	Total[c]	1,177,400	8.4	—	—
Bolivia	1976	Total	993,437	36.8	24.2	48.6
		Urban	176,748	15.2	6.2	23.2
		Rural	816,689	53.2	37.3	68.5
Brazil	1978	Total	16,223,404	23.9	22.0	25.7
		Urban	7,308,975	15.6	12.8	18.1
		Rural	8,914,429	42.4	40.9	43.9
Chile	1970	Total	594,749	11.0	10.1	11.8
		Urban	276,270	6.6	5.4	7.7
		Rural	318,479	25.6	23.6	27.9
Colombia	1981	Total	2,407,458	14.8	13.6	16.1
		Urban	923,430	9.0	—	—
		Rural	1,484,028	24.8	—	—
Costa Rica	1973	Total	121,312	11.6	11.4	11.8
		Urban	23,177	4.9	4.0	5.7
		Rural	98,135	17.0	16.6	17.5
Cuba	1979	Total	218,358	4.6	4.3	4.9
Dominican Republic[b]	1970	Total	678,910*	32.8	31.2	34.3
		Urban	165,841	19.0	—	—
		Rural	517,796	43.4	—	—
Ecuador	1974	Total	932,723	25.8	21.8	29.6
		Urban	153,280	9.7	6.9	12.2
		Rural	779,443	38.2	32.3	44.4
El Salvador	1975	Total[a]	1,064,159	38.0	34.5	41.1
		Urban	216,593	18.0	12.7	22.2
		Rural	847,566	53.0	48.9	57.2
Guatemala	1973	Total	1,528,732*	54.0	46.4	61.5
		Urban	291,380	28.2	20.0	35.5
		Rural	1,235,220	68.6	59.9	77.6
Haiti	1971	Total	2,005,052	78.7	73.8	83.1

TABLE 1—*continued*

Country	Year	Category	Illiterate Population Total (N)	Percentage of Total Population		
				Total	Male	Female
Honduras	1974	Total	594,194	43.1	41.1	44.9
		Urban	99,015	21.1	17.6	24.0
		Rural	495,179	54.4	52.1	56.8
Mexico	1980	Total	9,400,000	19.0	16.7	21.2
Nicaragua[d]	1971	Total	410,755	42.5	42.0	42.9
		Urban	94,319	19.5	16.1	22.1
		Rural	316,436	65.4	63.8	67.0
Panama	1980	Total	166,669*	15.4	14.7	16.0
		Urban	26,221	6.3	5.6	7.0
		Rural	149,162	38.1	35.5	41.1
Paraguay	1972	Total	256,690	19.9	14.9	24.5
		Urban	61,570	11.4	7.4	14.7
		Rural	195,120	25.9	19.7	32.3
Peru	1972	Total	2,062,870*	27.5	16.7	38.2
		Urban	586,191	12.6	5.9	19.1
		Rural	1,454,676	50.9	32.9	69.2
Uruguay	1975	Total	124,664*	6.1	6.6	5.7
		Urban	87,500	5.2	5.1	5.2
		Rural	37,000	11.0	12.6	8.6
Venezuela	1971	Total	1,373,561	23.5	20.3	26.6

Source: Statistical Abstract of Latin America, vol. 25 (Los Angeles: University of California, 1987), 148.

[a]Data refer to age 10 and over.

[b]Excluding 8 percent of the population unspecified as to literacy or illiteracy.

[c]Data refer to age 18 and over.

[d]In 1980, after the National Literacy Campaign, the Ministry of Education estimated that of the 722,431 illiterates identified, in the census of October 1979, 130,372 were "analfabetos inaptos," and 406,056 were made literate, leaving only 186,003 "analfabetos aptos" (or 12.96 percent of the population of 10 years and over).

*Urban and rural do not equal the total.

than 5 percent of the population in the tertiary system. Women make up one-half or less of this student population at the entry point, but many fewer finish their degrees. Women tend to concentrate in the humanities and the social sciences.

At present, as universities retrench because of government cuts to their budgets and as family incomes fall, it is becoming more difficult for women to complete university degrees. Under such circumstances, if, as a recent World Bank report recommends, subsidies for higher education decline further, women will lose out even more. Because this is such an important issue, it is worth analyzing more closely.

It is true, as many of the essays in this book report, that the formal schooling system in the developing countries, especially at the university level, have increasingly become "credentialing" institutions. Indeed, this formal system continues to be the major, and sometimes only, channel for social and political mobility for individuals. If this upward mobility channel is closed, societies in the region would become more rigidly stratified, and efforts aimed at achieving political democratization would be dampened.

Education, nonetheless, gives much more than just a means for political control or a "credential." It has an immediate effect on demographic trends. There is a close correlation between a woman's educational level and the number of children she bears: years of schooling decrease the number of children born. This correlation is even stronger with a woman's participation in the paid labor force. A recent and growing phenomenon of adolescent mothers in some countries of Latin America and the Caribbean has been closely linked to the dropout rates of girls in high schools or to their loss of interest in education as they perceive that it no longer ensures economic and social mobility. Once young women are caught in early motherhood it is almost certain that they will not go on to higher studies.

In such a context it is of great concern that public expenditure in education in Latin America has steadily declined since the beginning of the 1980s. Ominously, two-thirds of the countries stopped publishing figures on public education expenditures after 1984. As financing for formal education shrinks in many countries, other alternative forms of education are receiving attention.

Women and Nonformal Education

For many centuries knowledge in many Latin American and Caribbean countries has been preserved and transmitted through oral tradition and nonformal education. In slave communities on plantations in the West Indies and Brazil, in Indian villages in Middle America and the Andes, in older barrios in capital cities, highly complex systems of oral communication of myths, techniques, cultural identity, and moral values were developed. Women have played a critical role in such communication, since they have been at the center of family, kin, and barrio networks, acting as guardians of traditional values and communicators of social news.

Today the schools and the mass media are substituting for such networks; consequently, women, especially in the small village, or barrio, are losing major parts of their role in the transmission of social judgments and information. Most important, they are also losing control of the transmission of values to the younger generations, especially regarding moral norms and social identity. Nor are the schools attending to these concerns. Instead, the mass media is taking on this role, having little or no accountability to society as a whole. Consequently, in many areas of Latin America and the Caribbean—and, according to recent literature, in industrialized countries as well[10]—there is a growing sense of cultural anomie, the symptoms of which are loss of cultural identity, of "sense of place," empty consumerism, and, probably, secondary effects related to corruption and violence.

Fundamentalist groups in Latin America are using this situation to argue that religious education, stressing moral and personal values, should be reinstated. Part of current arguments for the privatization of education run along these lines. However attractive such proposals appear from a financial perspective, it must be recalled that, in Latin America at least, it was traditional Catholic education that gave support to rigidly stratified oligarchic systems in which women were particularly oppressed and, in many instances, excluded from formal education. A regression toward patriarchal and authoritarian values would only clash with women's hopes for advancement as well as with the new democratic outlook of most societies in the region today. Fortunately, there are alternatives to a return to traditional education.

Alternative Education and Traditional Knowledge

In the last few decades many groups in Latin America and the Caribbean have been leaders in exploring new ways to revitalize schooling and to establish alternative ways of learning. It began in the 1960s when Paulo Freire shocked the educational establishment with his book *Pedagogy of the Oppressed*,[11] in which he deconstructed the old authoritarian form of education and proposed a freer and more creative process of learning. Out of his teachings grew the mass movement toward *concientización*, or consciousness raising, which political activists, social scientists, and adherents of the Theology of Liberation took to many regions of Latin America during the 1970s.

Another school of thought that also developed in Latin America was the major critique of education led by Ivan Illich.[12] While others proposed only a more benign form of education, Illich and those working with him demanded a more radical form of "deschooling" society.

The arguments of both Freire and Illich coincide with those of recent groups, which stress that a wealth of "popular knowledge" exists that provides a basis for alternative education.[13] As cultural change sweeps over countries of the region as well as other Third World regions, on the crest of the new wave of telecommunications, extremely valuable traditional intellectual resources are being lost. People are becoming poorer in knowledge and, what is even worse, *poorer in the confidence that they can continue to create knowledge.*

The whole range of dire consequences of this loss of knowledge and of the power to create knowledge, I believe, has not been seen in its full dimensions. The loss in the confidence to develop useful knowledge reacts reciprocally with the loss of a livelihood in a downward spiral of poverty, especially in rural areas and in the new urban areas. Rural women, those formidable sources of resilience, practical knowledge, emotional strength, and other-worldly wisdom, find their capacities and skills are undermined. In the current environment social prejudice and ignorance are destroying valuable local knowledge related to ecology, pharmacopoeia, botany, zoology, and agronomy and to subsistence techniques in hunting, gathering, and fishing. It is impossible, also, to assess the loss in human knowledge and expertise handed down over centuries about social interaction, personal relationships, and their psychological uses that have been vital for the social and cultural well-being of local societies. Self-reliant initiatives to alleviate poverty have to be backed by people with confidence in what they know and can continue to create. If this is lost, our hopes for true development will be irrevocably limited.

It is hard to exaggerate what this loss will mean in terms of our human future. It is surely the equivalent, in the realm of cultural diversity, of the irretrievable loss of species and genetic diversity that biologists warn us about. Knowledge is the backbone of a culture; if it is undermined, the whole social fabric of that culture will slowly fall apart.

This is the challenge of women's education in Latin America: constructing reformed educational systems that address our needs, preserve our heritage, and direct us to a future of greater equity and fuller participation. This will not occur if current policies to limit educational expenditures continue. But increased spending is a very limited response. Of far greater utility would be a reassessment of the kind of society we hope to construct and the type of education likely to promote it.

NOTES

1. For Latin America, see German Rama, *Education, Images and Styles of Development* (Santiago de Chile: UNESCO, 1978).

2. Cf. Jane Martin, "Excluding Women from the Educational Realm," *Harvard Educational Review* 52, no. 2 (1983): 133–48.

3. World Bank, *Poverty in Latin America: The Impact of Depression* (Washington, D.C.: World Bank, 1987), 11.

4. World Bank, *Poverty in Latin America*, 11.

5. Comisión Económica para América Latina y el Caribe (CEPAL), "Balance preliminar de la economía latinoamericana 1988," *Notas sobre la Economía y el Desarrollo* 470 (December 1988): 1.

6. Eduardo Garcia, "La Crisis económica y las políticas sociales en América Latina y el Caribe," conference given at Economic Commission for Latin America (ECLA), Santiago de Chile, 5 May 1989.

7. For an analysis of the effects of the economic crisis on women in five Latin American countries, see UNICEF, *The Invisible Adjustment* (New York: UNICEF, 1989).

8. UNICEF, *Invisible Adjustment*, 23.

9. UNICEF, *Invisible Adjustment*, 23; my emphasis.

10. Joshua Meyrowitz, *No Sense of Place: The Impact of Electronic Media on Social Behavior* (New York: Oxford University Press, 1985).

11. Paulo Freire, *Pedagogía del Oprimido* (Mexico: Siglo XXI, 1974).

12. Ivan Illich, *De-schooling Society* (New York: Harper and Row, 1971).

13. The term in Spanish is *saber popular*. The word *saber* encompasses a kind of knowledge that is also wisdom, as opposed to that of *conocimiento*, which is more mechanical knowledge. Also in Spanish *popular* has a positive connotation, referring to anything having to do with the people; it does not have the more commercial undertones of the term as used in English.

Citizenship and Education in Peru and Mexico: Political Challenges for the 1990s

Susan C. Bourque

The American public has watched in amazement the realignment of Soviet politics and the collapse of regimes in Eastern Europe. Nevertheless, the current upheavals in the formerly Communist world should not blind us to similar signals of discontent with the economic and political systems of the developing nations of the capitalist world.

During the 1980s past models of development and expectations for future economic growth have been drastically revised in Latin America. Spiraling inflation, mounting foreign debt, the violence of the international drug trade, and accelerating political terrorism have undermined the confident nation building of the post–World War II era. With real income levels in the region falling to 1960 levels, countries such as Mexico and Peru, which once staked their futures on massive investments in public education, have cut their national expenditures by draconian amounts.[1] This contraction of investment in public goods is occurring in countries whose populations have had far greater access to education than the preceding generation. More Latin Americans entered and completed primary and secondary school in the 1980s than had done so in the preceding quarter century, and an increasing proportion of the newly educated have been women.[2] Governments throughout the Americas face profound discontent from citizens who have become much more highly organized and politicized than they were a generation ago. This expansion and the challenges it poses are part of a fundamental reshaping of political life in the region.

In both Peru and Mexico the political parties that have struc-

tured participation for the past fifty years are now challenged by
popular movements, newly created political parties, and, in Peru,
terrorist organizations from both the Left and Right. The new
consciousness created by education for women has made Peruvian and Mexican women elements of the new political configura-
tions. Expanded educational opportunity has played a central role
in their political activism and has shaped their responses to the
current crises.

Education and National Development

In both Mexico and Peru educational opportunity assumed mythic
significance for the revolutionary national leaders. Postrevolutionary Mexican governments viewed the educational system as the
primary vehicle for nation building and the extension of schools
into the rural areas as the key to integration of the peasant and
indigenous population. The courtyard of the Ministry of Education in Mexico City bears testimony to the gendered component
of that vision. Decorated by Diego Rivera in the 1920s at the request of the great visionary of Mexican education, Jose Vasconce-
los, the murals include some of Rivera's strongest political statements. In contrast to these biting satires, Rivera's portrait of the
New School is idyllic. A young woman teacher stands in the fore-
ground of a cultivated field surrounded by a group of pupils clad
in the white cottons of the Mexican peasant. The students hold
books and slates and listen with undivided attention to the hand-
some young woman so clearly dedicated to her charges. A revolutionary soldier, ammunition belt crossing his chest, stands guard,
while in the background peasants harvest a field.

Rivera's idealized picture glosses over the actual experience of
rural female teachers, who were often harassed and assaulted in
the communities they served. But his mythic depiction is a correct
reflection of the hopes associated with public education and the
central role assigned to women in building the new structure.

Very quickly political pressures and economic constraints undermined the dream. As Mexico experienced rapid urbanization
and industrialization, planners redefined the goals of public education as the provision of the work force required for economic
growth, rather than the vehicle for creating greater equity.[3] Much

of the battle over educational content reflected postrevolutionary struggles between the Mexican government and the Catholic church and its middle-class supporters. These conflicts turned on the required use of a standard textbook in both public and private institutions. The political battles emphasized ideological controversies over how communism and socialism were treated in the textbooks and by and large left traditional gender roles unchallenged. Nevertheless, the submerged agenda of economic necessity meant that some aspects of the idealized role of women and the values associated with that role gave way in the face of the need for an educated population.

This utilitarian goal fostered expansion of the public education system, an expansion in which women participated, though there was little thought devoted to their expected use of education, except in traditional roles as mothers and teachers. The scale of the expansion is apparent in the doubling of those finishing elementary education in the 1970s and the 316 percent increase in enrollments in higher education between 1970 and 1984. This expansion of the public system, tellingly referred to as "massification," has occurred at the expense of quality. Today the public system is dominated by a vast government bureaucracy, the Ministry of Public Education (SEP), and the hemisphere's largest union, the National Union of Educational Workers.[4] Public confidence in the system has declined, to be replaced by widespread belief that the quality of education has deteriorated with increased access. To further cloud the picture public expenditures were radically reduced. Education, which claimed 21.1 percent of Mexico's public expenditures in 1975, now claims a mere 13 percent.[5]

In the 1990s the cast of characters involved in Mexican education had changed dramatically from Rivera's day. The rural school teacher was replaced by a male urban technocrat, located in the upper reaches of the Ministry of Education, far removed from students and classroom and surrounded instead by stacks of towering forms, timesheets, and endless paperwork.

A similar story may be told about the hopes and realities of expanding educational opportunity in Peru. Free public secondary education was introduced in 1966, expanding enrollments from 19 percent of the age cohort to 72 percent by 1985.[6] Over the same period expenditures on education fell from a high of 30 percent of the national budget in 1966 to an estimated 13 percent in the mid-1980s. Because expenditures have not kept pace with demand, one of the most pressing political issues for the squatter populations of Lima's ballooning "new towns," which house 30 percent of Lima's six million residents, has been the demand for schools and teachers.

As the pressures for access mount, the impact of the economic collapse of the 1980s has led to fundamental questioning of the current, much reduced level of educational expenditures. At the same time the declining quality of the system has led to escalating credential requirements for the simplest jobs.

Despite higher school enrollments for girls, gender inequities have not been eliminated. For Peru the differences between men and women are still striking, especially at the upper and lower ends of the educational scale.[7] At the primary level there were ninety-five girls for every one hundred boys enrolled and at the secondary level ninety-three girls for every one hundred boys. The percentage of the total age group enrolled at each level has expanded dramatically in the past twenty years. Hernán Fernández, director of Research at the Peruvian National Institute for Educational Research, reports: "In 1940, less than a third of school age children attended, by 1961 more than 53 percent attended and by the last national census nine of ten school age children attended. For women in 1981, 88 percent of girls from 6–14, and 52 percent of those 15–19 were in school."[8]

In Mexico, by 1985, illiteracy had been reduced to 9.7 percent among the total population, 7.7 percent among the males over fifteen, and 11.7 percent among the females. In 1982 for every one hundred boys enrolled at the primary level there were ninety-seven girls. At the secondary level there were ninety-six girls enrolled for every one hundred boys.[9] It is clear that, with each new generation, girls' school attendance has expanded.

One might argue that with continued government support the remaining discrepancies between men and women would disappear over time.[10] But the consensus that supported wider educational opportunity is under the strongest attack since expansion began in the 1940s. There are those today who argue that past policies to broaden educational opportunity have created today's economic and political problems. These critics argue that the quality of education has declined, the nation's development problems have remained unresolved, and schooling has created enormous financial burdens for government.[11] Reflecting on the current situation in Peru, Luis Pasara writes: "it's clear that education is a massive fraud. Spending ten years in primary and secondary school has no utility: you don't learn to read and write adequately and the four basic mathematic functions remain chancy operations. What's worse, not even university studies guarantee employment."[12] The critics note, correctly, that government expenditures go primarily for teachers' salaries and for the educational bureaucracy. These costs have swelled government payrolls, politicized employment, and created large, militant teachers' unions capable of paralyzing the school system in their efforts to extract their demands from government.

The democratization of Peruvian education in the 1960s and 1970s gave a much wider group of women access to higher education.[13] In 1987 26,000 women entered the university, compared to 39,000 men. Total university enrollment has grown from 30,000 in 1960 (23,000 men and 7,000 women) to 410,000 in 1987 (261,000 men and 149,000 women).

In Mexico there has been an equally dramatic increase in the number of women enrolled in higher education.[14] By 1985 men constituted 65.5 percent of those enrolled in higher education, and females constituted 34.5 percent. As the enrollment in higher education grew 4.19 times from 1969 to 1985, to a total of 779,511, the male university population grew 3.39 times and female university enrollment 9.4 times.

The multiplication of universities and students correlates with the declining prestige of the system and the widespread belief that universities have become diploma factories and credentialing systems, no longer graduating an educated elite nor guaranteeing employment to their graduates. For women who benefited from the expanded access the newly acquired university credential has often proved of limited value in the job market. Women have concentrated in sex-stereotyped fields such as nursing and teaching, in which salaries are low. In Peru in 1982 women constituted 99.5 percent of the nursing graduates, 98.7 percent of those in social work, 97 percent of the obstetrics graduates, 96 percent of those studying nutrition, 74.8 percent of those in pharmacology,

72.9 percent of the psychologists, and 57 percent of the education graduates.[15] A recent study of enrollment trends in Mexico found women opting for medicine and accounting, but, because these fields are also popular choices for men, women face stiff competition when they seek employment.[16]

Even with the expanded university systems most nations turn away substantial numbers of unsuccessful applicants who return to a glutted job market. Indeed, the paucity of jobs leads many young people to look for university places, lacking career opportunities elsewhere. Peter Cleaves concludes, "Many persons called university students in Mexico could as easily be classified as the hidden unemployed."[17]

Expectations of economic mobility accompany higher education, and the phrase "who studies, triumphs" characterized the beliefs of many Latin Americans. Those who gain university entrance and graduate hope for jobs commensurate with their educational achievement. When their employment and social expectations are unmet the resulting frustration has widespread political reverberations.[18] It is precisely this concern with the dangerous lack of fit between education and employment that has led many politicians to support financial cutbacks. This is an especially devastating development for women, who have gained increased access at the precise moment when economic and political conditions have led to calls for educational retrenchment and dramatic cuts in expenditures.

Perhaps the most chilling demonstration of this phenomenon is the situation that has developed in Peru. In that beleaguered nation economic collapse has combined with widespread political violence. The *Wall Street Journal* reported in 1990 that "in the past two years gross national product fell 22 percent while real income slumped 63 percent. Inflation topped 1,500 percent in 1988 and surpassed 3,500 percent in the past 12 months."[19] Twelve years of armed struggle have taken over twenty thousand lives and have cost the nation millions in destroyed property. For many Peruvians terrorism and education are interwoven at a variety of levels in Peru's dual political and economic crises.

Education is deemed to be the culprit for Peru's woes, from somewhat contradictory perspectives. On the one hand, access to higher education for the children of rural Andean peasants has been linked to the origins of Sendero Luminoso, the Shining Path movement. According to some analysts, young, educated, rural peasants became the backbone of the terrorist group when their hopes for economic and social mobility were frustrated by a shrinking economy and the persistent prejudice they encountered, despite a university degree.[20] The creation of rural universities did not eliminate the widespread belief that the education they offer and consequently the credentials of their graduates are inferior. In this instance the educational system is blamed for having created expectations that the social system did not fulfill.

Paradoxically, the educational system is also criticized for failing to absorb all those who aspire to it. In 1988, 331,330 Peruvians took the university entrance exams for the 70,429 spaces available. The 260,000 young people who did not gain entrance and remain unemployed are believed to be potential recruits for the various armed guerrilla groups.

Finally, the universities are accused of being "nurseries for revolutionaries," with students radicalized by leftist professors and "professional" students more concerned with political mobilization than with learning. This claim justified police raids of the five university campuses in Lima in 1987 and the arrest of some eight hundred university students and professors. It may also be a central consideration in the government's decision to slash university budgets. The dean of law at San Marcos remarked in 1989 that the university was being slowly strangled by lack of funds. Even more ominous have been recent cases of forced "disappearances" and attacks upon university personnel. The *Chronicle of Higher Education* reports "a wave of political violence and intimidation . . . focused on academic leaders and students" at San Cristobal Huamanga National University. Right-wing groups tied to the military are thought to be the perpetrators, but there are also those who credit Sendero Luminoso with the threats.[21]

Both universities and rural teachers are viewed as sources of Sendero Luminoso's membership. The leader of the Shining Path, Abimael Guzman, a former professor of philosophy at the University of Huamanga in highland Peru, used his teaching position to proselytize, recruit, and organize the terrorist movement. Additional evidence of the involvement of university graduates comes from a 1989 study, which noted the high levels of education among those convicted of terrorism. Thirty-six percent of those convicted from 1983 to 1986 had some university education, as compared to 3 percent of those convicted of assault and 8 percent of those sentenced for drug trafficking. These figures are even more striking in light of the fact that only 5 percent of the entire population, and only 8 percent of the economically active population above age fifteen, attains this educational level.[22]

Lima newspaper accounts of Sendero's methods also identify the secondary schools as the site for active recruitment of cadres. Mariella Balbi, a respected journalist from *Diario La República,* recently wrote: "Sendero has managed to infiltrate itself into 80% of the public high schools in the city of Huancayo (central sierra of Peru) and in the neighboring towns. . . . The situation in the high schools of Huancayo and the neighboring area is, to say the least, alarming. Utilizing the schools, Sendero Luminoso has found the way to have a 'bank' of recruits or sympathizers who will maintain the necessary ardor to carry out acts of intelligence, propaganda, support and . . . selective assassinations."[23]

Several analysts have also noted the relationship between the significant number of women identified as Sendero leaders and an increase in women's enrollment in the university in the late 1960s and 1970s. These observers have argued that young women found Sendero attractive because of the relative equality of women within the terrorist organization. They also note the number of women employed as rural school teachers, Sendero's dominance in the education department at the University of Huamanga, and its explicit strategy to use rural schools as a basis for recruitment. Women represented 16 percent of those sentenced for terrorism; 57 percent of those women had some university education, substantially higher than the comparable male figure of 31 percent.[24]

Among the women in Sendero's leadership Edith Lagos is perhaps best known. As a nineteen-year-old Senderista leader in Ayacucho, she led a daring prison break in the early days of the movement, and was subsequently killed while in police custody. Her funeral in September 1982 was attended by upwards of thirty thousand people in a city just twice that size. Edith Lagos and Carlota Tello were leaders of the major Regional Committee of Sendero in Ayacucho. Among the best-known women in the current structure is Laura Zambrano Padilla, or Comrade Meche, a former schoolteacher, arrested by the government in 1984. She was the head of Shining Path's military operation in Lima.[25] Sendero's leader, Abimael Guzman, was captured in 1992 along with three female members of the central committee. Following those arrests an exhaustive search began for four more women, all members of the central committee. Recent research on Sendero's internal structure indicates a central committee that was 56 percent female and a high incidence of women in regional leadership positions.[26]

Today one finds in Peru the educational system barraged by a growing chorus of critics. But those who claim the educational system is partially to blame for the growth of terrorism are especially troubling. The sources of Peru's insurgency are to be found in the profound neglect of the rural highlands and its population, rather than expanded educational access.[27] Nevertheless, those who link terrorism to education find their prescription to cut public funds for the university coincides with the desires of governments hard pressed to trim their budgets.[28]

For Peruvians and Mexicans and for many other Latin Americans the question remains: How will governments deal with the frustrations of the young if their policies do not generate the economic growth to provide employment? For women, in particular, the questions become: What are the implications of shrinking public services and narrowed educational and economic opportunities? The widespread disenchantment with the public education system has given new force to those who have argued for educational reform; that the current system is both costly and inadequate has created new openness to innovation. Among the innovators Latin American feminists with extensive experience in nonformal education have been particularly influential. They have linked reform in the public system to gender equity.

Gender and Educational Reform: Experiments with Nonformal Education

Prior to the 1980s most Latin American feminists despaired of the possibility of introducing discussions about the gendered basis of power and authority into the rigidly structured educational system.[29] As recent participants, they felt most schooling perpetuated sexist values, gave women a very limited sense of their potential, and reinforced class-based hierarchies. Moreover, because of its bureaucratic structure and entrenched unions, the formal system seemed particularly resistant to change. Instead, their initial efforts began in nonformal education, in which the possibilities for experimentation appeared to be far greater.

Their efforts were directed at women from the popular urban sectors, women with limited resources who missed the formal system or dropped out at an early stage. The nonformal programs became the principal link between feminists and the popular women's organizations. The programs they have developed suggest some alternatives for making the formal system more conducive to gender equity and in the current political environment have attracted new attention from the traditional political establishment. As a result of their activities, important lessons have been learned with implications for reworking the formal system. Governments, faced with discontent over the cost and performance of the state-supported educational network, have been willing to reexamine the lessons learned in the programs for low-income women.

Latin American feminist groups have concluded that nonformal education works best for women when the educational content clarifies women's contributions to the well-being of their families. These include both their unpaid work in child care and family and home maintenance as well as their contributions to the family economy, through their roles as agricultural workers (often unpaid), traders, and part-time workers in the informal economy. Portraying women as productive contributing members of families and society is essential to breaking cultural patterns that identify women as less important, less deserving human beings. Changing this evaluation improves women's self-esteem and helps decision makers and political leaders recognize the need for policies that take women's contributions into account.

Understanding the educational significance of this information, feminist organizations in Mexico and Peru (as well as in other Latin American countries) have documented women's contributions to economic productivity and petitioned government agencies to reflect these contributions in public policies. They have also fostered an awareness of inequities in intrafamily distributions of "entitlements," including education and recognition of the cultural and economic patterns that have sustained inequities.[30] Female university graduates and feminist research centers have been instrumental in pursuing the new research on women's lives, clarifying women's economic contributions, and pointing out the limits of current policies and the need for new ones. The results of these studies have been subjects of national level forums and the basis for lobbying policymakers and politicians.

The second pattern that has emerged in women's nonformal education has been the need to address domestic and sexual violence. Fear of sexual assault acts as a serious constraint on women of every social class and is among the most ubiquitous impediments to full participation. In Latin America fear of sexual assault affects the willingness of parents to send their daughters to school and the distance from home they will allow them to travel. It affects the kinds of employment a woman can safely pursue and her willingness to do so. Family violence and abusive attitudes toward women and children emerged in nonformal education programs as important constraints on women's self-conception and self-confidence. Addressing these issues became a central concern in the curriculum.

Domestic violence has now become part of the agenda for change in society at large. There is growing recognition that to secure lasting change these issues must be addressed much earlier in the life cycle and, therefore, in the curriculum of the formal education system. In a similar vein Peru and Brazil have created female police stations in which women can take a charge of rape or assault to officers, primarily female, trained to treat the crime and its victims with appropriate seriousness. The decision to establish women's police stations is a public policy victory for feminists, who had long campaigned for their creation. In Peru feminists were successful in part because they gained the support of a leading female politician from the governing party that championed their cause.[31] Significantly, the discussion of domestic violence and rape has moved from the confines of feminist publications such as *Viva* or *Manuela* in Peru or *Fem* in Mexico to the pages of the daily newspapers and the leading political journals. This recognition by male journalists and intellectuals of the wide-ranging significance of violence directed at women suggests acceptance of a key element in the feminist agenda for change.[32]

In the nonformal education programs developed for the squatter settlements of Lima, domestic violence, health, nutrition, human physiology, birth control, and women's legal rights are all included. Participants may also learn how to acquire low-interest group loans and how to keep books and calculate business expenses. There are no formal classrooms, rather small groups of eight to twelve women meet in a storefront or in a participant's living room. The courses are highly participatory, questions and exchange are encouraged, and teachers, who have relabeled themselves promoters, respond to frank questions in a forthright manner.[33]

Scholars often conceive of education as central to improving students' economic opportunities and enhancing their chances for economic productivity and social mobility. We see a different focus for women in the two dominant patterns in nonformal education. The nonformal courses seek change but primarily in self-esteem and in the ability to insist on greater consideration from those with whom one lives and works as well as from political institutions (bureaucracies, agencies, and political parties) and policymakers. Thus, the yardstick by which we measure the success of such programs may be less in terms of immediate economic return (though this may be a consequence or correlate of greater assertiveness and self-confidence) and more in terms of greater openness to political mobilization and participation.[34]

Nevertheless, despite the lessons learned in the development of nonformal education programs, they are a limited response to resolving gender inequality and educational reform. Structural constraints limit their effectiveness. Having no access to the state's tax base and lacking consistent financial support, these programs are dependent on the inspiration and money from a leadership group that is not necessarily self-renewing. These constraints have led women's groups in Peru to look anew at the public education system. They now grapple with how to transfer what they have learned in nonformal education to public systems, to focus new efforts on curriculum reform and the development of new programs to address the needs of girls.

Today educational reformers and feminists in Mexico, Peru,

and throughout Latin America look to an altered system in which both formal and nonformal education will be critical vehicles for the dissemination of nonsexist curricular materials shaping new patterns of behavior for both men and women. Educational forums are deemed essential to breaking the circular pattern of domination, economic dependency, and violence that have ensured women's subordination. Substantial reworking of the existing educational system implies continued and complex ties between women's organizations and the government. For many feminist groups this has meant constructing more extensive ties to governing elites and new links to political parties. Virginia Vargas, director of the Centro Flora Tristán, a leading Peruvian feminist organization, reflected on the government's key role in assisting the feminist agenda: "the state has the capacity to give public visibility to our demands, to generalize these at the societal level, thus contributing to changing the perception of the situation of women."[35]

A New Political Spectrum: Feminism and the Popular Movement

Political and economic conditions have converged in many Latin American countries to reshape the political spectrum, making women's organizations politically significant. This new configuration suggests developmental consequences quite different from the patterns that have previously characterized the relation between women's education and politics in the West.[36] Long considered a region especially prone to *machismo,* or unquestioned male dominance, paired with *marianismo,* or self-abnegation among women, the past twenty years have brought dramatic changes in the roles of many Latin American women. The heightened expectations that educational opportunity aroused (in both the formal and nonformal systems) has led to new levels and modes of political organization. Whether we speak of Mexico, Peru, Brazil, Costa Rica, Chile, the Dominican Republic, or Argentina, we find new political activism among women.

Some activism builds upon women's traditional roles in the family and extends those concerns into the public sphere, such as the demonstrations orchestrated by Argentine women protesting

the loss of children and loved ones through government organized "disappearances." Women also constitute a vital part of the
new social movements that have emerged to confront the consequences of the economic crisis or to meet community needs
caused by catastrophic events such as the 1985 earthquake in Mexico City. In addition to these groups, which extend women's traditional concerns to the public realm, a variety of feminist organizations committed to fundamental change in gender relations and
the elimination of inequality in women's status have developed.

Consequently, women's mobilization has emerged in a variety
of forms, shaped in part by social class and educational experience. No single unified or universal woman's movement has
taken shape; rather, one finds in both Peru and Mexico a range of
organizations, ideologies, and alliances. The women's organizations differ in their prescriptions for change and in the degree to
which they accept or challenge traditional gender roles and divisions of labor.[37]

The explicitly feminist groups in Peru and Mexico are quite
small (at times with an active membership under one hundred);
the popular women's organizations are large, with a potential
mass base in the tens of thousands. In the current context of
economic and political crisis the most intriguing alliance among
these groups is that constructed between middle-class moderate
and radical feminist groups and the popular organizations of poor
women. The difficulty in constructing such coalitions across significant class and social barriers cannot be underestimated. Moreover, these barriers are exacerbated by the initial resistance of
most women in the popular organizations to a feminist label.
Feminism has been branded antifamily for many Latin American
women; thus, for women in the popular movements struggling
to keep their families together, feminism did not appear to be
consistent with their values nor to address their needs. In a number of cases, especially in Peru, the gulf between these groups has
been bridged, and popular education has played a role in this
politically significant process.

The popular movement is composed of men and women of
limited resources, the poor and working class, known in Latin
America as the popular classes. Urbanization and democratization

have contributed to women's political participation in the popular movements. The prolonged struggles of recent migrants to obtain titles to land and access to urban services have often been waged by women. Similarly, the battle to feed children without the guarantees of even a subsistence economy has led women into new forms of community-level organization.

In Peru these groups emerged in response to the economic crisis of the late 1970s to meet the crushing problems of scarcity and to protest government policies that led to shortages. Women throughout the squatter settlements of Lima took part in the anti-government protests and dealt with the high price of food by organizing communal kitchens and participating in municipal milk distribution schemes. The communal kitchens allowed women to purchase food in bulk and cook meals on a rotating basis, thus allotting them time for other income-generating activities to support their families. The milk program distributed powdered milk to organized groups of mothers, who prepared it for preschool children and lactating women.[38] In their focus on food issues and the need to feed one's family these popular women's organizations are reminiscent of women's participation in the bread riots of early modern Europe.

In Mexico the popular movement is composed of working-class and poor women living in the newly settled marginal areas around Mexico City or in the deteriorating neighborhoods of the center city. Their activism also began with struggles for urban services and land titles. It is also part of the democratization of Mexican politics following the electoral and administrative reforms of the late 1970s. The debt crisis of 1982 and government austerity programs gave further form to discontent. The economic decline forced many women into marginal employment, and many joined popular movements in the aftermath of the 1985 earthquake and in the political mobilizations around the candidacy of Cuauhtémoc Cárdenas.[39]

Deteriorating economic conditions for the poor have given rise to increased political organization and protest in Mexico and Peru. This pattern has not escaped the attention of political parties. As the popular women's organizations have grown in size and persisted over time, competition for their votes and satisfying their needs have become factors in electoral politics. Both feminist groups and popular women's organizations have also found sympathizers among leading female politicians and bureaucrats. Politicians in both Peru and Mexico, increasingly baffled by seemingly intractable problems, heightened instability, and increased restiveness among their citizens, are anxious to pull the popular groups into the system. This has given women's organizations a political significance they had not previously enjoyed.

There are now many contenders for the allegiance of the popular women's organizations. In the 1985 Peruvian elections, Alan García's party, Alianza Popular Revolucionaria Americana (APRA), courted the communal kitchens with programs of stove and pot and pan distribution. As the economic crisis put an unprecedented 49 percent of Lima's female population into the economically active work force, the APRA government created the Temporary Income Support Program (PAIT) which gave adults three months of employment in urban cleanup. Eighty percent of the jobs went to women. APRA also sponsored the organization of mother's clubs, creating about two thousand of them by March 1987, with more than 120,000 women participating.[40]

Recognition of the significance of the women's popular organizations has also come from Sendero Luminoso, which has sought to eliminate them by intimidation. María Elena Moyano, president of the Federation of Popular Women of Villa El Salvador (a squatter settlement of over 100,000 in the southern section of Lima) received threats from Sendero and was brutally and publicly murdered in February 1992. Much of the leadership of the Popular Women's movement have had to flee the country or to increase their security precautions due to death threats from Sendero. Reacting to these tactics, *Manuela,* a publication of the feminist group Manuela Ramos, analyzes Sendero's position as follows:

> Sendero is opposed to the people organizing in pursuit of their needs. They think of the communal kitchens, local committees and milk distribution programs as "welfare" created to distract the people and prevent them from supporting revolution . . . . Sendero hopes to sow terror among the popular organizations and within women's organizations, so that their leaders are obligated to disactivate and abandon them.[41]

There can be little doubt that in Peru, where armed guerrilla movements are challenging government authority, or in Mexico, where the ruling party of the past seventy years is under its most serious electoral challenge, political leaders recognize the benefits of working with those who enjoy extensive ties to the popular sectors. Feminists as well have begun to recognize the need for more extensive ties to formal politics and to commit their energies to shaping state agencies and public policies.

Both the popular movement and the feminist organizations face questions about what would constitute the most effective ties to the political system. The women's organizations began in opposition to the established parties, protesting the "system's" failure to address their needs. To what extent will a feminist agenda be compromised if women are absorbed by the traditional parties? Alternatively, to what extent can women advance their agenda if they are not closely linked to the political system? The same questions hold true for the popular movements. Will they lose their vitality if they are absorbed into the traditional parties? Conversely, can they find common cause with the established parties to help those groups refocus the political agenda?

The State, Women's Education, and the New Politics

Latin American women have begun to take their concerns to the public arena, in which more far-reaching, systemic solutions can be considered and public funds can be committed to their resolution. This realignment comes from a deepened appreciation of the role of government policies in shaping relations within the home and family and a heightened awareness that piecemeal, stopgap solutions will not be as efficacious as efforts that could call upon public resources. Their change in focus occurs at a propitious moment, when many politicians and policymakers are beginning to recognize that their own best interests will be served by new attention to the issues raised by popular organizations.

This responsiveness has much to do with the changing nature of women's political organization. Urban life has coincided with new levels of political mobilization and participation for women, usually growing out of family and neighborhood concerns. Political elites under pressure for democratization have begun to see the concerns and demands of women as part of the political agenda to which they must respond. Recent elections in both Mexico and Peru have served notice to the dominant political parties that they have failed to maintain the allegiance of voters. Those parties are open, perhaps as never before, to women's organizations with policy alternatives and ties to popular organizations.

Mexico's governing party, the Partido Revolucionario Institucional (PRI), encountered vigorous opposition in the 1988 elections. In 1990 Peru's traditional parties learned the extent of the electorate's discontent, as Alberto Fujimori, an unknown political newcomer, put together his own party, Cambio 90, or "Change 90," and the public voted overwhelmingly for him. Both events provide new opportunities for women's organizations. While women's issues did not characterize the Fujimori campaign or the administration of Carlos Salinas, both are affected by the high levels of dissatisfaction expressed by popular movements, and both are aware of the political challenge posed by these groups as they are forced to confront the impact of past developmental strategies on their populations. Both leaders are aware that women are an important part of the popular movements and that their demands to feed and house their families are widely viewed as legitimate extensions of private concerns into public arenas. Nonformal education programs sponsored by feminist organizations have played a catalytic role in helping women from the popular organizations find new voices, identify the public content of their private concerns, and organize to defend those interests. Feminists are decidedly *not* setting the political agenda in Peru or Mexico, and dramatic change in gender relations of the sort envisioned by feminism does not appear to be part of the immediate future. Nevertheless, the unexpected coalitions between feminists and the popular social movements are redrawing the political landscape in both nations and forcing politicians to take women's political concerns into account as never before.[42]

A contemporary muralist who hoped to capture the complexity of education in Mexico or Peru in the 1990s would replace Rivera's idyllic rural scene with a sprawling urban settlement. The teacher would still be female, but, rather than a cornfield, her classroom would be in a storefront or a borrowed living room. Her students would be adult women from the popular classes, and the subject of study might well be birth control.

The challenges facing this teacher are formidable. On the one hand, she can count on the energies of other female volunteers committed to gender equity, who see education as part of the construction of a more just society. But she faces a contemporary scene in which poverty, violence, and subordination are part of daily life. Furthermore, her task must be performed in the shadow of a bloated and entrenched educational bureaucracy controlling the formal system and limiting access to the tax base. This teacher operates in a political climate in which governments are facing their most severe challenges. Conservative elites want to use the economic crisis to privatize educational structures and reduce the state's role in financing education. Even liberals ask if the models adopted in the past have served the national interest.

If serious reform becomes a possibility, the lessons learned from efforts in nonformal education might serve as a point of departure. Paradoxically, the dearth of public resources and the widespread fear of popular unrest have heightened the probability that politicians will look anew at this alternative.

NOTES

1. In Mexico from 3.1 percent of gross domestic product (GDP) to 2.6 percent; in Peru from 3.6 percent to 2.6 percent of a steeply declining GDP.

2. Figures are from *Statistical Yearbook for Latin America and the Caribbean* (New York: United Nations, 1988), 58, table 32 (Public Expenditure on Education); and *ECLA Statistical Yearbook of Latin America* (Santiago: UN/ECLA, 1987), 62. Estimates on the real value of Peru's GDP are from *Latin American Regional Reports*, Andean Group, RA 90-05, 28 June 1990, 4–5. For figures on actual expenditures, see James W. Wilkie, ed., *Statistical Abstract of Latin America* (Los Angeles: UCLA Latin American Center, 1989), vol. 27, chap. 9, 197, table 923 (Public Current Educational Expenditures).

3. As Soledad Loaeza makes clear, the goal of national allegiance as a product of the educational system never totally disappears. It figured prominently in the debates about the need for uniform national textbooks throughout the late 1950s and 1960s. See her discussion in *Clases Medias y Política en Mexico* (Mexico City: El Colegio de México, 1988). For a review of Mexican education policies and their relation to industrialization, see Jorge Padua, *Educación, industrialización y progreso técnico en México* (México: El Colegio de México y UNESCO, 1984).

4. Regina Cortina estimates the membership of Sindicato Nacional de Trabajadores de la Educación (SNTE) at 645,000, representing 40 percent of all public employees in Mexico. See Regina Cortina, "Gender and Power in the Teacher's Union of Mexico," *Mexican Studies* 6, no. 2 (Summer 1990): 242.

5. See Jorge Padua, "Los desafíos al sistema escolar formal en los albores del Siglo XXI" (Unpub. MS, El Colegio de México, 1988), 8.

6. See the discussion in Robert Drysdale and Robert Myers, "Continuity and Change: Peruvian Education," in *The Peruvian Experiment*, ed. Abraham Lowenthal (Princeton, N.J.: Princeton University Press, 1975); and Norman Gall, *Reforma Educativa Peruana* (Lima: Mosca Azul, 1974). Enrollment figures are from *Statistical Yearbook for Latin America and the Caribbean* (1988), 52, table 29 (Enrollment by Education Level).

7. In 1972, 5.9 percent of urban males over fifteen were illiterate in contrast to 19 percent of urban females. Fifty percent of the rural population over fifteen was illiterate; 32.9 percent of the males and 69.2 percent of the females. By 1985 the government reported only 15.2 percent of the over-fifteen population as illiterate, 8.5 percent of the men, but still 21.9 percent of the women. In 1987, 13 percent of the total population remained illiterate, 6.5 percent of the men and 20.1 percent of the women. In the rural areas 46 percent of the female population above fifteen remained illiterate.

8. Hernán Fernández, "Women's Educational Situation in Peru" (Paper prepared for the Mount Holyoke Conference on Worldwide Education for Women, South Hadley, Mass., November 1987).

9. Figures are from Yolanda de los Reyes, *La Desigualdad educativa de la mujer: El caso de México* (México: UNESCO, Oficina Regional de Educación para América Latina y el Caribe, 1983).

10. In Peru the continuing economic and political crisis is creating high levels of school desertion. After years of expanded educational participation the 1990s are witnessing declining numbers of students, who are dropping out to avoid the expense for their families.

11. See Peter Cleaves, *Professions and the State: The Mexican Case* (Tucson: University of Arizona Press, 1987), 43–57, for a full statement of this position. In the 1988 Mexican presidential campaign Carlos Salinas de Gortari, the Partido Revolucionario Institucional (PRI) candidate and the eventual winner, argued for careful scrutiny of expenditures for higher education, with future allocations going to the most efficient and useful programs. He also stressed the need for public universities to find alternative sources of funds. Cuauhtémoc Cárdenas defended university expansion. See the remarks of Carlos Salinas de Gortari on 26 April 1988 in Ciudad Obregón, Sonora, and those of Cuauhtémoc Cárdenas delivered at the Ciudad Universitaria of the Universidad Nacional Autónoma de México (UNAM) in Mexico City, as reported in *Universidad Futura* 1, no. 1 (November 1988–February 1989): 59–67.

12. Luis Pasara, "El Nuevo Perú profundo," *Caretas* (Lima), 10 April 1989, 45.

13. In Peru women represented 27 percent of the university population in 1960 and 34 percent in 1975. "In 1960, 1,500 women entered universities, a figure that increased 13 times to 19,000 by 1981. Annually, enrollment of women increased

by 12.4 percent, while the equivalent figure for men is 10.5 percent" (Fernández, "Women's Educational System," 3).

14. In 1969, of the 186,041 students enrolled, 82.7 percent were men, and 17.3 percent were women. By 1977 there were 351,617 students enrolled in higher education, 73.7 percent male and 27.3 percent female. Total enrollment increased 1.86 times, but male enrollment increased 1.58 times, while female enrollment increased 3.4 times.

15. Figures cited in Hernando Burgos, "La mujer en los nuevos tiempos," *Quehacer* (Lima) 66 (September–October 1990): 100.

16. See the discussion in Liliana Morales Hernandez, "La Mujer y la educación superior en México," *Universidad Futura* 1, no. 1 (1989): 68-77.

17. Cleaves, *Professions*, 44.

18. Modernization theorists, such as S. M. Lipset, predicted the possibility of this outcome in the 1960s, but planners hoped that economic growth—in part possible because of a more educated population—would absorb the new demand.

19. "Peruvians Brace for Fujishock as New President Confronts Economic Crisis, Determined Insurgents," *Wall Street Journal*, 27 July 1990, A8.

20. The most recent evidence for this thesis is provided by Denis Chávez de Paz, in *Juventud y terrorismo: características sociales de los condenados por terrorismo y otros delitos* (Lima: Instituto de Estudios Peruanos, 1989).

21. "Students and Academics in Peru Are Targets of Political Violence," *Chronicle of Higher Education*, 15 August 1990, A29.

22. See the discussion in Chávez de Paz, *Juventud y terrorismo*, 42–43.

23. Mariella Balbi, "Valle del Mantaro: despensa de la subversión," *Diario La República*, 28 January 1990, 16–17. On the same theme, see the analysis of Manuel Jesús Granados, "Sí, senores, ésto es Sendero," *Diario La República*, 12 March 1989, 13–15.

24. Chávez de Paz, *Juventud y terrorismo*, 44.

25. For a further account of the role of women in Sendero and an analysis of its early feminist position, see Carol Andreas, *When Women Rebel* (Westport, Conn.: Lawrence Hill, 1985), 178–92. For a more recent assessment, see Rosa Mavila, "Pasado y presente de las mujeres de la guerra," *Quehacer* (Lima) 79 (September 1992): 44–53.

26. A brigade of Sendero women controlled a cell block at the high-security Castro Castro prison, and they figured among those killed in the Fujimori government's attempt to reassert control in May 1992. See the reports in "Inicio del fin de Sendero," *Resumen Semanal* (Lima), 13, no. 572: 1–2.

27. For discussion of the origins of Sendero Luminoso, see Cynthia McClintock, "Why Peasants Rebel: The Case of Peru's Sendero Luminoso," *World Politics* 37 (1984): 48–84; and David Scott Palmer, "Rebellion in Rural Peru: The Origins and Evolution of Sendero Luminoso," *Comparative Politics* 18, no. 2 (1986): 127–46.

28. *ECLA Statistical Yearbook of Latin America* (Santiago: UN/ECLA, 1987), 62.

29. See Nelly Stromquist's article on nonformal education, "Women and Illiteracy: The Interplay of Gender Subordination and Poverty," *Comparative Education Review* 34, no. 1 (February 1990): 95–111.

30. Amartya Sen has quantified the impact of this pattern and its devastating

impact on women in various regions of the world. See his discussion in "Women's Survival as a Development Problem," *Bulletin of the American Academy of Arts and Sciences* 63, no. 2 (November 1989): 14–29.

31. Berta Gonzáles Posada, a congressional representative and member of Apra, was responsible for organizing parliamentary support. See the account in *Quehacer* (Lima), 64 (June 1990): 89. The idea for the police stations came from feminist initiatives in Brazil, but Mexican feminists have also written about the need for such units, and Peruvians established their own in 1988. In its first twelve months the women's police stations in Peru received more than 4,100 denunciations.

32. See the accounts in *Uno más uno, El Día,* and *La Jornada,* April and May 1990, for Mexico; and *Quehacer,* June 1990, for Peru.

33. Two recent studies describe this process in Lima, Peru. See Christina Hee Pederson, *Nunca Antes me habían enseñado eso* (Lima: Lilith Ediciones, 1988); and Carmen Montero "Le dije lo que quise" (Lima: Sumbi, 1989).

34. There are very real limits to the political mobilization and gender consciousness that results from nonformal education efforts, particularly from a feminist perspective. Despite the emphasis on revaluing women's economic contributions, women as well as men are hesitant about reassigning the traditional division of labor. Women value their roles within the family and would be reluctant to entrust the care of children to men. Belief in women's innate capacities to nurture and their psychological and emotional differences from men are deeply embedded and embraced by many Latin American women as well as men. This sets very important limits on the strength of alliances likely between feminist groups and popular women's organizations. On this issue see especially Cecilia Blondet, *Las Mujeres y el poder* (Lima: Instituto de Estudios Peruanos, 1991); and Maruja Barrig, ed., *De Vecinas a Ciudadanas* (Lima: SUMBI [Servicios Urbanos y Mujeres de Bajos Ingresos], 1988).

35. See *Aporte de la rebeldía de las mujeres* (Lima: Flora Tristán, 1989), 139. For the history of the feminist movement in Peru see Virginia Vargas, *Como Cambiar el Mundo Sin Perdernos* (Lima: Flora Tristán, 1992).

36. Contributing to the change have been widened educational opportunities for women, the economic crisis, rapid urbanization, increased democratization, the growth of popular movements, and the influence of the United Nations (UN) Decade for Women. The UN Decade for Women was instrumental in providing financial support for work with women's organizations. A great deal of this support came through nongovernment organizations (NGOs). A recent study found over seven hundred such organizations in Lima alone and also noted that NGOs are an important source of employment for social science graduates of Peruvian universities. See Maruja Barrig, "The Difficult Equilibrium between Bread and Roses: Women's Organizations and the Transition from Dictatorship to Democracy in Peru," in *The Women's Movement in Latin America: Feminism and the Transition to Democracy,* ed. Jane Jaquette (Boston: Unwin Hyman, 1989).

37. One might categorize them as follows: (1) radical feminist organizations espousing change in the social and economic system as well as in gender relations; (2) moderate feminist organizations willing to accept the existing economic

system but committed to ameliorative change in state policy toward women, for example, ending discriminatory laws and practices and expanding women's leadership and participation (included in this category are the growing number of research centers and women's studies programs whose publications help illuminate women's experience); (3) women's organizations with class-based interests, committed to the status quo and the existing system of gender roles, which use both to seek power and influence (these are often associated with the women's branch of conservative political parties); and (4) popular women's organizations created in response to the economic crisis and concerned with maternal and food issues.

38. By 1986 the milk distribution program was based on 7,500 neighborhood programs, and 1985 estimates put the number of communal kitchens at 715. See Barrig, "Difficult Equilibrium."

39. Cárdenas was critical of former President Miguel de la Madrid's acceptance of the International Monetary Fund's policies. Support for the Cárdenas candidacy reflected protest against the PRIs internal candidate selection processes and the austerity programs. For discussion of women's roles in the aftermath of the earthquake, see Alejandra Massolo and Martha Schteingart, eds., *Participación social, reconstrucción y mujer: El sismo de 1985* (Mexico City: PIEM, El Colegio de México UNICEF, Documentos de Trabajo no. 1, 1987). For a discussion of the new social movements and their implications for Mexican politics, see Susan Eckstein, "Formal versus Substantive Democracy: Poor People's Politics in Mexico City," *Mexican Studies* 6, no. 2 (Summer 1990): 213–40.

40. See the full discussion of the political implications of these programs in Barrig, "Difficult Equilibrium," 144–45.

41. "Lo que todas debemos saber sobre Sendero Luminoso," *Manuela* 8, nos. 133–34 (November 1989): 9–10.

42. Here is the vision of change as expressed by Virginia Vargas of Peru's Centro Flora Tristán: "the pressure and exchange between the feminist movement and the State, political parties, the Church and public institutions, for measures in favor of equality, is part of a political strategy . . . a strategy which tends toward the democratization and decentralization of the state and of society" (Vargas, *El aporte de la rebeldía de las mujeres*, 43).

Persistent Inequalities in Women's Education in Peru

HERNÁN FERNÁNDEZ

In Peru equality of educational opportunity is not guaranteed by the incorporation of children into public schools. There are marked inequalities in resources, quality of curriculum, and school conditions throughout the nation. The dramatic increase in schooling over the past twenty-five years takes on new meaning when we evaluate the great disparities in teaching conditions. Only 16 percent of local schools have a full complement of water, drainage, and electricity (44 percent in the urban areas and 2 percent in the rural). Many schools lack elementary teaching materials from chalk to maps, and adequate science laboratories do not exist outside Lima's elite schools. Almost one-third of the students in rural areas attend only up to the fourth grade of primary school.

To make matters worse, public expenditure for education shows a decisive decrease in real value. What was spent on each student in 1982 was less than half of what was spent in 1963. Compounding this decline is the drop in family expenditures for education; in metropolitan Lima this decreased on the order of 23 percent between 1972 and 1978. The situation is yet again worse in the rural area.

Families in Lima spent on average 4.2 times more than families in the countryside.[1] These conditions reflect the sharp class and regional stratification of Peruvian education. It is no surprise that the educational experience of boys and girls from the popular classes is markedly different from the experience of the children of the elite.

The vast majority of Peruvian children attend the national system of state-supported schools. Administration and curriculum are centralized through the Ministry of Education. Instruction in public schools is free; the state covers the cost of personnel and school maintenance. But the level and quality of state support has shown a marked decline.

Approximately 15 percent of the student population attend private schools. In contrast to the public system, private schools (located in Lima and the most prosperous provincial cities) often have excellent facilities, fine foreign language teaching, principally in English, and are very much in demand by the elite. With the exception of a few parochial schools for children from the popular sectors, private schools charge parents hefty tuition (pegged to the U.S. dollar). This system is also stratified, with a range of schools with different tuition rates available to the middle class and above.[2]

Social class also affects the students' experiences at school. Economic responsibilities seldom affect the school performance of children from the middle and upper classes. In the popular sectors the majority of boys and girls experience difficulties at school that derive from their economic situation, such as lack of books, having to help out at home, and having to work.

In all social groups a greater number of girls must help out at home, and this affects their school performance. The cultural standard that assigns domestic work to women operates at all social levels. In the case of women from the popular sectors what complicates matters is not just domestic work in a woman's own home but also the domestic work she does for other families. The majority of poor women begin their work lives as maids. As more middle-class women enter the paid labor force, in part a product of greater levels of education, there will be an even greater demand for domestic workers and a greater likelihood that girls from households with limited resources will forgo schooling for renumerative domestic service.

Women's work (including domestic service) begins at an early age. In a study of Peruvian peasant women Violeta Sara-Lafosse found that "female child labor occurs in more than two-thirds of the groups studied, and reaches 80% in the area of Cuzco, where 31% of the girls begin work at the age of 7."[3]

Class-based educational inequalities occur at the earliest ages. Students from the popular classes tend to be on average two and a half years behind in their schooling, and students from rural areas are even further behind. Fifty-four percent of rural women are more than three years behind the normal age for their year in school.[4]

Economic status also affects the probability that a child will remain in school. In a study of low-income women 42 percent of the 684 peasant women interviewed reported they were forced to leave school because of their responsibilities in agriculture and domestic work. In a study of 230 self-employed seamstresses the most important reasons reported for giving up studies were illness and personal reasons (33 percent) or a lack of economic resources and hence the need to work (27 percent).[5]

Enduring Gender Issues in Education

Teaching is shaped by the dominant values (whether manifest or latent) in society. In Peru this propagates prejudices against women. Even teachers have an image that favors male students over female students. Primary textbooks also convey distinct images of men and women. Woman's image is oriented toward the home and man's toward work. Moreover, important messages about authority and leadership and the appropriateness of these characteristics to each sex are communicated in the classroom through textbooks. For instance, males outnumber females in "giving orders" at a ratio of 5 to 1. Females "assist others" in nineteen cases, and no male represents this stance.[6] In four textbooks widely used in the first grades of primary school, the woman is characterized as a fastidious protector of her children, who worries about the family, sacrifices herself for her own children, is religious, fights for her own children, and is helpful. The male characteristics include making decisions, governing the country, organizing himself and others, ordering, constructing, and creating things, and giving his life for his country.[7]

With these images conveyed through textbooks the classroom experience runs counter to the goal of redefining more just and equitable roles between men and women. Furthermore, these texts misrepresent women's active and essential roles in rural and urban society.[8]

The Educational Challenge for Adult Women

For the adult working-class woman returning to school requires a Herculean effort. That schools have been created for adult women is not enough. There are schools that offer night classes especially geared for domestic servants; nevertheless, many of these schools have fewer students than spaces available. Many female domestic workers report that their desire to attend is blocked by their employers. The following account reflects the difficulties that many poor women face in their quest for schooling:

> I studied at night, after putting my baby to sleep, she and my second daughter already having eaten. I went to school pregnant. With the first baby, they performed a Cesarian section on me and I didn't have the energy to do anything. Then the boss gave me a month's leave, and a friend lent me her notebooks during the day.... Then my husband said to me: "But how can you do this, these stupid things, if you are ill?" But I continued. I finished primary and then secondary school having my three young children. Then I studied to be a nurse's assistant.[9]

The number of adult women attending school in the formal system is minimal. Instead, nonformal education programs are providing most of the educational opportunities available to adult women. Significant changes are taking place in these nonformal programs, most of which are sponsored by private voluntary organizations. In many cases women participate in nonformal education courses, despite the resistance of their spouses. A teacher in a school for adults in a marginal district of Lima points out: "there are women who attend all of their classes in spite of the fact that their husbands don't want them to. Once they begin to learn they don't want to give up."[10]

We need to know much more about how the formal educational system can respond to the great desire of adult women to educate themselves. Although feminist organizations have played a significant and innovative role through nonformal educational programs, the link to the formal system still needs to be constructed.

Assessing Education's Impact

Education in Peru seems to be carried along by inertia. We are aware of its growth, but we do not know its effects. One of the most important but least studied aspects of education is the effect that it has on individuals. It is helpful to ask, "What purpose does a Peruvian woman's years of schooling serve?"

At a minimum we know that the growing presence of women in school demonstrates that their role in society is in the process of being redefined. Thousands of young Peruvian women now have expectations of paid work that contradict the traditional view that women should restrict their sphere of action to the home.

We can hope that education, especially at its highest levels, will provide a wider worldview, a greater capacity for abstract reasoning, a broader view of the conception of oneself and of society, and better and more varied forms of communication. A greater level of education can lead women to reflect upon their situation and help them move toward transforming their place in society. The development of feminism in Peru is related to the notable increase of women in Peruvian universities following the decade of the 1960s.

The most educated women have fewer children, marry at a later age, and know more about, are more efficient in, and more disposed to the use of contraceptives. Thus, women with advanced levels of education have an average of 2.7 children, whereas women without such education have 6.2 children.[11] The effects of a higher level of education are reflected also in the income of working women. Data from the 1981 census for metropolitan Lima indicate that the average monthly income for women with advanced education was three times that of women without education.[12] Education probably has effects on family organization as well. Recent studies indicate that a wife's level of instruction affects the structure of authority within the family. A lack of education in the mother favors the continuation of patriarchal families.[13]

Education has significant effects on the most disadvantaged groups of women. Studies of the domestic workers of Lima show that education develops a woman's personal sense of security. Evening schools for domestic servants provide a safe place where these young women can meet other domestic workers; these schools offer the possibility of developing friendships, exchanges of experiences, and mutual support. While the quality of instruction may be elementary and inadequate, attending the schools leads to enhanced self-confidence among the young women, and in some cases it prepares them to work in other occupations. The domestic worker's school experiences also help bridge the gap between rural life and a new urban identity.[14]

For vast numbers of women in the rural and marginal urban sectors one important aspect of their subordinate position is limited verbal expression. Perhaps the most dramatic expression of women's submission is silence. This silence has limited women's leadership in community life in both rural and urban Peru. Overcoming women's subordination in the home, where a woman often found herself in a state of virtual servility, is related to women's increased wage-earning capacity. But this has not always been translated into public leadership.

The most notable changes in women's popular participation have been made in the cities. The increase in marginal districts, composed largely of migrants from the country, has led to multiple forms of mobilization. First migrants gained the physical space to establish dwellings through land invasions. Then came their struggles for basic services of water, sewage, electricity, schools, medical posts, and transportation. Subsequently, against the background of collective poverty, exacerbated by the economic crises of the 1980s, the new urbanites established community kitchens. Women have been a major force in these movements, as much because of their economic situation as for their gender. But this organizational experience appears to be the key to changing women's status and has translated into greater political participation. In one instance women who had been involved in a nonformal education project to produce soap operas with a political message moved on to wider community involvement.[15]

Feminist organizations are significant leaders in popular education. These groups have taken on the challenge of collaborating with women from the popular sectors, confronting the enormous distances in communication with those with whom they share only their gender, not social class, nor, in many cases, race. In opposition to the practice of the formal educational system, which puts so much emphasis on concrete results and the retention of information, the feminist "capacitators" have sought instead to emphasize the participation and incorporation of their students in the learning process.

There are some important success stories among the women of the popular sectors who have taken the courses provided by the feminist organizations. Recuperating their own history, the women begin to see how their childhood experiences have marked their behavior as adults. The majority point out that, as children, they learned to approach the world timidly. Exposure to the popular education courses has brought about changes in the women's relationships with their partners and their children; it has reinforced their self-esteem and broadened their knowledge of their own sexuality. With respect to self-image, almost all of their positive self-images are linked to new ties to neighborhood organizations and to their struggles as women. They have learned to say: "We are fighters, we work a great deal."

Final Remarks

The challenge for education is linked to the hope for a better future. It is not surprising that the motivation for education is so vital in women. Thinking about a better future has something to do with a hard and difficult present. But, in order for the challenge of education to be meaningful, one must understand its limits, effects, and possibilities. To be in favor of extended educational services and improving the quality of teaching can be good ends in themselves, but they are also rather general standards and can be sources of confusion. To have blind faith in education without being critical of its practice can be the best way to waste resources and increase frustration.

Despite official declarations and curricular aims, social inequalities and prejudices will be reproduced in school unless concrete efforts are made to alter this process. Educational strategies and policies for women must be related to the social groups and generation from which the students come. Planning an educational program for adult women from marginal districts or for peasant women with low levels of education is not the same as thinking about the educational needs of young women in the middle and upper classes. But, despite these distinctions, there is a common problem that operates against women of every social sector: once women are excluded from the educational system they become far less effective participants in any other aspect of society that requires educational achievement.

Among adult urban women who have had little education, lack of time and material resources make it impossible for them to complete their formal studies. The options for further training include nonformal education organized through groups such as mother's clubs, communal cooking groups, and neighborhood and district organizations. Among these women there is now a rich array of experiences in which they have won the right to speak and have been recognized by their spouses as participants in community meetings. These women have transcended the limitations of the home to confront situations that affect them as a group. They have learned to express themselves and have practiced many forms of communication in imaginative ways: through bulletins, radio soap operas, and theater.[16]

The extension of these activities is extremely important for attaining more dignified, respectful levels of life for the most marginal groups of women. But the search for solutions cannot be limited to education and training, however important those may be. Alleviating the dire economic circumstances in which the majority of the Peruvian population finds itself must be at the center of women's popular education programs.[17]

The other area that calls for vigorous new intervention is in the formal education system. Millions of children and adolescent students each day attend a vast network of thousands of schools scattered throughout the country. Thousands of teachers follow a program developed by the technobureaucracy of the Ministry of Education. It is thus imperative to act from within the formal educational system, to take part in curricular plans, and to improve the quality of teaching. Educating children is not limited to ensuring entrance into schools; it also involves active support and care in the management of those institutions. Popular organizations, which have been so effective in supplying nonformal education, now need to turn their energies toward reforming the formal system.

NOTES

1. Hernán Fernández, "Aspectos sociales y económicos de la educación en el Perú," in *Problemas Poblacionales Peruanos II*, ed. Roger Guerra Garcia (Lima: Asociación Multidisciplinaria para la Investigación y Docencia en Población, 1986).

2. There is some indication that the economic crisis has affected the less elite private schools attended by children of the middle class; parents unable to pay tuitions (which have risen to keep pace with skyrocketing inflation) are withdrawing their children and registering them in public schools. This in turn increases the pressure on the public system.

3. Violeta Sara-Lafosse, Carmen Chira, and Amelia Fort, "Valor del trabajo de la mujer en al agro y en la producción domiciliaria para la industria de confecciones," in *Participación Económica y Social de la mujer Peruana* (Lima: UNICEF, 1981), 37.

4. Hernán Fernández and Carmen Montero, *Desigualdades en el acceso a la escuela: Análisis de la cobertura y atraso escolar* (Lima: Instituto Nacional de Investigación y Desarrollo de la Educación, 1982).

5. Violeta Sara-Lafosse, "Comedores comunales: La mujer frente a la crisis" (Lima: SUMBI, 1984).

6. Jeanine Anderson, "Imágenes de la familia en los textos y la vida escolares" (Paper presented at the seminar on Education and Society, Peruvian Association for the Development of Social Sciences, Lima, 1985), 7.

7. María Carmen Masilla, "Aprendiendo a ser mujer," *Debates en sociología* (Lima), no. 9 (1983).

8. Susan C. Bourque and Kay B. Warren, *Women of the Andes* (Ann Arbor: University of Michigan Press, 1981).

9. Maruja Barrig, *Las obreras* (Lima: Asociación de Defensa y Capacitación Legal, 1986), 58.

10. Susana Checa, Virginia Guzmán, and Virginia Vargas, "Evaluación del impacto de los programas básicos integrados en la mujer: Las comunidades campesinas de Puno; los PP.JJ. del cono sur," *Participación Económica y Social de la mujer Peruana* (Lima: UNICEF, 1981), 335.

11. National Office of Statistics, *Encuesta Nacional de Fecundidad del Perú, 1977–1978* (Lima: Instituto Nacional de Planificación, 1979).

12. Marfil Francke, *Mujer, Población y Desarrollo,* in Roger Guerra García, ed., *Problemas Poblacionales Peruanos II* (Lima: Asociación Multidisciplinaria para la Investigación y Docencia en Población, 1986).

13. Maruja Barrig, *Convivir: La pareja en la probreza,* ed. Mosca Azul (Lima: Peru, 1982), 32; Violeta Sara-Lafosse, "La mujer y la familia en contextos sociales diferentes," AMIDEP Seminario de Investigaciones Sociales acerca de la Mujer (Cuzco: Universidad Nacional San Antonia Abad, 1978); and Kornelius Vermunt et al., *Opiniones y actitudes frente a la procreación en el estrato bajo de Lima Metropolitana* (Mimeo, CISEPA, Lima, 1967).

14. Rosa M. Alfaro, *De la Conquista de la ciudad a la apropiación de la palabra* (Lima: TAREA, Asociación de Publicaciones Educativas, 1987), 109.

15. Alfaro, *De la Conquista de la ciudad,* 286.

16. Carmen Lora, Cecilia Barrenechea, and Frine Santisteban, *Mujer: víctima de opresión, portadora de liberación* (Lima, 1985); Alfaro, *De la Conquista de la ciudad;* and Cecilia Blondet, "Nuevas formas de hacer política: las amas de casa populares," *Allpanchis* (Cusco, Peru) 21, no. 25 (1985).

17. Christina Heé Pedersen, *Nunca antes me habían enseñado eso* (Lima: Capacitación feminista, Ediciones Lilith, 1988), 238.

Alternative Education for Women in Peru

VIRGINIA VARGAS

The women's movement in Peru is composed of many organizations, united in their common commitment to fostering varied and creative forms of participation. All seek to end women's historical neglect by the political, social, and economic order. At the popular level, in the sprawling squatter settlements of Lima, many women have banded together for their family's survival to make new demands in the labor market; others have turned the political organizations seeking their votes into arenas in which they can discuss women's marginal situation. Women from the middle classes are questioning their situation in the workplace; many more are struggling in union assemblies, and in their families, for personal and collective advancement. Feminist groups have also expanded their activities into the economic and political life of the nation, territories usually reserved for men.

The many forms of the women's movement illustrate Peru's complex and diverse social, political, and economic dynamics, possibly more so than any other movement. Amid all their diversity, however, two things define their commonality: they each begin with an initial rebelliousness, and they all emphasize the daily circumstances of women's lives as the basis for learning and creating political consciousness. The needs of women vary enormously, but through these organizations and their activities women are questioning the most evident aspects of their subordination, displaying an enormous potential to develop new forms of expression and new social practices to question the current social, political, and economic structures.

Many centers and institutions try to assist women through educational programs. The various feminist centers and groups do extensive educational work with slum residents, workers, farmers, and housemaids. Through women's daily struggles and concrete needs these groups attempt to strengthen women's awareness that the oppressive structures they face discriminate on the basis of gender and that these structures are linked to other dominating structures in society.[1]

Programs are usually led by "promoters" who also prepare the content of the classes and workshops.[2] The promoters become the connection between women. They are a kind of "transmission belt" for the processes, experiences, and practices of the various women's organizations; they are fundamental in explaining and promoting gender demands to those who direct their work. The promoters are professionals with university educations or substantial training and experience; most have worked in leftist parties. Generally, they are relatively young women, who, through their work with women from many social levels, have come to question women's condition. Although an important sector of this group hold feminist positions, others have advanced only so far as their respective class position or the approval of men allows.

The feminist education that the feminist groups promote is a political practice borne out of women's desire to build a women's movement, with all the personal commitment that this implies. In this respect it is different from many other types of education. We attempt to establish democratic practices in our educational program that are neither vertical, idealistic, or materialistic. Experience has demonstrated that feminist educators and those being educated are involved in an active and mutually rewarding relationship. Both the instructors and the trainees have different bodies of knowledge, and the objective is to integrate the two, saving what is of value and discarding the oppressive concepts about women that we have internalized. Education is not simply a matter of imparting knowledge; rather, it is a process by which life experiences are integrated with scientific information and by which a new, rich knowledge capable of integrating different realities is produced.

By concentrating on gender oppression, we do not mean to imply that there are no other kinds of oppression. Nevertheless, we do believe that women's subordination is the first and most general power relationship in every society. The subversive aspect of feminist capacitation is in its attack on the most deeply rooted oppression in societies. In doing this it reveals other forms of domination at work.

At the same time our broader political task is to go beyond revealing oppression and to search for alternative proposals for real, possible change. We have added new themes to public debate and have demonstrated their political content. When we politicize what is private we reveal that the same power relationships in society as a whole are found within our intimate and private relationships. Feminist capacitation deals with daily living, with explaining the politics of interpersonal relations. This is part of its subversive strength.

We are sowing autonomy and confidence in women so they can shed their inhibitions and free themselves from fears built up over centuries of oppression and discrimination. Within feminist capacitation programs women are allowed the freedom of speech that has been denied them in the past because they were women. Recovering the right to speak goes far beyond the speech itself; it represents recognition of dignity, needs, and demands.

Behavior that we may believe to be personal and private is actually a consequence of the structures that formed us and that we propose to change. We take this to mean that our job is to weaken all that has oppressed and discriminated against women and made us the "second sex," or "the others." Sexuality divides the world and its relationships. Our bodies have been seized and with them our freedom of movement and our capacity to decide. Once we lose our power to decide, we lose our bodies, our sexuality, our reproductive options and are unable to develop as free and autonomous beings. So the issue of sexuality must be raised, regardless of the chosen theme for discussion—it is fundamental to our understanding of women's relationships with the surrounding world. We believe that feminist education will lead us to question power imbalances, domination, oppression, and discrimination against women.

Our subordination lies fundamentally in our fragmented consciousnesses, where gender awareness has been twisted by the messages and traditions received from the church, political parties, schools, and mass media, all of which serve other interests. We seek to liberate the whole of women's identity. Therefore, our programs must consider the political scene and its effect upon women and their problems from a feminist perspective.

Feminist Education's Contribution to Formal Education

While there have been some advances, our efforts to develop an alternative feminist education have been largely ignored by the government, in spite of women's enormous educational needs. Feminist education should not be the exclusive job of private centers and institutions. It is the responsibility of the government to respond to its people's educational needs, and feminist education should be incorporated into all levels of the educational system for both men and women.

It is also fundamental that formal education, which reaches a great segment of the population, be seen as terrain for confrontation and change. Feminist education is now directed toward adult women, but it is important that children start to form new values so that the relationship between the sexes can change. It will not be easy to accomplish this. The feminist movement's relationship with the state has been a difficult one, mainly because women's issues have never been a priority for the government. Currently, some government sectors have begun to act: the National Commission on Women's Rights has been formed, which includes among its members a representative of each public ministry. A Women's Consultative Council has been formed in the National Planning Institute (INP), which has begun to discuss short-term plans for women and medium- and long-term political alignments.

In its program for education and training the INP's national plan includes the following: a consideration of gender issues in its curricula for adult education, reading instruction, and early education; training teachers in matters related to the issue of gender; incorporating the concept of gender in nonschool educational programs; organizing a seminar for professionals in the public and private sectors to plan women's development; and, finally, formulating alternative programming for radio, press, and television. Members of the women's movement must urge the government to implement these proposals.

Our experience indicates that schools can create an adequate environment and space for women when the teachers are committed to the communities in which they teach. A study made in Pamplona Alta to measure the impact of basic night education programs for workers revealed that most of the students enrolled were women; one of their main interests was to acquire more knowledge for better job performance (most were semi-illiterate, door-to-door salespeople); another interest was to approach the educational level of their children, who had elementary and secondary instruction and who felt a degree of contempt for their less-educated mothers.[3]

The women in these basic education programs changed their attitudes and their self-perceptions; the teachers discovered new ways to approach their students. Education, from this perspective, is a social practice, one in which, "by the processes of teaching and learning, human beings acquire and develop knowledge, attitudes, and abilities related to their material and spiritual needs."[4]

If education is a social practice, then it must also work toward changing reality. In this respect the contributions of alternative feminist education to formal education are:

—Designing content according to women's reality and their local and regional differences, and determining what power mechanisms directly or indirectly affect women's lives.
—Establishing the everyday experiences of women as the context for change.
—Demanding curriculum diversity that matches the ethnic, linguistic, cultural, and social diversity of the students. This requires a theoretical structure that questions patriarchy and communicates to women that they need not wrestle with their problems in isolation, that they are problems all of society must solve.
—Refusing to separate those who teach from those who receive instruction. This goes beyond the concept of democratic education and recognizes that education should also educate the educator.
—Promoting education that does not limit its priorities to knowledge but also considers the personal and social development of women.

Feminist education, when rooted in these principles and practices, can be a vehicle for the release and strengthening of women's potential. It can help women evaluate and overcome the mechanisms of oppression, and it can offer an alternative perspective for social change throughout society.

NOTES

1. Among the Peruvian feminist groups dedicated to education are the "Flora Tristán" Peruvian Woman's Center and the "Manuela Ramos" movement. Both work with women in the slums, promoting workshops on health, sexuality, and education. The "Aurora Vivar" Association deals with female workers; the CESIP-Woman directs its actions toward organized women through workshops and courses on women's struggles; and the Woman and Society Association and the Peru Woman Association are two other important organizations in the women's movement.

There are similar organizations in some of the provinces, including the Amauta Association in Cusco, the Woman's Office in Chimbote, the Arequipena Woman's Center in Arequipa, the Micaela Bastidas Association in Trujillo, the Women's Democratic Front of Cajamarca, and the Woman's Area of the Ideas Center of Piura. All promote an understanding of women's reality and strengthen local women's movements through educational action.

2. Promoters are the "facilitators" or "teachers" who establish the pedagogical relationship with the women, presenting classes or workshop and maintaining permanent contact with the group to which the actions are directed.

3. Virginia Guzmán, Susana Checa, and Virginia Vargas, "Evaluación del impacto de los programas de servicios básicos integrados en la mujer," *Participación económica y social de la mujer en el Perú* (Lima: UNICEF, 1981).

4. Sigfredo Chiroque, *Usos y abusos de la tecnología educativa* (Lima: Autoeducación, 1987).

Education, Race, and Inequality in Brazil

FÚLVIA ROSEMBERG

The underprivileged population is serviced by underprivileged schools.

In Brazil a woman has held the post of minister of education, and women have been, and still are, in charge of state and municipal education offices. Women have figured prominently in the formation of educational policies and in the administration of the country's educational system. In 1980 women accounted for 87 percent of Brazilian teachers,[1] and half of all Brazilian students were women in 1982. In spite of these facts and figures suggesting positive trends, I will argue that the Brazilian formal education system discriminates against women. How can this apparent paradox be explained?

In Brazil, as in other countries around the world, sexual discrimination in education has shifted. Rather than hindering women's access to schooling, discrimination now affects those within the system. Although access to education has increased admirably in Brazil, the education of men and women is fundamentally different. Despite the principle of coeducation, schools are a veritable sexual ghetto. Brazilian schools reinforce sexual stereotypes in their curricular materials, and the values transmitted by teachers reflect sexist values. I will argue that there is a direct link between the sex-biased content of schools and women's experience in the Brazilian labor market, where even with the same level of education, women consistently earn less than men.

The Politics of Brazilian Education

Over the past several decades Brazil has embraced a project for national development that has led to intense urbanization and the pursuit of a modern, expanding economy. Brazilians have responded to the economic, social, and cultural demands that urbanization creates by expanding educational opportunities and reforming an educational system that had been inadequate for centuries.

Brazil has partially succeeded in democratizing and modernizing education. The ratio of schooled individuals to the general population has jumped from 9.05 per 100 in 1940 to 28.56 in 1989. But, despite advances in enrollments, persistent and crucial distortions remain. The level of education in Brazil remains low. The population five years and older has on the average only 3.9 years of schooling. Some estimate that one-fifth of Brazilians ten years of age and older cannot read or write. Even among youths age fifteen to twenty-four, the most literate age group, the illiteracy rate was a high 9.6 percent in 1989.[2] In 1989, 17 percent of Brazilian children between the ages of seven and fourteen did not have access to a school.[3] Out of every one hundred students five years and older, only 6 percent were at university.[4] As in other dimensions of social life, educational opportunities are not equally distributed among the different segments of Brazil's population. White, urban residents in the south have access to the best education. There is also a strong correlation between education and a family's socioeconomic status. In essence, despite educational reforms and the relative increase of educational opportunities, the Brazilian system of education still withholds education from large segments of the population and favors others, conferring an elite status on a fortunate few.

This pattern forces us to reconsider the progressive assumption that widened educational opportunity would automatically lead to increased opportunities for all. Indeed, some scholars have begun to ask to what extent the educational system perpetuates inequalities. They note that budgetary resources are not equally distributed among the levels of education, nor are they allocated on the basis of the percentage of the school population at each level. In 1985 federal and state departmental resources bound for education were distributed as follows: 62.2 percent were destined for the primary system (which receives 86.0 percent of the Brazilian students); 10.3 percent for the secondary system (which receives 9.5 percent of the students) and 27.5 percent for higher education (which serves only 4.4 percent of the students). Underlying the preference for supporting the public university system is the tendency of Brazilian families with high incomes to send their children to private schools (with higher educational standards and prestige) at the primary and secondary level and then on to the public universities.

Furthermore, there are enormous inequalities in expenditures per student at the primary level among the Brazilian states. In the richest states of the south and southeast the expenditure per student exceeded U.S. $120.00, while in the poorest states of the north and northeast it was about U.S. $50.00. This inequality shows up dramatically in the classroom. In a sample of five hundred public schools in northeast Brazil 34 percent of the classrooms did not have a table for the teacher.[5]

The Study of Women's Education

There has been only limited scholarly attention to women's education in Brazil. The few surveys that exist concentrate on limited themes and were usually done in conjunction with studies of general education. Many of them were fashioned directly or indirectly by theoretical models that assume that the goal of education is the production of skilled labor.[6] Often this approach ignores intervening variables such as the availability of economic resources and employment. Similarly most theoretical models assume that schooling has the same significance for men and women, an assumption that seems problematic at best.

Analyzing the specifics of women's education is clearly not a priority for researchers, nor for the government agencies that are responsible for funding research. General research pertaining to the Brazilian woman is equally limited. "Woman and work" was the main theme of research until the end of the 1970s.[7] In addition, Brazilian educational statistics were not always broken down by gender, and this has retarded research.

The absence of studies, census information, and research pertaining to the educational situation of black women is even more striking.[8] Researchers have seldom debated racial discrimination. Until recently white scholars practically ignored the specific conditions of discrimination suffered by black Brazilian women. The absence of debate is generated in part by the widespread myth that Brazil is the kingdom of racial democracy—why discuss something that is not a problem? Why investigate racial differences in the kingdom of racial equality, if that will call attention to discrimination? Only six of Brazil's nine national censuses have gathered information on race, and even that information was nonspecific. Ministry of Education officials do not include the racial origins of students and teachers in their annual reports on Brazil's education system.[9]

The Brazilian system of education also conceals its prejudice against blacks by subordinating racial discrimination to class origin. The reasoning is that, since most of the black population is poor, observed differences between blacks and whites can be attributed to poverty, not to race. This thrusts racial discrimination in education into limbo and begs the issue of educational priorities.

With these caveats let me summarize what we do know about women's education and the impact of race on education in Brazil.

Schooling and Literacy
Women have benefited from the expansion of education in Brazil and now participate in the school system in the same proportions as men. In 1980, 50.0 percent of the twenty-six million students in Brazil were women. Although women have yet to enter all levels of education in the same numbers as men, statistics indicate a tendency toward equalization. In 1980, 33.3 percent more women and 26.5 percent more men entered all levels of education than in 1970.

Women also account for much of the increase in literacy over the past several decades.[10] While 8.2 percent more men were literate than women in 1940, the percentage difference in 1982 was a mere 0.4 percent for the population five years of age and older. As in other Latin American countries, the Brazilian women who are most likely to be illiterate are those who are poor, older, black, and who live in rural regions. Some 1982 figures illuminate this point:

1. In the Northeast one of every two women is illiterate, compared to the state of São Paulo, in which one in five women is illiterate.[11]
2. In rural areas one in two women is illiterate, compared to urban areas, in which one in five women is illiterate.[12]
3. Illiteracy is most prevalent among Brazilians fifty years of age and older, 38 percent of whom are illiterate, while the group with the highest rate of literacy is women between the ages of fifteen and nineteen, only 11 percent of whom are illiterate.

The most recent figures for illiteracy broken down by race have not been published. It is possible, however, to extract information from the number of people five years of age and older who in 1980 declared that they had no schooling or less than one year: 18.4 percent of white men, 21.4 percent of white women, 47.6 percent of black men, and 47.6 percent of black women.

Instruction
The level of instruction (years of school completed) is extremely low for both male and female populations; nonetheless, it has been increasing slowly. Statistics indicate that men and women have almost equal access to education, yet significant differences persist among the races. On the average black women remain in school for 2.2 years, while white women remain in school for 3.2 years.

A recent series of studies shows that the labor market does not give consistent recognition to the education acquired by different segments of the population. Women are paid less than men, even when they have the same education, and the "contrast between salaries for men and women is even clearer when dealing with those who have secondary and university educations."[13]

Although education grants black Brazilians social mobility, it does not guarantee them the same benefits enjoyed by whites.[14] Whites not only make more money than blacks of the same educational level, but the difference between the races increases with the level of education.[15]

Data pertaining to years of education, earnings, sex, and racial origins for the state of São Paulo show that for each level of education there is a consistent salary hierarchy: white men are at the top, followed by black men, white women, and, finally, receiving the lowest salaries, black women. In other words, the earnings of white women and black women are lower than those of white men and black men with the same education.

Race and gender intersect in a persistent pattern when we consider the following comparisons:[16]

1. The greatest discrepancy in earnings appears in a comparison of the earnings of white men and black women, especially in jobs requiring higher education. In the economically active population (EAP) with the highest degree of schooling, black women earn 30.5 percent of what white men earn.
2. The smallest discrepancy in salary appears in the comparison of white women and black women, even among those with high levels of education.
3. For all levels of education the difference between the salaries of white men and black men is less than the difference between the salaries of white men and white women.
4. The difference between the salaries of white men and white women is greater than the difference between the salaries of black men and black women. White women earn less than 50 percent of what white men earn, while black women earn slightly more than 50 percent of what black men earn.

These global comparisons mask important differences in the experiences of males and females, blacks and whites. When differential work hours or years of experience fail to explain salary differentials, some scholars have been led to argue that salary differences are due to discrimination within the labor market.[17] Wage inequality may also reflect discrimination in the educational system, since whites and blacks, men and women, do not go to the same schools, just as the poor do not attend the same schools as the rich. The same educational level can conceal enormous differences in training, quality of instruction, and curriculum content. The "underprivileged population" is usually serviced by "underprivileged schools" that are unable to offer adequate learning.[18] Similarly, many more black students attend poor-quality schools than do whites. As a result, the educational system provides white students with better training, so whites have an advantage when competing for jobs.[19]

Schools play an important role in maintaining the sex and race wage differentials by creating educational ghettos. While previous studies have shown that the educational system discriminated against women by preventing them access to schooling, sexual discrimination now seems to affect those within the educational system by supporting fundamental differences in societal expectations for men and women. Men tend to enter technical and scientific fields, while women enter such fields as the humanities, education, and health. The Brazilian educational system continues to prepare women for occupations of lower social and economical prestige and thus is implicated in the persistent discrimination against women.

Why does this segregation happen? First, some structural determinants must be taken into account: sophisticated technical courses are usually offered in the large urban centers. This usually means that rural youngsters who wish to attend these schools must move to the cities. This places limits on women's opportunities. A young girl living alone in a big city, in which there are considerably higher indices of violence, is considered to be at risk and in a threatening situation.

Second, education lays a comfortable trap for women. Given that women's professional futures are obscure and uncertain and the parameters set by family obligations are concrete, women demonstrate a powerful sense of reality when they search for courses that enable them to acquire multivalent competence. If their choice is between a low salary and unemployment, choosing the former might be viewed as a survival strategy. Given the current economic and social conditions in Brazil, choosing flexibility may be viewed as increasing a woman's options and providing multiple professional choices. A degree in the liberal arts or humanities prepares students for many types of jobs. Since, however, jobs in the humanities are not specialized, and there is a large work force available to fulfill them, they do not pay as much as jobs that require technical knowledge, most of which are held by technically trained men. Women also continue to reason that, even if they are unable to find employment, the knowledge acquired in a general humanities-based educational program will be useful in their domestic work within their own families and with their own children, making use, for example, of concepts of pedagogy, nursing, or psychology.

Racism and Sexism in Schools

Returning to the initial question of how racism and sexism are perpetuated in the Brazilian school system, let us consider each in turn. In regard to racism, as one researcher has written:

> When a social organization is racist, it not only displays discriminatory practices but also limits the motivation and aspirations of blacks. The black population's social mobility is limited both by overt discrimination and by an internalized negative self image. This unfavorable view begins in school textbooks, and is pervasively conveyed by the racist aesthetics of the mass media. Thus, there is a mutual reinforcement of discriminatory practices. Blacks tend to avoid discriminatory situations and expressions of symbolic violence against themselves. This has the effect of regulating their aspirations, and as a consequence, the dominant racial group has been able to impose its definitions of the "appropriate place" for colored people.[20]

In regard to sexism, the differential socialization of the sexes, giving women an expressive role and men an instrumental one, limits women's expectations and motivation toward their performances in adulthood. Educational structures are also responsible for transmitting bipolar sexual models. In addition, sexist patterns exist in student-teacher relationships, which not only reflect society's discriminatory values but those of the educational system as well. There is also evidence that the curricula and didactic material utilized at all educational levels, from preschools to universities, discriminate against women. Women's organizations in Brazil have therefore organized special "days" designated within the schools to be devoted to correcting the bias clearly present in curricular materials.

Thinking about the Future

To locate the school's responsibility in the fabrication of "black people's place" and "women's work" does not mean to ignore the role of other institutions in perpetuating social inequalities. Nevertheless, the schools are not neutral. Substantial changes toward equality of educational opportunities will not be achieved solely through the expansion of registration in schools or in the number of years of mandatory education. The Brazilian educational system must recognize the existence of economic, racial, and sexual discrimination and act to end it. Given that blacks and women are often channeled into fields of learning that prepare them for jobs that pay less than those held by white males, there would be little sense in establishing racial and sexual quotas in universities. Since women and blacks often receive academic preparation that is inferior to that of white males, there would be little sense in establishing labor quotas. Rather, equal education must begin with fundamental changes in the content of education, in the values and ideas that the educational system communicates.

One important area for action in Brazil is the education of female teachers about the need for curricular change. This might begin with an effort to make explicit the present economic, sexual, and racial inequalities in our society and in the educational system itself. It would also necessitate developing an adequate teacher's training program, curricular reorganization, and didactic materials to transmit new standards of racial and human relationships. The new curriculum should allow children and young people to develop comportment patterns to strengthen their racial and sexual identity. It would allow students to follow their individual destinies, even if these are not similar to the ones prescribed by the dominant ideology.

If these initiatives in the national educational plan give rise to new interests, strengthen the identity of women and blacks, and help in the formulation of new life projects, then structural plans will be essential in order to make these projects real. If educational democracy is to be achieved, national plans must include a more equalitarian geographic distribution of schools, both with respect to quality and curricular variety. Such a plan would enable the child who lives in the outskirts of São Paulo or in the rural northeast to attend a school with adequate human and material supplies and a young girl living in a small country town to have access to a diversified curriculum, by which she could study both the liberal arts and also the sciences and technology. In addition, the provision of a high-quality daycare network will be essential. It is the only way to prevent young mothers from having to choose between motherhood and a professional career.

Meanwhile, in the absence of such reforms the gap in employment opportunities for women compared to men, continues to widen, and the potential for women, seemingly apparent in Brazil's educational statistics, cannot be realized. If this gap is not closed, the potential benefits for women gleaned in the new emphasis on women's legal rights and in feminist efforts to confront the problems of Brazil's culture of violence against women will not be realized.

NOTES

1. These figures and others presented throughout this chapter come from the 1970 and 1980 demographic censuses and the 1982 Pesquisa Nacional por Amostra de Domicílio (PNAD), the Brazilian household survey, wherever another source is not stated.

2. Fúlvia Rosemberg, "Gender Subordination and Literacy," in Eve Malmquist, ed., *Women and Literacy Development in the Third World* (Linköping, Sweden: Linköping University, 1992), 302.

3. PNAD 1989.

4. PNAD 1987.

5. Instituto de Planejamento econômico e social (IPEA), *Educacão e Cultura—1987: Situacão e políticas governamentais* (Brasília, 1988), 87, 91.

6. Claudio L. Salm, *Escola e trabalho* (São Paulo: Brasiliense, 1980), 28.

7. Albertina de Oliveira Costa et al., "Pesquisa sobre mulher no Brasil—do limbo ao gueto?" *Cadernos de Pesquisa* 54 (1985): 5–15.

8. Currently, sectors of civil society concerned about racist manifestations in Brazil have used the expression "black populations" when referring to blacks and mulattoes. This integration of the two groups recognizes that racial-social, economic, cultural, educational, and symbolic discrimination—contrary to general assumption—does not spare offspring of mixed marriages.

9. The Statistics Service of Education and Culture, connected with the Ministry of Education (SEEC/MEC), is responsible for educational statistics at the federal level.

10. The 1970 and 1980 censuses considered literate all people able to read and write at least a simple note in their known language.

11. Figures are for the population five years of age and older.

12. Figures are for the population five years of age or older.

13. Cristina Bruschini, *Mulher e trabalho: uma avaliação da decada da mulher, 1975 a 1985 (São Paulo: Nobel,* 1985), 52.

14. Carlos A. Hasenbalg, "1976—As desigualdades sociais revisitadas," in *Movimentos sociais urbanos, minorias étnicas e outros estudos* (Brasília: ANPOCS, 1983) (Ciências Sociais Hoje, vol. 2), 183; Sueli Carneiro and Thereza Santos, *Mulher*

negra: Política governamental e a mulher (São Paulo: Nobel/Conselho Estadual da Condigáo Feminina, 1985 [Década da Mulher]), 6.

15. Lucia Elena Oliveira et al., *O lugar do negro na força de trabalho* (Rio de Janeiro: IBGE, 1985); Hasenbalg, "1976—As desigualdades sociais revisitadas"; Nelson do Valle Silva, "O preço da cor: diferenciais raciais na distribuição da renda no Brasil," *Pesquisa Planejamento Econômico* (Rio de Janeiro) 10, no. 1 (1980): 21–44.

16. These figures immediately confirm comments already made by Carlos Hasenbalg and Nelson do Valle Silva (*Industrialização, emprego e estratificação social no Brasil* [Rio de Janeiro: IUPERJ, 1984], 42): "Considering the different positions white women and black men hold as family providers and the low earnings black women contribute to the family's support, it is possible to conclude that there is strong interracial disparity in the distribution of family earnings."

They do not, however, validate the hierarchy of privileges for the four populational segments, based on race and sex association, currently promoted (Hasenbalg and Silva, *Industrialização;* Sueli Carneior and Thereza Santos, *Mulher negra*) white men, white women, black men, and black women. On the contrary, they suggest that, in spite of equal educational opportunities for men and women, and the ever greater access of white women to higher levels of education, the labor market still treats all women as second-class workers.

17. Cristina Bruschini, in *Mulher e trabalho* (Woman and Work), points to occupational segregation as one of the factors responsible for salary variance observed between the sexes: "As long as job-openings for women are very limited and the number of workers grows, female salaries will continue to be proportionately smaller than those of men. There are too many workers available for 'women's jobs' at the same time that the positions carry less prestige because they reflect women's position in society" (50, 51).

Nelson do Valle Silva's studies are also directed to interpreting salary differences between whites and blacks in the light of racial discriminations by the labor market. In the conclusion of his study about black men residing in greater Rio de Janeiro, the author states:

These observations have some theoretical and practical implications. Although inferences taken from data for the period can be very risky, the data does not support the hypothesis that, when non-whites [meaning here the black racial segment] invest in education, imposed obstacles will be removed. On the contrary, they seem to indicate that, at least short term, as long as the *market structures* are maintained, the salary differential between races can increase when non-whites increase their educational level, as the figures show that these differentials increase as the degree of schooling does. Therefore, prospects of racial equality in Brazil seem quite remote, a fact reinforced by the extraordinary tenacity of the "racial democracy" myth. ("O preco da cor: diferenciais raciais na distribuicao da renda no Brasil," *Pesquisa Planejamento Econômico* [Rio de Janeiro] 10, no. 1 [1980]: 43; my emphasis.)

18. Maria Malta Campos ("*Escola e participação popular:* a luta por—educação elementar em dois bairros de São Paulo." [São Paulo: USP, 1982], 341), research-

ing the struggle for elementary education in two neighborhoods adjacent to São Paulo, also verifies that "the one-school appearance is deceiving": "It actually uncovers various possible routes, maintained by various mechanisms considered 'inefficient' or 'poorly adjusted' but integral parts of a class-determined society's educational system."

19. Fúlvia Rosemberg et al., *Diagnóstico sobre a situação educacional de negros (pretos e pardos) no Estado de São Paulo* (São Paulo: Fundação Carlos Chagas, 1986).

20. Carlos A. Hasenbalg, "Raca, classe e mobilidade," in *Lugar de negro*, ed. Zelia Gonzalez and Carlos A. Hasenbalg (Rio de Janeiro: Marco Zero, 1982), 91.

Part 4
Methodological and Comparative Considerations

The Economics of Women's Schooling

T. PAUL SCHULTZ

There are two major barriers to effective public policy on women's education in the low-income world. Both involve the transfer to low-income societies of concepts and models central to economics. Standard methods of accounting for economic growth have masked the high returns, both individual and social, resulting in societies from investments to increase women's productivity. The use of information in economic accounts derived solely from monetized activities systematically understates the benefits, both individual and social, that flow from investing in women's education.[1]

While indicators drawn strictly from the marketplace lead to misreporting of the true results of investment in women's skills, there is another conceptual barrier to effective public policy regarding women's education. Because most policymakers operate with an oversimplified view of the family and its dynamics, they fail to take into account its internal conflicts and the family functions that in many societies results in the subordination of women. Historians of the family have made us see that this much romanticized and mythological social institution functioned very differently in the past from the idealized family of Western social science. The precise forms of family conflict may vary, and gender roles may differ across cultures, but today in general it is possible to see family and kin relationships as involving trade-offs between conflicting interests of family members within all cultural contexts. Yet when economists talk about the role of the family in developing countries most still assume single-generation nuclear families and discuss family economic choices as though the family were a perfectly altruistic institution guided by a unified decision maker.

A realistic discussion of family relations, Western or non-Western, must recognize and explain the causes of the inequality between women and men and the varying forms this inequality takes. The standard economic explanations for the differing status of women and men are of two kinds. The first takes into account only those activities to which cash values can be assigned and thus assumes that women participate only infrequently in productive labor. But, even allowing for this bias, and accepting its relegation of women to less productive labor, it is still hard to explain, for example, why there is so great a difference between investment in the training and education of men compared with women in so much of Africa and southern and western Asia, whereas these differences are narrower in Latin America and eastern Asia.

A second type of economic explanation for the difference in investment in men's skills compared with the investment made in women rests upon theories about family behavior. Kin networks have many social, economic, and psychic functions. One of the most important functions of such networks is economic, providing through the vehicle of the family a mechanism for old-age insurance, a pooling of economic resources to minimize risk, and a framework for specialized skill training, both across and between generations.

Families, it is argued, make their investment in skill training in those family members who are thought to offer the decision makers in the family the highest possible returns. The returns on investment in the skills of sons, therefore, are thought to offer a higher return than investment in daughters. When custom decrees that sons must make higher remittances than daughters to sustain their parents in old age, educating males is thought to be a stronger form of risk insurance. Thus, the family functions as a prudential institution, investing in those members (male) who will deliver through personal service the kind of risk management transferred in the West to commercial or government insurance institutions. Since risk management is an important function in any society, differential investment in males is legitimized.

Such legitimation is persuasive, however, only to the degree that we accept the standard market-oriented measures to evaluate human productivity. The long-standing bias in economics toward market activities and cash transactions as the only "real" producers of "value" means that nonmarket (home) production by Third World women does not figure in calculations of family income or of gross national product (GNP). Yet research on family and child health and welfare clearly indicates that women's nonmarket production is highly significant for family health and welfare.

Our bias toward the market as the economic basis for measuring value leads to decisions on investment in developing countries that misallocate resources in three fundamental ways. First, although a large share of total production in low-income countries is carried out in the home, the production and dissemination of new technology is almost entirely channeled toward market production. Such investment, sustained over time, is a powerful force in redistributing personal income, a force that works systematically to disadvantage women. Because women's time is consumed by fetching and carrying fuel and water, preparing and cooking food, and caring for children, women would gain significantly from the development and dissemination of technologies to improve their efficiency in market or home production. Improved domestic technologies suitable for small-scale use would free time for market production, education, and the acquisition of new skills.

Since women are tied to their domestic base, their access to the labor market is limited compared to men, and their opportunities for learning new skills, especially those bearing on new market-oriented technology, are slight. Yet they are arguably just as much in need of new technological skills as the male workers who qualify for special training programs. Until very recently, we had few ways of assessing the returns on investment in such education for women because the product of their work was for home consumption.

Third, and most important, women have less access to schooling and health care than men in some developing countries, possibly because the economic return on their access to education is not accurately reflected by current economic measures based only on paid work. We should assess the returns on education based upon our understanding of the increase in productivity of the individual's time, regardless of whether it is allocated to market or nonmarket production. Since about one-half the world's men and two-thirds of the world's women do not receive a wage, we need to develop more satisfactory measures of the productivity of this substantial portion of the world's population. Conceptually and statistically satisfactory methods have been developed, only very recently, for estimating the rates of return on education for all persons. These show that the returns on investment in women's education in many low-income countries are significantly higher than those for men.[2] Even so, statistical measures of increased productivity still do not allow us to assign a cash value to reduced child mortality, decreased unwanted births, and increased childhood schooling, all closely correlated with women's experience of schooling but unrelated to our traditional concepts of production.

Why, then, if improved productivity and multiple social benefits accompany women's education, does the public sector fail so repeatedly to undertake programs of investment in it and in the technologies that would increase the efficiency of women's labor? The case of agricultural education in sub-Saharan Africa offers a striking illustration of the problem. Here, where women are responsible for much of the agricultural production, the staff of agricultural extension agencies is predominantly male and serves male farmers. Thus, whether extension agencies transmit information about agricultural technology, home sanitation, family planning services, or schooling, their message is delivered mainly to men by men. We might expect that a different staffing pattern would produce a different result, but there have been few experiments of this kind funded through the $5 billion a year spent worldwide on agricultural extension programs.[3]

Similarly, most agricultural research on improved plant and animal varieties and production techniques is focused on cash crops, which in low-income countries are managed primarily by men. Commercial interests are excellent lobbyists, and governments have a strong incentive to promote both national revenues and foreign exchange earnings, hence their tendency to invest in agricultural education for men. As a consequence, the productivity of men has increased more rapidly than that of women in most agricultural societies, although basic domestic food resources are produced predominantly by the labor of women.

Following the onset of severe famines in Africa, the bias in research and education toward fostering cash crops has been somewhat reduced. Research on improving the production of the food staples eaten by the poor—such as cassava, pulses, sorghum, potatoes, and yams—has been increasing, as has the effort to provide appropriate education for agricultural communities reliant on these food sources.

Nonetheless, the tendency in Africa for large-scale, sophisticated agricultural technology to displace traditional female farmers continues, even though there is now a spirited debate about whether food production may be better stimulated by promoting small-scale farming. At present, precisely because women farmers have so little education in comparison to men, new technologies benefit men disproportionately because they have the educational attainment to acquire the needed new skills.[4]

Similar biases derived from market economy limit women's access to credit in low-income countries and hence their ability to invest in new technologies, whether as farmers or as urban producers. In most parts of the developing world women are at a disadvantage in obtaining credit because their nonmarket production cannot be attached by creditors. Moreover, many women have traditional rights of use over the land they farm but not of the individual title, which allows the provision of collateral for loans. Effective responses to this situation require departures from traditional credit transactions. The Grameen Bank of Bangladesh is frequently cited as the model for innovative credit institutions adapted to the mores and resources of the society they must serve. In mid-1988 the Bank had branches in 10 percent of the villages of Bangladesh and made 70 percent of its loans to women having use of less than half an acre of land. Because individuals lack collateral, borrowers must seek credit as a community. Individuals then face community pressures to repay loans, which are then recycled to other community members. To date the Bank has had few nonperforming loans, and its community approach has resulted in considerable strengthening of the economic productivity of female borrowers.

If we leave the realm of public sector initiatives and study family investment in education, we see that the family's function as a prudential institution operates to restrict private investment in women's education, in favor of men. Therefore, no matter how desirable the individual and social benefits of promoting women's skills, their development will still be stunted unless we can devise ways to prompt different allocations of educational investment by families. It is in this area that we encounter the knotty problem of understanding the dynamics of internal family decision making. The best formulation of this question, given our current knowledge of the family dynamics, is to ask what are the major factors determining a family's investments in the education and health of its children.

Many social welfare policies have foundered on the rock of this difficult behavioral question. Any given family coordinates the use of its members' time and resources in parallel processes of market and nonmarket production. Transfers of resources to a given family for any externally directed purpose may or may not achieve the desired goal, because the family may reallocate its resources in a compensatory fashion. For instance, free school lunches may or may not increase a child's level of nutrition, depending on whether the child's family then reduces or holds level the ration of food available at home.

Any public policy initiative designed to achieve a redistribution of family resources will undoubtedly be resisted by those negatively affected. Thus, the effort to encourage the schooling of women unleashes an internal political process within families as well as among those interest groups in society who stand to gain or lose by a reallocation of public goods.

There are certainly reasons to reassess the neoclassical economic framework that has depicted the family as behaving as though it pursues a single set of agreed-upon goals. Clearly, spouses will have divergent interests in family decisions about expenditures according to the resources, both market and nonmarket, that they bring to the family. Evidence from Brazil suggests that for women who hold jobs that permit them to exert control over their earnings and have greater nonearned income sources, their families will invest more extensively in child health, nutrition, and education than families of identical income in which women have no such independent resources. Their bargaining position is improved in family resource allocation, while the family's long-term interest clearly takes account of its females as valuable resources.[5]

If we must modify the neoclassical formulation of the family as a unit engaged in satisfying a single set of goals, in favor of one in which members bargain on the basis of different power relationships, we must also reconsider the stereotypical view of the family as "normally" a male-headed institution. Clearly, one way people express their choice of life-style and consumption patterns is in the form of families they establish. Therefore, the demonstrable increase in the number of female-headed households observable in many countries warrants careful study. In south Asia and Latin America, for instance, women's control of the resources of domestic production has been accompanied by a rise in female-headed households, in which women allocate family resources on their own. We have yet to understand what this phenomenon may mean for future public and private investment in women's education.[6]

This trend should surely be borne in mind by development agencies and foundations working to improve women's welfare and status in low-income countries. Such agencies often invest in fostering female-directed institutions or in promoting family planning, rather than in education per se. But we should question this allocation. Unless women have productive opportunities other than childbearing, control over unwanted fertility may only marginally reduce their high fertility levels. The availability of low-cost means of birth control does not necessarily ensure low birthrates. In societies in which women have less schooling than men it is likely that both women and men will want to have many children and that women will have little ability to influence family resource allocations. By way of contrast, it is clear that the benefits that accrue through reducing child mortality, increasing child schooling, broadening the taxable base of waged employment, and reducing fertility are demonstrably greater from educating women than from educating men.[7]

When such policy goals are accepted there are relatively simple public initiatives that can be taken to intensify their effect. Uncertainty and risk lead families in many low-income countries to pool their risk across the extended family. Parent-arranged marriages for daughters may be designed to mitigate the family's risk from local crop failure. Crop insurance programs can remove this underlying economic motive for marriage and permit female children more years of education. Social insurance to meet the hazards of illness and old age can also influence the way the extended family behaves and allow women greater opportunities to develop marketable skills. In short, by changing the external environment through the creation of prudential institutions, we may be able to change the internal dynamics of family decision making in favor of the investment in women's education known to produce high social and economic returns.

But, if we continue to transfer Western accounting methods and attitudes about "paid" work to low-income countries, we will not achieve effective public policy to secure these clearly desirable objectives. Nor, if we persist in the neoclassical economic view of the family, will we develop the insight into the functioning of the family that will be necessary to redirect family decision making to favor investment in women's skills.

If we want to understand the outcomes of development investments, we must, following the experience of sub-Saharan Africa, pay careful attention to the gender components of our aid delivery systems and outcomes. Once we begin to rethink our ways of counting the productive forces in society and to revise our view of the idealized family, we will begin to collect our data about the outcomes of women's education in ways that will confirm its potential for generating social and economic benefits for current and future generations.

NOTES

1. T. Paul Schultz, "Investments in the Schooling and Health of Women and Men" (Paper presented at the conference on Women's Human Capital Development, Bellagio, Italy, 18–22 May 1992).

2. Illustrated by data from Thailand, Peru, Ivory Coast, Philippines, and Indonesia, in Schultz, "Investments."

3. R. E. Evenson, "Agricultural Extension and Women Farmers: Evidence from Kenya and Burkina Faso," Economic Growth Center, Yale University, 1992.

4. C. H. Gladwin and D. McMillan, "Is a Turnaround in Africa Possible without Helping African Women to Farm?" *Economic Development and Cultural Change* 37, no. 2 (1989): 345–70.

5. D. Thomas, "Intrahousehold Resource Allocation," *Journal of Human Resources* 25, no. 4 (Fall 1990): 635–64.

6. T. Paul Schultz, "Women and Development: Objective, Framework and Policy," Working Paper (WPS-200), Women in Development Division, Population and Human Resource Department, World Bank, Washington, D.C., 1989.

7. Schultz, "Women and Development."

Rethinking the Impact
of Women's Education

Jill Ker Conway

When Westerners speak about improving educational opportunities for women, our received myths shape the conversation. We often misconstrue the real forces that led to the rise in Western women's status in the late eighteenth and early nineteenth century, an improvement usually linked by historians to the results of educational opportunity. Only in very recent years have historians begun to study the outcomes of education, rather than the simple fact of access; the outcomes indicate what the real consequences of the rise of public education in the West were, in particular, the real consequences for women.[1] When these are examined it becomes clear how problematic the belief is that education increased women's economic opportunity and led males to concede them greater equality.

Historians have argued that the rise of public education in Prussia, the United States, and Great Britain shaped the modern industrial work force. But what precisely does that mean? When we speak of education and its role in the development of the Western industrial work force we are really talking about the preparation of men for the factories and machine shops of the later industrial revolution, a preparation in which women were restricted to a newly defined domestic realm. The transportation revolution—the bridges, railroads, and canals that made up the communications network of the modern state—were built by semiliterate laborers, immigrants in the United States, and displaced rural workers in England and Europe. It was in the laying out of roads and bridges and in the design and fabrication of improved steam engines to power early factories that literacy and numeracy were required.[2]

Studies have now demonstrated that the acquisition of literacy by the masses was not necessarily the outcome of the development of state-financed public education in the West.[3] Additionally, the acquisition of literacy had little correlation with subsequent earnings in industrializing Western states.[4] Certainly for women, literacy brought no change in the traditional pattern of their earnings, always predictably about one-half to two-thirds those of men with equivalent levels of preparation. Industrialization offered women new areas of employment but not the chance to improve their status relative to men.[5] They could serve as unskilled laborers in factories, as teachers and nurses, and in clerical roles, but these were all poorly compensated because of the oversupply of female workers.

How, then, should we understand the significance of women's access to public education, achieved in the 1840s in the northeast United States, in the 1870s in England, and in the 1880s throughout Europe? What did learning basic reading, writing, and arithmetic mean for working-class, middle-class, and elite women? Contrary to the received version of educational history, we know that women's entry into the industrial work force did not improve their status and that, until the arrival of the modern women's professions, education gave single or widowed women of the middle class only the marginal role of governess or the chancy career of a popular writer. On the other hand, for elite women education offered new routes to learning and fueled the drive for social reforms such as the campaign for the humane treatment of prostitutes or for the development of dispensaries for poor women. It also prompted educational innovation such as the opening of higher educational institutions for women.

Nevertheless, despite these significant changes, the impact of women's entry into higher education was by no means as striking during the first one hundred years of access, as the proponents of university education for women claimed. This was particularly the case in the United States because the curriculum of public higher education was sex typed, offering female undergraduates such fields as home economics, food sciences, and nursing education, extensions of women's traditional roles, rather than exposure to abstract theoretical knowledge. Most public and private professional schools discriminated in the admission of women so that access to undergraduate education could not be translated into entry into the prestigious, highly paid professions of law, medicine, engineering, or business. Formal professional training in teaching, nursing, social work, and librarianship was quickly introduced as the numbers of young women entering higher education increased. These lower-status professions were not research based, and their practitioners were assumed to enter them for the emotional rewards involved, rather than for the high earnings.

In the realm of politics modern democratic societies, beginning with France and the United States, first segregated middle- and upper-class women in a separate domestic sphere, supposedly governed by emotion, and later granted them the franchise on the basis of assumed maternal interests, rather than on the recognition of universal human rights. Women were citizens, but only in respect of their maternal functions, and their supposed domestic sphere remained separate from the world of political contention.

Humanitarian concern with the abolition of subordinate statuses, such as that of slavery, spilled over to affect people's awareness of women's inferior political and civil rights.[6] In both England and the United States it was the reform activities of educated women that politicized them and set them upon the long and bitterly disputed road to women's suffrage and the political rights of full citizens. These reform movements had little effect, however, on women's economic status. Their earnings in the helping professions and in the service sector of the economy continued to lag far behind those of males with the same level of education, even after the achievement of suffrage.[7] After the loss of one and a half million male lives during World War I, however, demography rather than abstract justice prompted the opening up of new opportunities for women. Women still remained clustered in the teaching profession and in the same textile and clothing industries familiar in other industrial countries, although Frenchwomen could enter into government service and did so particularly after the baccalaureate degree was opened to them in 1924.

In Germany, where demographic decline was less striking and less feared than in France, the Prussian male bureaucratic tradition remained firmly established, leaving teaching as the only professional activity available to educated women. Since the Prussian bureaucratic state ruled out voluntarism as a sphere of activity for educated women, the Frauenbewegung leadership and rank and file were drawn almost exclusively from the pool of female teachers, eager to increase educational opportunity as an avenue to improving women's status.

In Western Europe and the United States the segregation of educated women within the conjugal family meant that their unpaid labor in child care and domestic tasks was performed with a level of understanding of hygiene and economic efficiency that helped control population growth and fostered the development of a predictable domestic consumer sector of the economy. Later in the twentieth century the pool of educated women took up the slack in professional employment created by the mobilization of men for the twentieth century's mass wars, and two-career families eased the economic adjustments that followed those disastrously wasteful conflicts.

But, on balance, we have to concede that, during the first century in which it was available to women, access to formal education did not undermine the misogynist bias of Western culture, nor did it enable women to secure political or economic equality with men. Discrimination persists in a sex-segregated labor force and is reinforced by a physical and cultural environment that separates women from the workplace and restricts their mobility.[8] The secularizing of Western attitudes to marriage has not diminished the belief that child care is uniquely a woman's responsibility, an assumption that combines with segregated labor markets and restricted mobility to produce the impoverishment of women who are single heads of families.[9] Individualism has given educated women in the United States and Western Europe the aspiration to control their fertility and acceptance of work outside the home, but it has also left them devoid of real community supports when marriages are dissolved, and their limited earning capacity (relative to men) must provide food, shelter, and child support.

The authors in this volume who write about their expectations for women's education in Africa, Latin America, and south and east Asia see many of the same patterns emerging. They are not interested in recapitulating the same pattern of women's education but often seek to achieve differing goals within their own countries and regions. Pioneers of education for women in Europe and the United States have expected it to transform Western society. The authors here hope that education will conserve valued aspects of women's precolonial and traditional roles, raise women's political consciousness, and help preserve the natural environment.

The context in which these reformers think about education for women is in many respects utterly unlike that of the United States. American women were politicized by the abolition movement and by the battles for the suffrage and for reproductive rights. The vote and many fundamental legal rights were accorded to Indian and African women during the process of securing independence, but the political consciousness necessary to exercise those rights still exists only among elites, while the "decolonization" stimulated by rejection of the West has revived religious and social conservatism at the popular level. In conservative Islamic societies the possibility of cooperation with a state intent on returning women to the Islamic family law, administered by mullahs, seems so remote that educational reformers focus on voluntarism and on the creation of a nonformal educational system aimed at conferring minimal literacy. Since they cannot assume a beneficent state, much of their educational work must be directed toward the political consciousness raising that will mobilize women to claim the rights formally granted them but rarely exercised.

In India, where child marriage and the dowry system still operate and where there is great respect for Hindu, Muslim, or Parsee culture, the aim of reformers is to secure education in the skills necessary for family health and to mobilize women politically for the preservation of the natural environment, which is the source of women's traditional crafts and of their herbal medicines. Indian educational reformers emphasize, however, that the educational process designed to transmit this knowledge must not devalue or, in the name of progress, trivialize the traditional knowledge and skills of village women. These traditional skills give them a responsibility for the natural environment and a body of information about living in balance with the environment that no one wants to see devalued or lost.

Many Indian reformers do not want to see the face-to-face village community disappear, and those represented in this volume want to retain India's tradition of self-employment. Their task is to make women question patriarchy and to muster the political will to fight it, without copying a model of development that has been notably unsuccessful in ending Western women's subordination. Some educators favor increasing women's opportunities for self-employment through access to distant markets for their crafts or agricultural produce. Others question whether increasing women's cash income results in improved family living standards, when tradition makes the males in the family the disposers of cash income. All are agreed that improving women's status requires a curriculum that tackles the politics of family life head-on and gives women a better understanding of the economics of agricultural or craft production.

In Latin America internal migration has created vast "new settlements" in which a substantial number of squatter families are female headed. In these new settlements on the outskirts of huge urban aggregations such as São Paulo or Lima, the skills needed for survival are economic, political, and medical. Since there is no likelihood that the formal economy will grow fast enough to provide satisfactory employment for rural women newly arrived in the cities, the skills conveyed by formal education do not contribute to solving their most fundamental economic problems.

Women in the new settlements need to know how to develop the entrepreneurial outlook to make their way within the informal economy, how to deal with Latin male *machismo*, how to manage family hygiene and diet in the urban setting, and how to avoid repeated pregnancies. Here also reformers want to convey these skills while sustaining respect for the culture of indigenous peoples, whose agriculture and knowledge of native plants constitute a valuable heritage.

In Africa, where women produce 80 percent of the region's food, women's most pressing need is for agricultural education. They also need the political skills to maintain their traditional rights over land, in the face of Western-style development, with its stress on exportable cash crops cultivated by males and its relegation of female food producers to marginal land. Here the conflict between women's traditional roles and Western-style "development" presents itself in the most unambiguous terms. The issues of development strategy here raised are at the center of

African women's political consciousness. They give primacy to environmental issues and to sustaining their roles as food producers. They are committed to preserving women's traditional knowledge of the environment, along with their now politicized role as its preserver.

The curriculum of the formal system of education, copied from the West, does not convey this kind of knowledge, nor, indeed, do its materials acknowledge women's roles as food producers. In this setting reformers seek to train women agricultural extension workers and to develop texts that acknowledge and build upon women's environmental concerns, both in the present and in traditional culture.

In general, migration in the Third World makes women de facto heads of families. In Africa this is the result of male migration to employment in mining or commercial agriculture. In Latin America the major population movements have been from rural poverty to squatter settlements. In southern and Southeast Asia the female-headed family is more likely to be the result of war and famine, and the squatter settlements have grown up reflecting religious and political conflicts (between India and Pakistan, between contending regimes in Vietnam and Cambodia, in Iran, and in Afghanistan). Because public sector efforts to build employment have been aimed at males, and because international refugee relief programs often sponsor male employment, women's working life takes place within the nonformal or informal economy.

Women everywhere use their access to schooling to improve their knowledge of health and sanitation and to exercise more prudential judgment about family size. But in Africa the consequences of the AIDS epidemic, the results of warfare, and the sexual mores that typically accompany a migratory male work force combine to make the health problems facing women of a different order of severity and danger than those of any Western society during urbanization and modernization. The world travel industry is exporting these health hazards to Asian women in the "entertainment industry," an enterprise in commercialized sex unlike the prostitution of early Western industrial cities, because of its scale, its international ramifications, and the deadly disease that accompanies it. Moreover, literacy and health education alone will not enable women in these settings to improve family health. Only sustained political mobilization and an international humanitarian movement comparable to the nineteenth-century revulsion against slavery will end the sexual exploitation of women and girls in this global industry.[10]

In the Third World low-income female entrepreneurs must create their own small enterprises within the informal economy, for rates of growth in the formal sector, private or public, have not, and likely will not soon, accommodate their labor. As efforts at self-employment programs for women in the Indian subcontinent, Africa, and Latin America have shown, the creation of new opportunities for earnings for women who must gather fuel, carry water long distances, and eke a meager food supply from inadequate soil merely extends an already exhaustingly long working day. Moreover, in families in which there is a male present, custom and family power relationships often dictate that males control cash resources. Thus, education that helps a woman produce and market a traditional craft does not improve her or her family's health, unless she gains the political training to resist traditional family allocations of resources.

While we might expect the task of female reformers intent on overcoming the injustices of this system to be relatively easy, there are powerful cultural forces working in opposition to change. The desire to de-Westernize Third World countries by mobilizing women around the values of traditional culture make the abandonment of practices such as child marriage and the dowry system unlikely. The current trend to de-Westernize is one of the most dynamic political forces operating in Third World countries, reinforcing the power of the mullahs against a shah in Iran, supporting Afghan resistance against Communist rule, and encouraging Indians to revive the crafts once displaced by the products of Manchester and Birmingham and leading them to reassert the power of ancient cultures devalued by imperialism. The rejection of the West also applies to Western-style feminism. The majority of Third World women see the family and kin networks as valuable prudential institutions, providing supports for widows and accepting responsibility for children. They may see supports for child rearing as nonexistent in Western society, in which divorced and abandoned women face isolation as well as poverty. Some Third World women activists are unconvinced that

Western technology and productivity have been beneficial to the developed world, since their environmental and human costs have been ignored or undervalued. Many also find Western-style materialism and individualism unattractive.

Moreover, reproductive technologies have different meanings in different cultural contexts. In India, for example, the ability to establish the sex of a fetus has resulted in very high rates of abortion for female fetuses. Cultural pressure to abort females makes the question of access to safe abortion assume an entirely different meaning for Indian women. It may not signify the right of women to reproductive freedom but, rather, illustrates the low value assigned to female offspring within many subcultures. Pressure from women's groups has led to legislation forbidding the use of prenatal testing to establish the sex of a fetus if the sole purpose is to decide whether or not to elect abortion, but there remain serious problems with enforcing this law.

When these differences have been spelled out there are, nonetheless, many similarities among women concerning their experience of access to education. Such access has produced the same outcome, reduced fertility, for women throughout the world. The growth of cities has exerted the same pull on rural women seeking a better life for themselves and their children, in every corner of the globe. Thus, women who are single parents are clustered in the poorest slums of every large city of Western and Third World countries alike. Many observers have commented on the extent to which female heads of families living in extreme urban poverty develop the same coping strategies and rely on the same networks, whether the urban slum be part of New York or New Delhi. In either setting isolated women find honorary aunts and devise new forms of "kin" networks.

The educational reformers writing in this volume share a concern for improving women's status that is directed toward building a better society by stressing community values and by elevating the importance of women's traditional concerns in political and economic life. They hope to develop a system of education for their societies that would convey the skills realistically required to deal effectively with the environments and range of opportunities women face in the struggle to feed, shelter, and clothe their families.

Many of these women reject Western aspirations for rapid economic growth. Most see population control as the key to an acceptable future. Their utopian dreams are for a more slowly growing population, combined with an ethos of living in balance with the environment and a rejection of Western-style consumption as a long-term goal. They hope for a more productive agricultural and village sector of the economy developed through agricultural education for women, the retention of natural seed stocks, and the rejection of genetically engineered hybrids and their accompanying chemical fertilizers.

Given these objectives, what returns might we expect to see on further investment in women's education were such an investment made according to the priorities of female educational reformers? We might expect to see the returns on investment in women's education appearing in reduced fertility, improved family and maternal health, and fewer costs incurred by environmental degradation. We might also see the preservation of women's traditional knowledge of herbal medicine, informed by careful analysis of dosage and by improved hygiene as a form of import substitution for more costly, and often inappropriate, forms of Western curative health technology. Obviously, Western public health innovations such as vaccines for contagious diseases are as valuable in Third World settings as in the West. Investment in women's education and access to knowledge about hygiene will, however, yield better long-term results than investment in costly Western health technology.

A sound assessment of the returns on investment in women's education in developing countries will nevertheless not be possible, while no value is attributed to their unpaid work as food producers, improvers of domestic hygiene, conservers and transmitters of craft traditions, and custodians of the natural environment. Since these areas of social and environmental policy are the focus of concern among politicized women in the developing world, their educational programs, of necessity, involve the mobilization of women in support of action to ensure an alternative path for the national economy from that followed by the Western industrialized nations.

With that goal in mind the educators and reformers writing in this volume suggest educational programs containing explicit political instruction, basic agricultural and environmental information, training in medicine and hygiene, and realistic instruction in gaining the best returns from work in the informal economy. The content of a female-shaped curriculum would certainly be more practical than literary, more political and hence more directed to analyzing women's actual situation than was the male-produced literary culture taught to women during the rise of public education in the West. This may mean that education as well as demographic change and patterns of migration, could, in fact, have a more immediate impact on women's social and economic status than did the literary and sex-typed curriculum to which women in the United States and Europe were exposed in the opening century of public education in those nations.

All policy debates about educational access, curriculum content, and systems of delivery are intensely political. They are components of a society's dreams for its future and key elements of the system by which a society grants or withholds its rewards. When Western women set out on their journey toward access to all levels of education, gender was seen as a basic biological category, which justified different levels of educational aspiration for women and men and different occupations for the two sexes. For the last thirty years Western scholars have been charting the history of ideas about gender as cultural categories in the West, categories that constrained what women studied, where they studied, and the occupations to which they aspired. Only major structural crises such as demographic disaster or wartime mobilization changed the interpretation of those categories in an economic environment in which expanding public and private sectors could employ (albeit marginally) or support as consumers in unpaid domestic work the rapidly increasing cohorts of women who gained formal education.

In the Third World rapid population growth, economic forces that promote female-headed families, a critical role in food production, and limited employment potential in either public or private sectors require women to become entrepreneurs and to find the means to sustain their families. The political conflicts that rage over their access to education have to do with who will control the product of their unpaid labor and whether new levels of skill in unpaid work can benefit dependent economies engaged in an enduring quest for substitutes to costly Western-style imports. Every effort to answer these questions must confront the emotionally charged question of de-Westernization. Does open acknowledgment of women as independent beings help or hinder progress toward a desired future? This is the essential question governing responses to feminist reformers in Western or non-Western societies, but its nuances are different where de-Westernization is the goal shared by feminists and antifeminists alike.

Giving women access to the skills and knowledge they need to maximize the returns on their labor seems like a simple task, but, in fact, in old world and new, in East and in West, in industrialized and in traditional economies, there is no more intensely politicized task. The difference for Third World women working on educational reform today, compared to their nineteenth-century European counterparts, is that women's productive labor is essential for feeding their societies, and women's traditional environmental concerns now intersect with a global environmental movement. Whether these trends give rise to access and a curriculum suited to the realities of women's lives will depend on the political will and astuteness of female Third World leaders and their allies.

NOTES

1. On this subject, see Todd W. Furniss and Patricia A. Graham, eds., *Women in Higher Education* (Washington, D.C.: American Council on Education, 1974); Patricia A. Graham, *Community and Class in American Education, 1865–1918* (New York: Wiley, 1974); Michael B. Katz, *The People of Hamilton, Canada West: Family and Class in a Mid Nineteenth Century City*, Studies in Urban History (Cambridge: Harvard University Press, 1976); Penina Glazer and Miriam Slater, *Unequal Partners* (Amherst: University of Massachusetts Press, 1989), examines the career opportunities and earnings of women physicians, social workers, research scientists and academics. Patricia Palmieri's *Adamless Eden*, to be published by Yale University Press in 1993, compares the earnings of female academics with those of their male counterparts.

2. See Brook Hindle, *Engines of Change: The American Industrial Revolution, 1790–1860* (Washington, D.C.: Smithsonian Institution Press, 1986); Raymond H. Merritt, *Engineering in American Society, 1850–1875* (Lexington: University Press of Kentucky, 1969); Monte A. Calvert, *The Mechanical Engineer in America, 1830–1910: Professional Careers in Conflict* (Baltimore: Johns Hopkins Press, 1967); Merritt Roe Smith, ed., *Military Enterprise and Technological Change: Perspectives on the American Experience* (Cambridge: M.I.T. Press, 1985).

3. François Furet and Jacques Ouzof point out in their study of the spread of literacy in France from the sixteenth century to the Republic of Jules Ferry that "both the chronology and the geography of French literacy are dependent less on the evolution of the school network than on the social history of France. The consequences of this are many and heavy. The obligation to gain admission to written culture was democratized first by Protestantism, and subsequently by the Counter-Reformation; but more than a condition of salvation, and for much longer, it represented the key to entry to the cultural model of the upper classes. Wherever we look, in every period, social stratification presides over the history of literacy." See François Furet and Jacques Ouzof, *Reading and Writing: Literacy in France from Calvin to Jules Ferry* (Cambridge: Cambridge University Press, 1982); see also *Daedalus* 119, no. 2 (Spring 1990), special issue on "Literacy in America."

4. Katz, *People of Hamilton.* Katz's study of the relationship between education and earnings for the population of the steel town of Hamilton, Ontario, illustrates in fine detail the more general conclusions of macro-studies of education and social mobility in nineteenth-century industrializing societies. See also Christopher Jencks and David Riesman, *The Academic Revolution* (Chicago: University of Chicago Press, 1977); and Stephan Thernstrom, *Poverty and Progress: Social Mobility in a Nineteenth Century City* (New York: Atheneum, 1964).

5. Joan Scott and Louise Tilly, *Women, Work and Family* (New York: Holt Rinehart, 1978).

6. The literature on women's battle for the vote in the West is vast. Ellen Carol DuBois, *Feminism and Suffrage: The Emergence of an Independent Women's Movement in America, 1848–1869* (Ithaca, N.Y.: Cornell University Press, 1978), provides a good overview of the origins of the movement in the United States and the reasons why the struggle was to become so protracted for American women. Maurice Duverger's, *The Political Role of Women* (Paris: UNESCO, 1955), is still a useful survey of women's achievement of political rights in the West. Janet Z. Giele and Audrey C. Smock, eds., *Women's Roles and Status in Eight Countries* (New York: John Wiley and Sons, 1977), provides valuable comparative perspectives.

7. Tilly and Scott, *Women, Work and Family,* provides a summary description of women's earnings in relation to men's during European industrialization. Barbara Franzoi, *At the Very Least She Pays the Rent: Women and German Industrialization, 1871–1914* (Westport, Conn.: Greenwood Press, 1985), gives detailed information for women's earnings during German industrialization. Valerie Kincade Oppenheimer, *The Female Labor Force in the United States: Demographic and Economic Factors Governing Its Growth and Changing Composition,* Population Monographs, series 5 (Berkeley: University of California Press, 1970), provides exhaustive information about occupational segregation in the United States.

8. The best exposition of the impact of residential segregation on women's economic and political life is Dolores Hayden's *The Grand Domestic Revolution: A History of Feminist Designs for American Homes, Neighbourhoods and Cities* (Cambridge: MIT Press, 1981).

9. See the volume on "Women and Poverty" in *Signs: Journal of Women in Culture and Society* 10, no. 2 (Winter 1984), especially the section by Mary Corco-

ran, "The Economic Fortunes of Women and Children: Lessons from the Panel Study of Income Dynamics."

10. Because of the long-standing presence of military bases and of the impact of the Korean and Vietnam wars, the global "entertainment industry" is particularly strongly established in the Philippines and Thailand.

Contributors

Lourdes Arizpe is the Director of the Mexican Institute of Anthropology and President of the International Association of Ethnologists, Sociologists and Anthropologists. Dr. Arizpe has been an advisor to the Secretary of Agrarian Reform and a consultant to the International Labor Organization.

Susan C. Bourque is the Esther B. Wiley Professor and Chair of the Government Department at Smith College. She is the Director of the Smith College Project on Women and Social Change.

Fay Chung is the Minister of State for National Affairs, Employment Creation and Cooperatives in Zimbabwe. Ms. Chung has served as Zimbabwe's Minister of Education, Director of the Zimbabwe Institute of Development Studies, and Chief Education Officer. Ms. Chung's first post in the Ministry of Education was as head of planning; during her tenure in that position, Zimbabwe's educational system tripled in size.

Jill Ker Conway is President Emerita of Smith College and currently teaches as a Visiting Scholar in the Program in Science, Technology, and Society at the Massachusetts Institute of Technology.

Neera Desai is Professor Emerita, Department of Sociology, and Honorary Director, Rural Development Project, Shreemati Natahibai Damodar Thackersey Women's University (S.N.D.T.), Bombay, India. Dr. Desai is the former Director of the Research Center for Women's Studies and has been appointed by the Indian Government to the Indian Association for Women's Studies.

Hernán Fernández is Director of Research at the National Institute of Investigation and Development of Education (INIDE), Lima, Peru. In addition to his duties at INIDE, Mr. Fernández is a member of the Andes Institute of Population and Development Studies, the Curricular Reform Commission, and the editorial committee of *Autoeducacion* magazine.

Devaki Jain is Director of the Institute of Social Studies Trust, New Delhi, India. She is a member of the Advisory Committee on the Development of Women and Children in Rural Areas to the Ministry of Rural Development and a member of the Indian Government's Standing Committee on Women's Education.

Kabiru Kinyanjui is the Senior Program Officer, School Policy Program, International Development Research Center, Nairobi, Kenya. In addition to his duties at the institute, Dr. Kinyanjui supervises graduate students in the departments of Economics and Sociology at the university and also trains development workers for nongovernment organizations.

In-ho Lee is Professor of History at Seoul National University, Seoul, Republic of Korea. Since 1979 she has taught at Seoul National University. Dr. Lee belongs to the Korean and American Historical Associations and serves on the Board of the Korean Academic Research Council as well as the Women's Hotline. She is a columnist for the *Chosun Ilbo* newspaper.

Vina Mazumdar is the Director of the Center for Women's Development Studies, New Delhi, India. Dr. Mazumdar is a member of the National Commission on Self-Employed Women, the Committee on the Status of Women in India. She has been Secretary of the Committee on the Status of Women in India, Director of the Indian Council of Social Science Research, and a member of several planning groups, most recently in the Ministry of Rural Development.

Khawar Mumtaz is a coordinator of Shirkat Gah Women's Resource Center's Lahore office. Ms. Mumtaz is a founding member of Women's Action Forum, Lahore Chapter, and is a member of the Human Rights Commission of Pakistan. Coauthor of an award-winning book on the women's movement in Pakistan, she has a number of other publications to her name on women, development, and the environment.

Dorothy L. Njeuma is the Technical Advisor to the Minister of Higher Education and Scientific Research in Cameroon. Dr. Njeuma, a scientist, became Vice Minister of Education in 1975 and, with one brief interruption, has worked in government ever since. Over the course of her career in public life, she has formulated educational policy, led the Cameroon delegation to several UNESCO conferences, and in 1983 she was made an officer of the Cameroon Order of Valour.

Fúlvia Rosemberg is a Research Scientist at the Carlos Chagas Foundation and Professor of Psychology, Pontifícia University, São Paulo, Brazil. Dr. Rosemberg is also Counselor to the State Secretary for Child Welfare and directs a research project on the education of blacks sponsored by the Brazilian Department of Education.

T. Paul Schultz is the Malcolm K. Brachman Professor of Economics and Director of the Economic Growth Center at Yale University. He has studied and taught the economics of individual and family behavior. The main focus of his current research is the causes and consequences of human capital investment in women.

Farida Shaheed is a coordinator of Shirkat Gah Women's Resource Center's Lahore office, and the regional coordinator of the international network Women Living under Muslim Laws (WLUML). She is a founding member of Women's Action Forum, Karachi and Lahore, Pakistan. Ms. Shaheed is the coauthor of an award-winning book on the women's movement in Pakistan and has authored a number of other publications on women and development.

Amaryllis Tiglao Torres is Professor of Community Development at the Institute of Social Work and Community Development, University of the Philippines, and Director of the Office of Research Coordination. Outside academia Dr. Torres is a Consultant to the Population Center Foundation.

Virginia Vargas is Director of the Flora Tristan Center of the Peruvian Woman in Lima, Peru. Ms. Vargas has been a leader of the feminist movement in Peru since the mid-1970s and the founder and director of the Flora Tristan Center. She is also a well-known authority on the women's movement in Latin America and the author of several collections on women, gender, and development.